Guilt, Shame, and Anxiety

Guilt, Shame, and Anxiety

Understanding and Overcoming Negative Emotions

Peter R. Breggin, MD

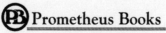 Prometheus Books

59 John Glenn Drive
Amherst, New York 14228

Published 2014 by Prometheus Books

Cover image © Bigstock
Cover design by Grace M. Conti-Zilsberger

Inquiries should be addressed to
Prometheus Books
59 John Glenn Drive
Amherst, New York 14228
VOICE: 716–691–0133
FAX: 716–691–0137
WWW.PROMETHEUSBOOKS.COM

18 17 16 15   5 4 3 2

Library of Congress Cataloging-in-Publication Data

Breggin, Peter Roger, 1936-
    Guilt, shame, and anxiety : understanding and overcoming negative emotions / by Peter R. Breggin, MD.
        pages cm
    Includes bibliographical references and index.
    ISBN 978-1-61614-149-3 (paperback) — ISBN 978-1-61614-721-1 (ebook)
    1. Emotions. 2. Guilt. 3. Shame. 4. Anxiety. I. Title.

BF531.B735 2014
152.4—dc23

                                                                                2014023875

Printed in the United States of America

Once again for my wife, Ginger,
A starburst of intelligence and integrity in the universe
And a never-ending source of love, support, and guidance in my life

CONTENTS

PART 3. FREEDOM TO LOVE

FOREWORD

This is an important book. It introduces a new and convincing theory about the origins of our most painful and self-destructive emotions and applies this insight to how we can improve our lives. If you think that nothing new can be written about the human condition, you have a surprise waiting for you. *Guilt, Shame, and Anxiety* is a book of breathtaking originality. It is filled with unique insights and innovative procedures that can transform our lives, relationships, and worldviews.

In March 1887, Charles Darwin met with ornithologist John Gould, who had been studying Darwin's bird specimens from his trip to the Galapagos Islands. Darwin left the meeting convinced that transmutation was responsible for the presence of similar but distinct species on the different islands. The dogma of "species barrier" had been shattered; instead, he concluded that species are not immutable. Nonetheless, Darwin waited several decades before he published his theory of evolution and then did so because another naturalist, Alfred Russel Wallace, was about to publish a similar theory. Darwin knew that his ideas would meet with stiff resistance from many powerful groups. In fact, they still do; many Americans, including prominent political figures, reject the theory of evolution outright.

Even so, Darwinian evolution is seen as the cornerstone of contemporary biology, and its influence cannot be overestimated. In the words of Michael Shermer, "Evolution matters because science matters. Science matters because it is the preeminent story of our age, an epic saga about who we are, where we came from, and where we are going."[1] Peter Breggin has mined Darwin's writings, and those who came after him, to propose a unique but crucial insight, namely that humanity's "negative legacy emotions," the residue of its evolutionary past, are at the root of many if not most contemporary personal, social, and political conflicts.

In this remarkable book, Peter Breggin takes his readers on a step-by-step journey to help them identify and replace this negativity with life-affirming attitudes and values that will enhance their well-being and happiness. Humans may be both the most violent and the most social of all creatures. What other species kills so many of their own kind? What other species reaches out to help numerous others survive and prosper? Breggin describes how guilt, shame, and anxiety serve an adaptive evolutionary function by inhibiting willfulness and violence in personal and family relationships. These negative legacy emotions make children compliant and are easily triggered in childhood, especially by deprivation and abuse as well as by conflicts later in life.

Breggin recommends liberating oneself from this negative legacy by identifying the emotion, rejecting its influence, and replacing it with common sense, rational values, and empathic love. His emphasis on love is in accord with an underappreciated aspect of Darwin's work. Darwin's book *The Descent of Man* mentions "survival of the fittest" two times, once derisively. But David Loye's computer search identified ninety-five instances of the word *love*.[2] Natural selection favored those who were able to give aid to each other, as this would give them an advantage over other tribal groups. Breggin has followed this often-neglected aspect of Darwinian thought, emphasizing traits that can be found in many nonhuman species that foster social support.

There are other ways in which the behavior of other animals can be instructive. Breggin tells the story of his two dogs, Blue and Cavie, both of whom were exposed outdoors to a lightning bolt that illuminated the neighborhood. Cavie never recovered and ducked for shelter whenever there was the merest rumble of thunder. Blue, however, was unfazed by the lightning and had no hesitation in walking about during a thunderstorm. In my experience with children and adults faced with trauma, I have seen similar differences. One war veteran will return from a combat situation emotionally shattered, with all the symptoms of posttraumatic stress, while his buddy will assimilate the horror and return to the battlefield the next day. Both are examples of the difference between an event and an experience. As Epictetus famously wrote, it is not what happens to us that is as important as how we react to what happens, an aphorism repeated over the ages by Marcus Aurelius, Alfred Korzybski, Aldous Huxley, and Albert Ellis. Therefore, I have written about potentially "traumatizing events" that often—but not always—lead to "traumatic experiences."[3] There cannot be a "traumatic event" because events are psychologically neutral. But many people's reactions trigger negative legacy emotions, often those that were evoked during childhood and adolescence, laying the groundwork for what later becomes post-traumatic stress with its accompanying panoply of repetitive nightmares, emotional numbing, severe anxiety, and "flashbacks." Oftentimes, guilt is part of the matrix and can lead to suicide, just as shame, when it occurs, can lead to antisocial acts. Breggin's self-help exercises can be especially useful for posttraumatic stress survivors and their families.

Breggin is a well-known and respected psychiatric reformer who for decades has taken on the "psychopharmaceutical complex" as well as the simplistic explanations of human behavior proffered by "neuromania." Instead of buying into the proposition that one's neurology controls one's actions, he cites research that demonstrates that human activity, especially spiritual practices, can alter brain function.

I agree with Breggin's description of spirituality as a worldview that encompasses something beyond oneself. This would include interaction with God, the "higher self," a noble cause, or the cosmos itself. In any event, the importance of spirituality has long been emphasized by humanistic and transpersonal psychotherapists and has finally been acknowledged by mainstream mental-health care providers.

In this book, Breggin provides a developmental roadmap that begins with self-examination, proceeds with self-determination, and concludes with self-learning, a process that can keep his readers from relapsing into subjective helplessness in all its forms. Indeed, *Guilt, Shame, and Anxiety* is a paean to the human spirit and what it can accomplish in a world that is badly but not fatally tattered. Most remarkably, he sheds light on the prehistoric origins of our most punishing and disabling emotions, examines how they result from contradictions within our human nature, and shows the way to overcome these negative legacy emotions through knowledge, wisdom, and effort.

Stanley Krippner, PhD
Professor of Psychology
Saybrook University
Oakland, California
Award for Distinguished Lifetime Contributions to Humanistic Psychology,
    Division 32, American Psychological Association, 2013

PART 1.

UNDERSTANDING NEGATIVE
LEGACY EMOTIONS

INTRODUCTION TO PART 1

Relationship is in our DNA. Each of us is born with an irresistible desire to relate to other human beings. By the time we are two or three, our brains have grown twice as large, much of it in response to the people around us, making us inseparable from each other. We are made of each other. Both physically and emotionally, we can and do complete and inspire each other's lives.

Yet willfulness and violence are also in our DNA. Each of us is born with impulses to inflict devastating harm upon other creatures and other people, including our family members. Both physically and emotionally, we can and do tear each other apart.

We are potentially the most loving and the most violent creatures on Earth. Given our passion for physical and emotional intimacy, and given our tendency to react to each other with willful aggression, nature faced a daunting task: how to keep us from destroying each other within our families.

Chapter 1

THE MOST VIOLENT AND MOST LOVING CREATURE ON EARTH

A life-changing birth occurred on the planet about 190 million years ago, when dinosaurs roamed the earth. Beneath their pounding feet, huddled close to the ground, the first tiny shrewlike creature brought forth an infant and began suckling her young. Her body was no larger than a child's pinkie, but this furry little mammal embodied a huge leap in biological evolution that would eventually result in our remarkable human capacities for emotional intimacy and social life—and for emotional suffering.[1]

That early ancestor of ours was a pioneer in intimate relationships. As the original mammalian mother, she was the first to participate in the most remarkable and life-sustaining relationship ever created—nursing a helpless, dependent infant toward eventual independence and maturity. Birds, for example, may sit on their offspring to keep them warm, fuss over them to keep them clean, chirp at them to stimulate receptivity for food, and nourish them with regurgitated food. Much more intimate, this new mammalian relationship involved the mother manufacturing nourishment and feeding it to her offspring directly from her own body in the closest possible physical proximity for an extended period. This put into motion a new branch of biological evolution that would eventually lead to our unique craving to relate to each other despite the uncertainty and emotional pain that our relationships so often cause.

All that began with a finger-sized animal nursing its young? Yes, all that and more, including the capacity for painful emotions that is implanted in every human being. That relationship brought about an emotional closeness never before known on Earth, a closeness that would culminate in human nature and human relationships. It would eventually expand beyond cooperation and empathy within the family and come to include our moral and spiritual values.

SO VIOLENT AND YET SO LOVING

From fossil records nearly half a million years old, we know that our ancestors were able to band together in small groups to attack ancient elephants many times the size of the modern version of this great animal.[2] Like us, our ancestors were relatively thin-skinned and thin-skulled. They lacked fangs, claws, tusks, or hooves with which to tear apart or bash in their prey. They could not rip jugular arteries and crush bones with their jaws, nor could they sprint with the speed of a cheetah. Yet these physically puny creatures attacked behemoths with pointed sticks—a feat that must have required ferocity and tenacity unmatched in the animal kingdom.

Assaulting great beasts in small hunting parties also required cooperation and subtle communication. It demanded self-sacrifice and courageous commitment to each other and to the survival of family and clan. Meanwhile, women, children, and the infirm back home had to defend themselves from predators and marauders. Then, as now, adults of both genders readily gave their lives to serve the community, once again confirming our enormous innate capacities for both aggression and love.

Our ancestors had the capacity to cooperate in unleashing violence on giant prey. That exemplifies what every child brought into the world at that prehistoric time—and what every child continues to bring into the modern world. Since long before we evolved into *Homo sapiens*, every humanlike and human child has been born with enormously conflicted capacities for close-knit social relationships and for incredible aggression.[3]

Built-in aggression in combination with built-in social cooperation was necessary for hunting and for defending ourselves and our families from predatory animals. There is also compelling evidence that, much like today, we were warriors against our own kind, but necessarily on a smaller scale.[4] Our capacity for aggression may explain why *Homo sapiens* became the only group from among many humanlike relatives to survive the evolutionary process.

We humans have always been both predator and prey. We have hunted other creatures, and other creatures have hunted us. Our capacity for aggression gave us prehistoric advantages as both predator and prey. As predator, our ability to unleash violence enabled us to slay giant animals for meat and to defeat human and animal competitors for scarce resources, such as large game and territories in which to gather food and find shelter. As prey, our aggressiveness enabled us to defend our families and ourselves from animal predators and other humans.[5]

No other social creature is as violent as we are. No other violent creature is as social as we are. This innate and seemingly impossible conflict continues to affect the lives of every one of us.

BEING SO SOCIAL HAS ITS HAZARDS

We evolved biologically as social creatures with innate urges to be cooperative, empathic, and loving.[6] This knowledge has become commonplace in more recent social and biological sciences, while empathy is increasingly seen as the central healing aspect of psychotherapy.[7]

Our thin and tender skin was probably not an accident in our evolutionary development—a flaw or glitch in natural selection that makes us vulnerable to injury and disease. Our skin enables us to be profoundly nurtured in childhood through intimate physical contact and to be further strengthened in adulthood by additional intimate physical contact in our affectionate relationships.[8] When nursing our young or making love, we are skin-to-skin—as physically close as we can get.

Some researchers have concluded that our sensitivity to touch plays a key role in our ability to feel empathy.[9] Evolution has packaged us with a highly sensitive, tender film of skin in order for us to be vulnerable to each other, to desire touching from each other, and to enhance our ability to communicate empathy and love.

Without the capacity for love and empathy built into our brains and bodies, even into our skin, we could not have survived in prehistoric times. Having neither fur nor hide to protect us, and lacking horns, claws, or huge canines with which to fight, we developed strength in numbers, which requires that we bond together to understand and meet each other's needs.

As human beings who evolved with two conflicting inborn tendencies—one for closeness and love, the other for willfulness and violence—we faced the necessity of controlling our violent reactivity in order to live in close-knit families and clans. Living in a cave or in a small array of huts, or sleeping beside each other around a campfire, we had the strong desire to share life with one another and, especially when frustrated, to tear each other apart.

If biological evolution and natural selection had not found a counterbalance to restrain or inhibit extreme self-assertion and aggression within the family and clan, we would not be here today.[10] Our inherent aggressive tendencies would have wrecked our most intimate and important relationships, as they still can do in modern life. We would not have been able to raise our children without many of them being sexually assaulted or beaten by other children and adults, as still too often happens today. We would not have been able to live in extended families and clans without turning on each other as murderously as we turn on strangers or people who look different. Without inbred restraints on our willfulness and aggression, we would have perished like so many of nature's "mistakes."

In primitive societies, individuals who were more innately inhibited by guilt, shame, and anxiety more easily avoided destructive interactions in their close relationships. Through biological evolution, the inhibition induced by these emotions favored these individuals' survival and the survival of their mates and children. This, in turn, gave them an advantage in passing on their genes to their offspring. Genetic lines with an innate capacity for these inhibitory emotions flourished in competition with their rivals.

As some families and societies developed larger numbers of individuals biologically primed for guilt, shame, and anxiety, they gained survival and procreation advantages over families and societies without these inhibitions.[11] Most or all human beings in every culture developed the capacity to experience powerful inhibitor emotions that dampened or controlled their willfulness and aggression in personal conflicts.[12] Guilt, shame, and anxiety preserved and promoted the human race despite its volatile and conflicting combination of sociability and violence.

BIOLOGICAL EVOLUTION AND NATURAL SELECTION RESULT IN NEGATIVE LEGACY EMOTIONS

In order for us to manage our willfulness and aggression within the closeness of our families and small communities, evolution endowed us with powerful inhibitory feelings as built-in defenses against our potential for self-assertiveness and even violence in close personal and familial relationships. I use the term *negative legacy emotions* to designate this new theory about the evolutionary function of guilt, shame, and anxiety. These emotions are *negative* because they are suppressive and because they have many harmful consequences. They are *legacy* emotions built into our brains and bodies, then triggered and shaped during childhood and adolescence. As adults, we experience these emotions as an inheritance of emotional "baggage," burdens that seem at times alien and at other times natural to us. They are leftovers from humanity's evolutionary past that no longer serve adaptive functions.[13] In this concept of negative legacy emotions, we will find an answer to why we humans *inevitably* suffer psychologically or emotionally in ways and degrees unlike any other creature on Earth.

Nature built guilt, shame, and anxiety into the fabric of our brains, minds, and family life as suppressors of our self-assertion and aggression, especially in our closer affiliations. Biological evolution by means of natural selection made it inevitable that when experiencing emotional or physical intimacy and love, we would also tend to react with powerful emotional inhibitions on our self-assertiveness and aggression.

A YOUNGSTER WHITTLING A SPEAR

Imagine a boy living fifty thousand years ago, with a brain already as fully evolved, complex, and subtle as ours. As he whittles a stick while sitting around the campfire with his family, he happily imagines how he will someday be like his father, who fiercely and bravely hunts great beasts to bring home huge chunks of savory meat. Nursed and nurtured by his mother and raised in an extended family and perhaps a clan, the boy is very social and loves his family, including his sometimes-annoying little brother. Yet, as he looks at his little brother across the flickering fire, the impulse crosses his mind to practice his hunting skills on him.

With his stick now whittled to a point, the boy imagines creeping close to his little brother to spring upon him with his weapon. At the instant he gets ready to hurl his hunting spear, he notices his father looking at him. He cannot quite read his father's expression, but a dreadful feeling overcomes him. A reflexive emotional paralysis prevents him from carrying out his urge to turn his brother into prey. He does not understand the emotion, and later on, he will not remember feeling it, but it stops him dead in his tracks. Negative legacy emotions of guilt, shame, or anxiety, or a mixture of them, paralyze him. These inhibitory emotions were built into the boy biologically. Otherwise, early humans, especially children, would have been much less able to modify their self-assertive and aggressive drives to conform to the necessities of living in close contact within the family, clan, or tribe.

Depending on the boy's circumstances and experiences in his family, his dread that his father would retaliate against or even kill him could have triggered the primitive emotions that stopped him from assaulting his little brother. This paralyzing feeling would probably be experienced as a mixture of guilt and anxiety. As an alternative, he may have remembered how much his father and mother adored his little brother and then imagined how they would reject or abandon him for harming him. His anticipation of rejection and abandonment would probably have triggered shame, and anxiety in him.

From a more positive perspective, the boy with the spear is old enough to feel emotionally attached and empathic toward his younger brother, and this, too, could have helped to inhibit his violent actions. However, empathy would not have the same stunning, paralyzing impact as guilt, shame, and anxiety.

Could simple *fear* of the consequences have stopped the boy from assaulting his little brother? Could he have realized that his dad might retaliate, making the boy afraid to harm his brother in front of him? If simple fear were at work, there would be no *built-in* inhibition. When his father is not around, the boy might not feel so constrained. He could then harm his brother, and, with sufficient guile, he might make it look like someone else did it. A child who learned to respond in such a fashion would become what psychiatry used to label a psychopath or sociopath and now diagnoses with antisocial personality disorder. Evolution built into us something much more socially effective in the form of negative legacy emotions that we carry with us all the time.

In the future, when the boy considers asserting himself in an aggressive fashion in the family, he will reexperience these feelings in the fabric of brain, body, and mind as painful emotions over which he has no power. They will seem like emotional reflexes or reactions wholly beyond his control. He will probably feel them without any memory of the event by the campfire or of earlier events that stimulated and channeled these emotional reactions. Like most people today who feel demoralized by their emotions, he will have little or no idea what is really happening to him.

Although abusive treatment by parents will amplify these painful emotions in children, children themselves are biologically primed to feel them in their daily lives. Self-suppressive legacy emotions will be triggered in children and teenagers during routine conflicts in the home, potentially crushing their self-assertive and aggressive impulses. Although these feelings seem to arise in childhood and adolescence, biological evolution originally embedded them in us.

WHAT IS AN EMOTION?

An *emotion* as used in this book is more than a feeling. Guilt, shame, and anxiety are emotional experiences that combine feelings, thoughts, and judgments or values and that drive us toward inhibiting ourselves or making choices that we did not initially wish to make. When we say to ourselves, "I should feel guilty when I do something selfish," we are naming a *feeling*. We are also connecting the feeling of guilt to *thoughts* about how we should and should not behave. We are further making a judgment or asserting a value that it is bad and selfish to do what we are contemplating. Ultimately, this combination of feelings, thoughts, and judgments is likely to lead to a *choice*, such as "I won't be selfish" or "I won't think selfish thoughts." This can lead to a specific *decision*, such not as to grab candy from another child or, more positively, to share candy with another child.

Our complex emotional processes can be negative, as in hatred, or positive, as in love. They can be self-suppressive, as in guilt, shame, and anxiety. They can be relatively unconscious or conscious. We are probably most effective and happiest when conscious positive emotions are motivating us.

THE INFANT'S NATURAL DRIVES RUN INTO TROUBLE

Toddlers and older children demonstrate a strong desire to feel closeness and, at times, empathy with other children and adults. A two-year-old is capable of reaching out to a sad or crying child with a toy or a hug. These positive emotions play a role in preventing children from unleashing willfulness and aggressiveness on others. But, as every parent knows, the strength of a temper tantrum can easily override the prosocial inclinations of any child.

Children enormously desire close and satisfying relationships with each other and especially with their parents. This social drive is the most powerful force in human life. But infants and children lack the experience and the cognitive abilities to fully grasp the need to inhibit themselves in many situations. Biologically, they lack the frontal-lobe and overall brain development necessary for self-discipline and self-control in moments of frustration. Some of the most important parenting involves the work of teaching our children responsibility and self-discipline in their early years.

A baby's cry is a thoughtless, uninhibited demand for attention. In an instant, especially when frustrated, the most gentle and loving child can become wholly self-centered and very aggressive. Anyone who has cared for toddlers knows how quickly even the most seemingly compliant child can turn into a raging little monster in need of the most skilled adult management. From biting the nipple during breastfeeding to hitting, kicking, and throwing objects at siblings or parents, infants and children display a built-in potential for violence that especially comes out when facing frustration in their intimate relationships.

Often, the imposition of guilt, shame, and anxiety will take place in response to nonviolent or even nonaggressive behaviors. Sometimes, the child's willfulness will be tempered by the hard realities of life, such as falling to the floor while joyfully running in the house or tumbling off a chair when bravely trying to climb onto the table. More often, the toddler will be thwarted by siblings and parents who want to protect him or resent the chaos he is creating. As a result, if the child falls while running about in the living room or while climbing the chair in the kitchen, the negative or restraining responses from those around him will often trigger feelings of guilt, shame, or anxiety.

If guilt, shame, and anxiety serve any useful purpose, it is to help control willfulness and aggression in small children. But the child will not have the understanding or wisdom to draw thoughtful conclusions such as, "Life goes better for everyone in the family, including me, when I control my impulses and play with more restraint." If the child is able to formulate any explanation, it will not be consistent with mature adult ethics. Often, the experience will become embedded in the youngster's unconscious mind, perhaps building an association between "having fun" and "getting hurt" or "getting punished" or "making Mommy mad at me" or "Daddy making a scary, angry face at me." Infants and toddlers will be stopped dead in their tracks by painful emotions without being able to grasp what is happening to them in the midst of asserting or simply enjoying themselves.

DEVELOPING CHRONIC ANGER AND NUMBNESS

The human heritage of painful emotions becomes especially disabling when children endure trauma and misfortunes such as accidents or illness; bullying; death or loss of siblings or nurturing adults; family conflict; or physical, emotional, or sexual abuse. When these trauma-stimulated emotions become unbearable, the brain and mind of the child, and later of the adult, will try to drive them out of consciousness. Instead of feeling guilt, shame, and anxiety, we end up feeling chronically angry or persistently numb and out of touch with ourselves.

When referring to "negative legacy emotions," I usually intend to include not only guilt, shame, and anxiety but also feelings of emotional numbness and extreme or chronic anger. Negative legacy emotions include guilt, shame, and anxiety, as well as the self-defeating anger and numbness that they often result in.

ABOUT SIMPLIFYING COMPLEX ISSUES

For practical purposes, a number of drives or instincts will here be treated as easily divisible and defined. In reality, however, the inborn capacities for violence, sociability, and painful emotions often reflect a complex of related emotional phenomena. For example, aggression, violence, self-assertion, and willfulness are discussed as if they are one general tendency, but they could also be analyzed as somewhat-separate expressions of human nature. My goal is to present this information in the simplest and most usable form while still basing it in science—ultimately, with the aim of promoting emotional liberation from negative legacy emotions in our personal lives.

GREAT VARIETY IN HOW EACH OF US EXPERIENCES NEGATIVE EMOTIONS

Our individual emotional profiles vary a great deal from person to person. Some of us react predominantly with guilt; others, with shame; and still others, with anxiety. Some of us end up hiding the painful feelings beneath anger or emotional numbness. But all of us suffer to some degree from these negative emotional reactions.

Negative emotions often occur simultaneously in combinations. Beyond that, the dominance of one emotion or another can change over a lifetime. Nonetheless, as we learn to identify our pattern of guilt, shame, and anxiety, as well as anger and emotional numbness, we are likely to find that we have a particular tendency to react with one of these emotions in particular.

WE ARE SIMPLE AND YET COMPLICATED

Almost everything about being human is complex and individualistic, including our emotional life. Yet our self-defeating emotions have a certain simplicity about them. They are simple enough to be programmed into our biology by evolution and simple enough to be triggered and inculcated into infants and pre-verbal children who cannot yet reason or make informed judgments about their emotions. As a result, the ways people experience guilt, shame, and anxiety look much more the same from person to person than their more individualistic and creative qualities.

When people blush with shame or tremble with anxiety, we know exactly what they are feeling. When they look guilty and express bad feelings about themselves, we also know what they are experiencing. It is far easier to grasp these negative experiences when we see them in others than it is to feel instantaneous understanding when someone tells us that he found the ability to overcome his negative emotions through prayer, meditation, reason, principled living, therapy, a religious experience, love, or some other positive approach to living.

The path upward toward increased personal responsibility and emotional freedom is far more unique and individualistic than the path downward into the negative emotions with which we all struggle in common. Part 2 of this book describes the three steps to emotional freedom, and Part 3 focuses on love. My suggested path to emotional well-being is informed by my personal and professional experience; I have no doubt that many other valid paths lead in this direction. I do believe that all of them require principled living, reason, and love.

Chapter 2

OUR HUMAN LEGACY
OF STONE AGE EMOTIONS

Most of our troubled and painful emotions are *prehistoric* in two senses of the word. They are prehistoric in the usual meaning because they were literally embedded in our brains and bodies during the long prehistoric period of mammalian and human evolution. They are part of our genetic heritage. We are able to feel guilt, shame, and anxiety because the capacity for feeling them is innate.

Patricia Churchland, who describes herself as a neurophilosopher, observes:

> Archeological evidence indicates that anatomically modern *Homo sapiens* existed in Africa about 300,000 years ago. . . . If we make the reasonable assumption that Middle Stone Age humans (300,000–50,000 years ago) had brains that, at birth, were pretty much like ours . . . then any story of the neural underpinnings of human morality should apply to them as well.[1]

TWO WAYS THAT NEGATIVE EMOTIONS ARE "PREHISTORIC"

Given that the biological evolution of human beings was more or less complete as long as three hundred thousand years ago, and even more certainly by fifty thousand years ago, then it is highly probable that when we were Stone Age people, we humans were experiencing guilt, shame, and anxiety, as well as chronic anger and numbing *much in their present form*. Our most disabling and disheartening emotions are indeed primitive Stone Age emotions. They are prehistoric in origin.[2]

Guilt, shame, and anxiety are also prehistoric in another, more subtle, sense. These emotions originated when we were so young that we have little or no memory of the events and circumstances that triggered and shaped them. In therapy, people usually have little or no consciousness of the origins of their

27

negative emotions in childhood until they put considerable effort and practice into recalling and understanding them. Even after working in therapy, people usually report very little memory of events before age four and only spotty memory of later childhood years.

When a family is brought together for a therapy session to discuss their varying viewpoints, people will describe painful events in the lives of family members who have no recollection of them, such as losing a loved relative, experiencing frightening surgery or an anxiety-provoking accident, being badly beaten by a parent, or fending off an inebriated father's sexual advances. Even after people are made aware of painful childhood events by siblings, parents, or other sources, their memories often remain lost or vague.

When we investigate our childhood memories, we will often find that we already had an established emotional profile of guilt, shame, or anxiety—or some combination—by the time of our earliest memories. As early as age two or three, and often around four or five, we may find that we were already feeling guilty, ashamed, or anxious in association with a new experience such as starting daycare. We may remember feeling guilty because a depressed parent made us feel to blame for his suffering. We may remember feeling ashamed when teased by siblings or classmates, or we may recall feeling anxiety over being left at pre-school for the first time by our mother or caregiver. Often, these emotions of guilt, shame, and anxiety will still be the dominant ones in adult life.

We may be able to recall critical moments in our childhood, especially with psychotherapy or self-help books, but the development of our most devastating and demoralizing emotions will commonly remain prehistoric: prior to memory and understanding. Not only early childhood memories but some painful adolescent memories and even adult memories can be suppressed and lost to consciousness.

In summary, guilt, shame, and anxiety are prehistoric in two ways. First, these emotions biologically evolved over millions of years, probably reaching their present form in us between fifty thousand and three hundred thousand years ago. Second, they are prehistoric because early childhood triggered them before we had mature understanding and often before we could form memories of most of what took place.

DEFINING AND DESCRIBING INSTINCTS

To provide variety and nuance, the terms *primitive, prehistoric, primeval, Stone Age, self-defeating, self-destructive, inhibitory, restraining,* and *demoralizing* will be used to designate or describe negative legacy emotions. These words indicate that negative legacy emotions are relics from biological evolution and that they are destructive to a mature, ethical life.

Another set of terms I will use somewhat interchangeably includes *innate, genetic, inherited, in our DNA,* and *embedded in our brains.* These terms indicate that a specific human capacity was built into our biology. However, the expression of this capacity is often modified by the environment and by human choice and effort. The capacity for language, for example, is innate but highly varied in its expression in cultures and individuals.

The term *instinct,* as defined in biology and applied in this book, will designate an inborn or genetic capacity for mental or behavioral activities that is characteristic of a species and commonly triggered and shaped in its expression by environmental factors or stimuli. The capacity is biological but is elicited and modified by the environment. This book will demonstrate that human beings inevitably struggle with a broad array of often-contradictory instinctual drives, including those associated with willfulness and aggression; with sociability, empathy, and love; and with guilt, shame, and anxiety. Human instincts include the socialization, sex, and hunger drives. More controversially, as others have also proposed, the capacities for speech, morality, and spirituality can be considered instinctual.

In earlier years, I found it demeaning to consider some of our most remarkable capacities, such as speech and spirituality, to be rooted in biology and instincts. But this only becomes demeaning if we use a rigid definition of instincts as *fixed* responses to *predetermined* environmental cues. Based on that rigid definition, hunger, thirst, and sex are not instincts in human beings because we are infinitely capable of modifying them. In the extreme, we can force ourselves to reject them so that we die of hunger or thirst or live celibate. Nor is it clear that hunger and sex are stronger instincts than language and spirituality; people at times find it easier to suppress hunger and sex than the desire to communicate and to feel spiritually connected to something greater than themselves. People commonly sacrifice their instincts for food and sex in the interest of higher ideals and spiritual aspirations.

THE INSTINCTUAL NATURE OF MORE PAINFUL AND OVERWHELMING EMOTIONS.

Guilt, shame, and anxiety are part of our genetic heritage or legacy. We are *able* to feel them because the potential for feeling them is innate in our brains and bodies. Our brains are primed to react with them, and our bodies are made to feel them. Environmental stimulation in childhood, usually in the form of inter-actions between us and other people, then elicits and helps to form the expres-sion of these innate emotions. In adulthood, these emotions can jerk us around, manipulating our behavior in the ways they were shaped to do so by biological evolution and our childhood experiences.

Our childhood and adolescent decisions also played a role in our moral development. We may have decided to be more like Mom or Dad or never to be like either of them. We may have decided to be like adults we met outside the family, such as another child's parents or a teacher, coach, hero in a book, or celebrity. But when making these choices, we were children or teenagers, lacking in mature adult insights and values. We may have chosen well, or not, and with good or bad consequences. As adults, we need to reassess these imma-ture decisions and the emotions that are still driving them.

Not only our brains but our entire bodies are constructed to respond to feelings of guilt, shame, and anxiety. Guilt often slows down physical responses, making us feel sluggish and ill. Shame lights up the face with a blush for the entire world to see. Shame also adversely affects the ability to stand tall or to look someone in the eye. Anxiety drives the sympathetic nervous system into high gear: a pounding heart; dilated pupils; increased blood flow to the muscles; and other signs of increased energy, alertness, and alarm (further discussed in chapter 16).

You and I did not freely choose these ways of reacting. They are part of our human inheritance; they are prehistoric emotional reactions that we humans have experienced for hundreds of thousands of years. Nonetheless, we can learn to modify our responses.

EMPATHY WAS NOT ENOUGH

During childhood and adolescence, we went through prolonged years when we were dependent and relatively helpless, making us want to be compliant with the adults around us, if only out of necessity. We also had an overriding desire for physical and emotional intimacy that is unique to human beings. This dependence and helplessness, or neediness, required that we inhibit our self-assertiveness and aggression.

From the first two or three years of life, our cravings for social relationship and our nascent empathy also encouraged us to get along in our families. These early manifestations of love softened our demanding and dangerous impulses.

Unfortunately, because humans have such a strong heritage of willfulness and aggression, neither our neediness nor our social impulses were sufficient to contain our potential destructiveness. To this day, these social feelings are often insufficient to prevent children from developing serious and potentially physical conflicts with each other and their parents or caregivers.

Natural selection promoted negative legacy emotions to fill the gap. The anxiety associated with separation and abandonment helps prevent dangerous conflict between children and their parents and caregivers. Similarly, guilt and shame inhibit innate tendencies toward willfulness and violence. For hundreds of thousands of years, this has taken place on an unconscious instinctual level as biological evolution's way of making children accommodate the adults upon whom they rely for loving care and guidance.

CULTURAL EVOLUTION MATTERS

Biological evolution involves genetic changes passed on from one generation to another by means of natural selection. *Culture* is "behavior that is taught and learned and varies among populations."[3] Culture occurs not only among humans but also among chimpanzees—and perhaps among our common ancestors. Among humans, cultural *evolution* involves the passing on of learned information, such as societal values and child-rearing practices, from generation to generation.

Culture can evolve on a local level, as the development of particular habits and attitudes in enclaves in mountain communities or on islands, and it can evolve on a national level in modern times. With our increasing capability to communicate globally, culture can evolve, sometimes in the blink of an eye, all around the world at once. This is in marked contrast to biological evolution through natural selection, which creeps along at a much slower pace as new genetic traits are passed on or dropped out from generation to generation.

Human culture has evolved over tens of thousands of years, but there is no guarantee that cultural evolution leads to human progress—for example, in creating more just, generous, or free societies. In modern times, we have continued to witness enormously destructive events such as ethnic cleansing and genocide, oppressive political regimes, and horrendous local and international wars.

Too often, culture piles onto the worst of biological evolution by creating overly authoritarian educational, religious, and political institutions that further reinforce guilt, shame, and anxiety, as well as anger and numbness. I will never forget a day trip I took with author Jeffrey Masson behind the Iron Curtain into East Berlin in 1988. From the drab and nearly empty stores to the teenagers who dared to risk being seen talking to us (Jeffrey speaks German), the entire culture seemed depressed and anxious.

A FLOOD OF INFLUENCES

Our social institutions flood children's lives in myriad negative ways, from bad lessons and traumatic experiences in daycare to violent video games, all of it typically absorbed without parental supervision or explanation.

The impact of cultural evolution and contemporary society on creating guilt, shame, and anxiety is too enormous a subject to address in depth, other than to emphasize its impact on childhood and child-rearing practices. During infancy and early childhood, when children develop much of their emotional profile, the family is the primary conveyer or implementer of cultural norms and values. If caregivers or daycare providers in part raise the children, then they too will have an impact.

As children grow older, television, movies, computer games, music, social networking, peers, and school increasingly influence them, for better or worse. Traumatic experiences inflicted outside the family by daycare providers, babysitters, or bullies can impair children's growth and development (see chapters 9 and 10). Racism, sexism, religious persecution, oppressive religious teachings, economic disparity, and myriad other injustices, inequalities, and prejudices also increase the impact of inhibitory, self-defeating emotions in growing children.

Some of these social influences, from daycare to computer games and television, can be positive and encourage a young person to mature into an adult who lives by reason, ethics, and love, but too few elements in the child's broader culture aim in this direction.

Despite this catalog of positive and negative cultural and societal influences, the quality of the home environment and the family's support or lack of support for the child's sense of worth remain pivotal in determining the direction and success of emotional growth. A solid, loving family with good values will help children to live positive lives in the face of negative pressures within their neighborhoods, their schools, and society.

HOW WE DIFFER FROM CROWS, WOLVES, DOGS, AND CHIMPANZEES

Consider some of the similarities among crows, wolves, dogs, chimpanzees, and humans. Each species socializes with and seems to enjoy the company of its own kind, and each cooperates with other members in activities such as raising a family, protecting themselves, and obtaining food. Each has the capacity for violence, and each must control its aggressive tendencies in relation to its own kind. These shared patterns of life, including the controls against aggression within a species, are the result of biological evolution. There is huge variation in how each species expresses and controls its conflicting aggressive and social drives. This, too, is based on biology and genetics.

We can see wisps of negative legacy emotions in animals. Jane Goodall has described similar emotions and their associated facial expressions, gestures, and vocalizations in chimpanzees.[4] Jeffrey Masson, who has written extensively about animal emotions, vividly describes subtle variations in negative emotion in many species.[5]

Anyone who has lived with dogs knows that our animal companions can show signs of painful, inhibitory emotions that bear some resemblance to guilt, shame, and anxiety and that arise during conflicts in their relationships with us, just as in our human relationships with each other. When dogs hang their heads or sulk, it immediately indicates to us that they feel guilty or ashamed for having "done something wrong." The nervousness they abruptly display as we begin packing travel bags suggests they are anxious about our leaving.

If we have two or more dogs, one of them is likely to assume a more submissive role, displaying behaviors that again seem to reflect inhibitory emotions similar to guilt, shame, or anxiety. Similar to their function among humans, these negative legacy emotions help to head off aggressive interactions within the "pack."

Without overly fussing about how closely animal emotions resemble ours, the existence of some negative legacy emotions in animals tends to confirm the evolutionary origin of these emotions. However, only in humans do they routinely influence, control, and even dominate our lives.

Beyond our emotional capacities, there is yet another and more important difference between humans and animals. In human life, individuality and choice play an enormous role in how we direct or redirect our built-in drives and how we advance and make the most of our emotional freedom.

TRANSCENDING OUR BIOLOGICAL DRIVES

Even animals can learn from experience to redirect or overcome aspects of their instinctual behavior. Individual crows, dogs, and chimpanzees express their emotions and intellect as unique and identifiable individuals, depending upon their genetic personalities, their environments, and perhaps even the choices they make. Nikolaas Tinbergen, a Nobel Prize–winning biologist and ornithologist, marvelously documented that even the instincts of a bird are not fully hardwired but vary individually, requiring environmental factors to stimulate and direct them, and can be somewhat modified by choices that the bird seems to make in the face of new challenges—for example, in the selection of unusual nesting materials or foods. Mockingbirds create new songs in mimicry of the animal and mechanical sounds that they hear in their environment. Perhaps there is an element of choice in this as well.

For animals, however, choice is limited, with very little imagining or planning the future. Human beings can transcend their biology to change how they react emotionally, how they think, and how they make conscious decisions.[6] The challenge and triumph of being human is to grow beyond the demoralizing and painful emotions from biological evolution and childhood in order to live a life that is happy and satisfying.

ACCENTUATING THE POSITIVE IS NOT ENOUGH

Roots of the self-help psychology movement lie deep in American culture and history, going back to the initial publication of Benjamin Franklin's *Autobiography* in 1771. During and after World War II, there was enormous growth in the field of humanistic psychology through the Western world. When I was a college student (1954–58) and then a medical student (1958–62), there were innumerable thought-provoking books about the importance of living by principles and for higher purposes.[7]

In recent years, superficial positive psychologies have replaced the rich drama of life that once was humanistic and existential psychology. These positive approaches lack understanding of what holds people back from living by their more positive feelings, thoughts, and values.[8] Understanding our negative legacy emotions can help us to triumph over and to transcend them in pursuit of a life based on self-determination; resilience; higher purposes; and love for others, life, God, or whatever source of spiritual fulfillment we seek.

Chapter 3

OUR BRAINS ARE MADE UP OF PEOPLE

From birth onward, our brain grows in response to our social life.[1]

OUR ASTOUNDING FIRST YEAR OF LIFE

Compared to other mammals, including primates, the human brain grows a great deal after the child's birth. Anthropologist Robert Martin observes that "after birth the pattern of human brain growth differs sharply from that of any other primate and any other mammal." He also notes that "human brain size increases almost fourfold after birth rather than merely doubling as in other primates." Further, "the human brain continues to show a rate of growth as fast as that of a fetus for a year after birth."[2]

Total brain volume increases by more than 100 percent in the first year of life.[3] This rapid brain growth in the first year results in a prolonged fetal-like development outside the womb. Martin estimates that breastfeeding, supplemented by other foods, lasted at least three years throughout most of our history as hunter-gatherers. He further observes, "As all parents know, human infants learn a great deal during the first year of life and already engage in sophisticated social exchanges. This feature was hugely influential in the gradual emergence of greater adaptability and behavioral flexibility during human evolution."[4]

There is a huge evolutionary advantage to such extensive postuterine brain development—the creation of the social brain. Prolonged rapid brain growth after birth creates a social brain made the infant's interactions with the mother, as well as with other caregivers and the overall environment. Instead of being born with a fully formed brain equipped to meet and react to specific stimuli and limited circumstances, we are born with a relatively immature brain that is primed to grow in response to the social world into which it enters.

During the first year of life, the nurturing experience is stitched into the biological fabric of our brain, creating our profound capacity and craving for social attachments or connectedness, for empathy, for touches and hugs, and for emotional and sexual intimacy. The human brain is a nurtured brain. It grows in the first years of life in response to intimate human contact and love.

At the same time, our negative legacy emotions are highly integrated into the anatomy and function of our brain. This occurs along with our more positive emotions and social experiences. Along with that, we are born with an unparalleled capacity for willfulness, aggression, and violence, which childhood can either ameliorate or exacerbate, depending on the quality of parenting and exposure to trauma.

THE INFANT'S EXTRAORDINARILY SENSITIVE BRAIN

Having a brain so immature and growing so rapidly can be a liability for the infant when neglect and abuse occur. Trauma and abuse experts Bruce Perry and John Marcellus explain:

> With optimal experiences, the brain develops healthy, flexible and diverse capabilities. When there is disruption of the timing, intensity, quality or quantity of normal developmental experiences, however, there may be devastating impact on neurodevelopment—and, thereby, function. For millions of abused and neglected children, the nature of their experiences adversely influences the development of their brains. During the traumatic experience, these children's brains are in a state of fear-related activation. This activation of key neural systems in the brain leads to adaptive changes in emotional, behavioral and cognitive functioning to promote survival. Yet, persisting or chronic activation of this adaptive fear response can result in the maladaptive persistence of a fear state.[5]

When babies experience deprivation and abuse during the first year, the expression of the basic instincts such as hunger, sex, and sociability is likely to be adversely affected.[6] An infant who is overstimulated by sexual abuse may struggle with control of sexual impulses later in life. An infant forced into a rigid feeding schedule may develop eating problems that persist into adulthood.

Since neglect and abuse occur at a high rate in the first year of life (see chapter 9), infants are at risk for having painful emotional reactions built into the fabric of their sensitive and malleable brains starting at birth. Many infants are abandoned for hours to cry alone. Too many are beaten and shaken in order to stifle their willful, imperative demands for food and attention. In addition, children in the first year of life are often tortured by physical and emotional pain associated with eating and sleeping difficulties, digestive problems, food and skin allergies, infections, and other afflictions. All these experiences affect the child's growing brain and mind.

Thus, during the first few years of life, we have been endowed by nature and by nurture with an infinitely complicated and, at times, conflicted human inheritance. No wonder being human is such a difficult task!

HOW RELATIONSHIPS MAKE OUR BRAINS GROW

The brain develops new neuronal connections and networks in response to the stimulation it receives from the outside world, including nurturing or the lack of it. Young animals and children develop more numerous and complex neural connections if they grow up in appropriately stimulating environments, resulting in increased cognitive abilities and intelligence.[7] This increased biological complexity in response to environmental stimulation is so dramatic that it is visible under a microscope in animal brains.[8]

Researcher Marian Diamond concludes, "We can now safely say that the basic concept of brain changes in response to enrichment hold true for a wide variety of animals and for humans."[9] Robert Martin points out that human babies "are undoubtedly preprogrammed to expect intensive physical contact" and that lack of it is a "major shock to the system."[10] It is an accepted fact in pediatrics that "inadequate nutrition and disturbed social interactions contribute to poor weight gain, delayed development, and abnormal behavior."[11]

The infant and child's brain has huge connectivity in the form of dendritic brain connections. Dendrites are the multiple-branched extensions of the nerve cell that receive impulses from adjacent neurons. Their density is several times greater in the infant and child than in the adult, allowing for increased, if not excess, brain capacity in the growing infant and child. This is followed by a major pruning-back of synaptic connections during adolescence, which continues to a lesser extent through the third decade of life before stabilizing.[12] Think of it—our brains continue to grow in complexity at least into our twenties, and after that, they continue to change in response to our choices, life experiences, and environments.

The process of brain growth and pruning in childhood takes place in response to the child's experiences, especially social relationships. It is required to fulfill our uniquely human potential as social beings who are able to communicate with signs and words, to be sensitive to the moods and viewpoints of others, to experience love, and, ultimately, to live cooperatively in human society. This was as true fifty thousand to three hundred thousand years ago, when the human brain reached approximately its current development.[13]

WHY SUCH A POWERFUL BRAIN?

A brain intended largely to relate to our family and clan was so powerful that it was eventually able to create the wheel, carts, cars, trains, planes, and rockets. It would eventually produce drawings on cave walls, followed by alphabets, the printing press, mass media, and computers. It would enable us to grow from laying down primitive bedding in a cave to building huts, houses, and skyscrapers, and even a temporary campsite on the moon. This brain would take us through the eras of smoke signals, telegraphs, telephones, fax machines, and Internet. It would lift us up from communicating with hand gestures, grunting, and a few spoken words to creating plays, novels, movies, symphonies, and extravaganzas that are seen simultaneously all around the globe, not to mention the radio waves we send deep into outer space and the social media matrix still rapidly evolving here on Earth.

The evolutionary history of our brain, with its enormous growth when we were living seemingly primitive lives, confirms that we were always social creatures living very complex lives and that most of our emotional success or failure depends on how we use our brains and minds to relate to each other.

In *The Minds of Birds*, naturalist and writer Alexander Skutch writes, "Life in complex societies tends to develop subtle relations between individuals, to sharpen intelligence, to promote communication, and to increase awareness of self in relation to others."[14] Human intelligence has probably grown in proportion to the unique, subtle, and complicated demands of our social lives.

Why did our brain develop such enormous capacities so long before civilization? This is astonishing to consider; compared to human beings today, there was seemingly very little to challenge that remarkable brain when it evolved to its current capacity so long ago. Wasn't there relatively little for it to do—at least, compared to today? There were no books to read, mathematics to learn, or computers and smartphones to operate. There was little or no technology, art, or civilization.

In their book *Born for Love*, science writer Maia Szalavitz and psychiatrist Bruce D. Perry observe that 150,000 years ago, we human beings were living in more complex and stimulating social relationships than today. In particular, children had much more opportunity for nurturing and, therefore, more to learn about human relationships:

> Humans have spent most of the past 150,000 years living in multi-generational, multifamily groups. These relatively small tribes were characterized by rich human interactions that aren't as present in developed Western societies. In these clans, the ratio of mature individuals to young children was roughly 4:1. That is, there were four caregiving individuals for every little one. Fathers, sisters, uncles, older cousins, aunties and other kin surrounded the children—and all of them could educate, discipline, nurture, and enrich. Two parents, many caregivers. That enriched social environment is what our brain expects.[15]

Their observations confirm that our brain developed to such a high degree tens of thousands of years ago in order to process our social relationships, including a childhood nurtured by an extended family and clan, and that these social relationships in childhood may have required more of our brains in the prehistoric past than today.

Szalavitz and Perry are emphasizing how modern children are deprived of nurturance they need in order to flourish and how too many adults also live in relative social isolation. As Ginger Breggin put in perspective for me, because humans are innately so social and so in need of companionship, many contemporary children and youth face potentially desperate degrees of isolation.[16] Untold numbers of tragedies result, including young people who are driven to violence and suicide and lives that are diminished by illegal drugs or psychiatric medications. Still others turn to online video games, compulsive texting, and other barely social interchanges for the minimal and often distorted satisfaction of their need for human companionship.

We are social beings; it is built into our biological fabric. Although we may want to deny it at times, we live and die by our social relationships. The worst of our stresses and traumas lie in our social relationships, but so does the great opportunity for healing.

COMPLEX BEYOND OUR IMAGINATION

Brain development in childhood depends enormously on the richness and quality of the nurturing. To make it more complicated, the quality of nurturing depends in part on hundreds of thousands of years of cultural evolution that have gone into creating and implementing child-rearing practices in the child's family and community.

Biologist Peter Richerson and evolutionary psychologist Robert Boyd place the evolution of culture or society on a par with biological evolution. *Culture* describes the civilization, intellectual achievements, customs, and values of a particular time or people. Culture is the influence of human history, past and present, upon a group of people. Culture enmeshes human beings in values and ideals that dramatically affect their behavior for better or worse. Nowhere is the impact of culture more marked than in child-rearing practices, which influence the child's development, including the child's brain and the future adult's capacity to thrive.

Biological evolution, cultural evolution, and child development all go into the creation, growth, and development of each human brain and mind. Throughout life, our brains and minds continue to be transformed by natural processes inherent in brain growth and by our personal experiences and decisions. We will never be able to understand the physical brain without taking into account how cultural evolution, child development, and adult life impact upon and direct its biological growth.

No wonder we have barely begun to explore the edges of neuroscience. Every single normal brain is the most complex space in the universe, probably even more complex than the whole of the inanimate physical universe put together. Maybe that is why we can think and talk and the cosmos cannot.

THE WHOLE BRAIN IS INVOLVED IN EVERYTHING WE DO

It has grown increasingly fashionable to claim that neuroscience explains one or another human attribute or difficulty by locating it in a specific part of the brain or even in a particular molecule, such as oxytocin (the "love" chemical) and dopamine (the "pleasure" chemical). Fortunately, there is now a healthy skeptical backlash.[17] Emotional responses are built into the whole brain. Understanding the human emotional landscape requires correspondingly holistic and comprehensive psychospiritual explanations and approaches.

Because of the complexity of our social brain, it will never be possible to locate one or another emotion in any specific biochemical process, module, connectome, or neural network in the human brain.[18] There are no known biochemical imbalances at the root of emotional, psychological, or psychiatric problems.[19] None.

We are bio-psychosocial beings of enormous complexity, and the relationship between our integrated bio-psychosocial functioning, especially in regard to brain function, defies current understanding. It will continue to do so, possibly forever. As of now, we have very little understanding about how the brain functions as a whole, how it expresses a personality, or how it relates to our emotional and mental lives.

Researcher Larry Swanson, in his twenty-five years devoted to the study of the brain, has found that "one thing seems obvious": that explaining any human activity, from eating and drinking to caring for our offspring, "really amounts to explaining how the entire nervous system is arranged and works as a whole."[20] Similarly, Szalavitz and Perry observe that the integrated nature of the brain makes it impossible to separate thoughts and feelings into separate functions. This is consistent with my working definition of an emotion (such as guilt, anxiety, or shame) as a combination of feelings, thoughts, and judgments or values.

The entire human brain has gone through biological evolution, including areas anatomically lower in the brain and evolutionarily older. Throughout biological evolution, the brain has grown as an integrated organ. As a result, the whole brain is involved in the creation of emotions, which are complex human responses made up of combined feelings, thoughts, and values, and the choices that flow from them.

Biological evolution—with all the contradictions and incompatibilities built into human nature—has also provided us with the potential to devote ourselves to our own moral, emotional, and spiritual development. The heart of this book is that we can rise above what nature and life have given or imposed upon us and instead learn to live by reason, love, and our highest ideals and purposes.

If you are having emotional struggles, including with severe psychiatric diagnoses such as major depressive disorder, bipolar disorder, or schizophrenia, there is nothing the matter with your particular genetic endowment or your brain. Your brain does not have a defect or biochemical imbalance in comparison to the brains of other people (see Appendix A). Our emotional struggles were built into all of us throughout millions of years of evolution and then amplified and manipulated in infancy, childhood, and adolescence. It is up to us to understand these inherent prehistoric problems in being human in order to triumph over and transcend them.

The following chapter looks more deeply into our violent nature—something every one of us needs to keep in constant awareness in order to defend ourselves and also to restrain ourselves.

Chapter 4

THE SOCIAL CARNIVORE
EMERGES FROM AFRICA

Homo erectus looked a lot like us. He can be traced back almost two million years, and his existence probably overlaps with ours. Hundreds of thousands of years ago, he was already killing and butchering large animals. As the first hunter-gatherer, he lived in small bands and probably had the capacity for speech. His jaw was already losing its massive earlier size and large canines, indicating a decline in his use of individual brute force for survival.[1] Yet he survived and eventually thrived among saber-toothed tigers and giant cheetahs. Yes, two million years ago, our ancestor *Homo erectus* was already struggling with the basic human dilemma of being the most violent and yet the most social creature on Earth.

Like us, *Homo erectus* was not strictly a carnivore but an omnivore who ate both meat and vegetation. But evolutionary biologists often refer to humans as carnivores to emphasize that we were more in competition for food with wolves and tigers than with horses and deer.

JUST HOW VIOLENT HAVE WE ALWAYS BEEN?

Remember the archaeological find in England indicating that 420,000 years ago, our ancestors—armed with pointed sticks—hunted, killed, and butchered prehistoric elephants four times larger than modern African elephants?[2] This is not an isolated archaeological discovery. Throughout Europe, there is evidence of early humans killing large herbivores with wooden spears and cutting up their meat with stone tools. Cave sites in Israel have revealed evidence for organized hunting of large animals and sharing of meat 250,000 to 400,000 years ago.[3]

Brian Hare, an evolutionary biologist, and Vanessa Woods, a scientist and journalist, conclude that when humans arrived in Europe, they were "the socially domi-nant carnivore."[4] Although Hare and Woods do not address the problem of our conflicted violent and social capacities, their phrase "socially dominant carnivore" captures those potentially conflicted aspects of human nature that to this day cause us such difficulty in our internal emotional conflicts and our personal relationships.[5]

Hare and Woods explain about the newly arrived human hunters, "Although not able to compete with other carnivores in terms of strength, they came in large numbers."[6] Hare and Woods do not emphasize the advantages of lan-guage and social cooperation, instead focusing on the fact that we humans lived together in larger numbers than Neanderthals and other carnivores of that era. They believe that our combination of ferocity and numbers, along with our ability to throw spears, made us so overwhelmingly superior as hunters that we literally "drove every other large carnivore except wolves to extinction."[7] Our prowess in bringing down giants like woolly mammoths and rhinos gave us such a competitive edge, in their opinion, that it led to the extinction of most other flesh-eating creatures, from saber-toothed tigers to Neanderthals. We weren't just the top of the food chain—we took over the food chain.

Anthropologists disagree about whether the Neanderthals disappeared approximately thirty thousand years ago because we outcompeted them for food, because they interbred with us, because they were annihilated by us, or some combination of the three. Writing for the *Smithsonian*, Joe Alper cites the nonviolent view and then counters with the view of archaeologist John Shea:

> "Brotherly love is not the way I'd describe any interaction between different groups of humans," Shea says. In fact, he speculates that modern humans were superior warriors and wiped out the Neanderthals. "Modern humans are very competitive and really good at using projectile weapons to kill from a dis-tance," he says, adding they also probably worked together better in large groups, providing a battlefield edge.[8]

Once again, the emphasis is upon our unique human combination of ferocity and social skills, as well as our ability to throw spears. However, the ability to hurl relatively puny sharpened wooden sticks (or even stone-tipped spears) against huge beasts with thick hides would itself have been useless if we not been able to do so in a ferocious and yet coordinated and organized fashion.

When you and I are suffering from guilt, shame, and anxiety as if these were our own personal cross to bear, keep in mind that our early human ancestors were almost certainly struggling with similar feelings hundreds of thousands of years ago or more. Early *Homo sapiens* was as willfully fierce and as cooperatively social as we are. Sitting around the campfire with their families a quarter million years ago, our ancestors were probably dealing with as many demoralizing emotions as we are as they tried to inhibit their ferocity while living in such emotional and physical intimacy with each other.

HOW WOMEN EXPRESS AGGRESSION AND VIOLENCE

Some researchers have tried to romanticize and reinterpret human history to make men the violent gender villains and women the peaceful victims. There can be no doubt that men as a group are much more *physically* violent than women, but there is little indication that women are any less aggressive in their basic nature. If only to deal with potentially violent males, women have always had to be aggressive enough to stand up for themselves and their children and to hold their own in dealing with males in their own families and clans. With the strongest males often away hunting or fighting, women have had to defend their homes and children from animal and human predators. When away from camp to carry out tasks such as gathering food and firewood, they also had to protect themselves and any children who accompanied them.

For lack of much prehistoric evidence, researchers have focused on violence as expressed in hunting and fighting, with the usual presumption that men were performing these tasks. But women must have struggled as much as men with the conflict between their willful and aggressive impulses and their loving and empathic emotions. Given that women have primary responsibility for the most challenging task of all—raising children—women on a daily basis have always been required to manage the stressors and provocations inherent in what may be the hardest, most frustrating, and potentially most important and rewarding job in the world. Anyone who helps or knows couples in conflict would be hard-pressed to say whether men or women express more anger in their family relationships. However, men are certainly far more physically and sexually abusive, and continued societal efforts must be made to educate boys and men to respect women and, when necessary, to protect them and to punish male violence against them.

VIOLENCE EVERYWHERE THROUGHOUT OUR HISTORY

Although there is inevitable disagreement among scientists who study the evolution of *Homo sapiens*, the scientific consensus is supported by common sense, indicating that we have been a violent species from the start.[9] Evidence for interhuman violence on a large scale can be found in human remains fifty thousand years ago.[10] Cognitive and experimental psychologist Steven Pinker has aroused controversy by arguing that, if anything, we have become *less* violent with increasing civilization.

Those of us who have taken guided tours of European historical landmarks such as palaces and castles are struck by the repeated tales of unrelenting violence and betrayal, generation after generation, not only between warring nations but within the royal families and domestic religious and political factions. Historical and even ancient writings confirm the impressions that we receive on these tours. Whether we begin with the Iliad and Odyssey or the Hebrew Bible, warfare is inextricable from the oldest stories of humankind. The New Testament, which focuses more upon love than the Old Testament does, nonetheless ends in a violent act of crucifixion that takes place amid political strife in Jewish lands occupied by Roman invaders.

LESSONS FROM BIRDS AND CHIMPS ON CONTROLLING VIOLENCE

Little grey-crowned babblers will huddle up to display against other babblers who come near their boundaries. These cooperative breeding associations of birds sometimes participate in internal disputes, but they rarely display the physical aggression toward one another that they do toward neighboring groups. Skutch observes, "The first point to be emphasized is the amity that prevails among all group members." To minimize "internal conflict," some birds develop a "rank order that assigns each a definite status in the group, and is preserved by means so subtle that they are difficult to detect."[11]

None of the bird groups described by Skutch are predators toward other birds. There are no hawks breeding in cooperative associations. If a powerful aggressive drive is innate in a species and integral to its survival, this aggression would be difficult to turn off for cooperative breeding. Chimpanzees, who also live in "cooperative associations" or tribes, exemplify this problem.

Researcher Jane Goodall, who studied them in their natural habitat, initially believed that the chimpanzees of Gombe were unlike human beings in their peace-loving social relationships. For years, she observed how the chimpanzees resolved conflicts without violence, often with hugs and mutual grooming. She thought our nearest animal relatives could provide a peaceful model for us.

Goodall identified many examples of empathy and generosity among the chimps, but also episodes of violence. In one case, two female chimps hunted down and killed the offspring of other mothers in the group. Another tragedy destroyed the idealistic hope that chimps do not go to war: One group of chimpanzees broke off from the main body and formed their own community. In a prolonged, bloody conflict lasting more than four years, the males of the original larger group of chimps "systematically hunted down and brutally attacked the members of the smaller Kahama community, until nearly all but the adolescent females had been killed or had disappeared."[12] Goodall had to accept that our nearest relatives, and her beloved cross-species friends, are more like us than she initially wanted to believe.

WHY GUILT, SHAME, AND ANXIETY DO NOT INHIBIT WARFARE

There is some debate over whether human beings conducted warfare, or intergroup violence, before the advent of farming. Anthropologists Douglas Fry and Patrik Söderberg, based on their study of modern primitive (foraging) societies, believe that before the advent of farming ten thousand years ago, human beings lived in too-small groups and had too little motivation to conduct wars against each other. Consistent with what I have observed in earlier sections of this book, I strongly suspect that they are wrong and that *Homo sapiens* probably attacked groups of Neanderthals and other humans, including other clans of *Homo sapiens*, even when operating in relatively small bands. The motivations would have included fear; access to scarce resources such as water; and the capture of women of childbearing age, much as Goodall's chimps seized "adolescent females."

However, the question of when warfare began in human history has little relevance to the concept of how negative legacy emotions developed. To this day, these otherwise powerful emotions have little impact on wars against people perceived as alien, different, or foreign. Natural selection did not promote these inhibitory emotions for that purpose. Human survival did not require that we give up fighting against other human groups; instead, our survival may have been enhanced by our warlike capacities. Our legacy of painful emotions biologically evolved to inhibit willfulness and violence *within the family and clan*.

Negative legacy emotions inhibit aggression in conflicts between single individuals known to each other or between small groups of familiar individuals, such as two siblings ganging up on a third sibling. Domestic relationships between couples and between adults and children most commonly trigger demoralizing, self-defeating emotional reactions. These emotions arise to contain the interpersonal expression of willfulness and violence. Consistent with this, Fry and Söderberg found that interpersonal violence persists among primitive societies that exist today, confirming that this kind of aggression was probably characteristic of prehistoric, pre-agrarian societies.

Most of our willful and aggressive tendencies manifest in more subtle ways than outright violence when we feel thwarted, irritated, or frustrated. We may tease. We may make a disgruntled grimace. We may express frustration. We may withdraw in anger.

However, even among relatively rational and loving couples, violence can quickly and unexpectedly come to a head. When a woman feels defensive and put down by her husband and then leaves the room, she is most likely removing herself before she says or does something too damaging to the relationship. When a man starts to feel guilty in a conversation with his wife, and he shuts down and refuses to respond, he, too, is trying to control an aggressive impulse. Our efforts to avoid expressing extreme willfulness or aggression in our intimate relationships often signal that we are dangerously angry.

The next chapter looks at our built-in drives for language, morality, and spirituality and how they help us as social beings.

Chapter 5

INSTINCTS FOR LANGUAGE, MORALITY, AND SPIRITUALITY

It may seem controversial, dismaying, and even degrading to think of ourselves as driven by many instincts, some of which relate to our cultural achievements. However, in animals and especially in humans, instinctual responses are not necessarily wholly determined in their expression by either genetic or environmental factors. Chapter 2 defined *instinct* as "an inborn or genetic capacity for mental or behavioral activities that is characteristic of a species and commonly triggered and shaped in its expression by environmental factors or stimuli." Humans, of course, have enormously wide latitude in choosing how to manage even their most primitive instincts, such as thirst, hunger, sex, and sociability.

I believe that our biologically driven or instinctual social life has three spectacular aspects: language, morality, and spirituality. The social brain has biologically evolved with these three capacities—language, morality, and spirituality—which are inborn but nonetheless find their expression in almost infinitely varied ways.

WHEN DID HUMANS START TALKING?

No one knows for sure how far back language began in the human species, but it may have started with *Homo erectus*, who spread humankind from Africa across the rest of the world some two million years ago.[1] Because the humanlike creature's brain was comparatively small, scientists remain in doubt about how much speech capability he really had. Biologists and textbook authors Jon C. Herron and Scott Freeman estimate that "spoken language arose sometime between 3.3 million and 530,000 million years ago."[2]

I have an intuition about dating the development of language. Our "controlled use of fire" dates back at least one million years.[3] Fire required social cooperation to keep it alive from day to day. People surely gathered around it to stay warm and safe at night. When I imagine my fellow human beings huddled around a fire a million or more years ago, it is hard to believe they weren't chatting up a storm. I would speculate that speech is at least as old as the campfire.

Speech makes cooperation so much easier in hunting and gathering—and in self-protection—that natural selection undoubtedly favored individuals who could communicate with sounds and words. Natural selection probably favored speech for many other purposes as well, including consummating sexual union and raising children.

YEARNING TO COMMUNICATE: THE INSTINCT FOR LANGUAGE

Language is a basic aspect of human social life. It can be viewed as an expression of the social instinct, but it will be treated separately here. A key to our unique social life is the ability to communicate through language. Herron and Freeman confirm that language is an instinct, "both innate and universal."[4] Individuals in every human society communicate by means of speech, as well as by means of gestures and other nonverbal cues or signals. Every child, unless suffering from severe deprivation and mental distress, quickly learns to talk with little or no direct help from other children or adults. The child hears speech and then automatically—that is, instinctually—begins to mimic and to learn how to speak.

As a psychiatrist and therapist, I have long been aware that while speaking comes easily and naturally to children, reading, writing, and the use of more abstract symbols like mathematics do not. Talking comes almost as naturally as walking, while these other endeavors can be extremely difficult and require years to learn, with widely varying results from one child to another. Being able to speak is built biologically into the human brain and into the function of the lungs, larynx, tongue, mouth, and lips to create vocal sounds, and aside from people with certain emotional or physical disabilities, all learn to speak well enough to communicate with others.

Language is inseparable from our social nature and is perhaps the most complex and subtle expression of that overall built-in social instinct that drives us to relate to each other. Human language has been compared to birdsong, which often functions among birds to attract mates, protect territories, or warn other birds of imminent danger. But birds cannot elaborate the kinds of meanings we can.

Meaningful speech requires substantial frontal-lobe and limbic-system functioning—and probably the whole of the evolved brain. While destruction of relatively discrete areas of the brain—for example, by a stroke—can rob us of the ability to speak, the actual generation of *meaningful* speech requires the concerted effort of the whole brain, which creates or enables the expression of our full human capability. Speech is an important reason why our social brains were already so fully developed 150,000 years ago.

THE INSTINCT FOR MORALITY VS. RATIONALLY CHOSEN ETHICS

Morality, as an aspect of our social instincts, appears in every human culture, and its expression begins in early childhood. Children begin to express empathy at about one year, perhaps ahead of when they begin to feel guilt and shame, but not before they can feel anxiety.[5] The empathy expressed by a toddler by sharing a cookie or a hug with a needy friend can grow into a morality of care. Every small child probably at some point complains, "That's not fair." This can foreshadow the later development of mature concepts of justice.

Being *moral*, as used in this book, means adhering to social norms for good behavior, in contrast to choosing a rational set of values to live by. As noted, guilt, shame, and anxiety probably play the dominant role in the development of morality, especially in childhood. These biologically driven emotional reactions are then modified and redirected by cultural evolution, including societal, institutional, religious, and family values. As a result, morality usually consists of a hodgepodge of disorganized values—some that enhance life and some that do not.

Unlike being moral, being *ethical* requires us to choose a mature and rational set of principles for guiding our behavior. The capacity for empathy is probably the most essential innate source of an ethical approach to living.[6] Empathy leads children at an early age to want to share with others and to soothe their suffering. Since the capacity for empathy results from biological evolution and natural selection, it seems reasonable to conclude that good ethics can have biological roots; however, we must use reason to choose which of our biological impulses to live by and how to apply them.

Without distinguishing between morality and ethics, psychologist and specialist in child development Jerome Kagan confirms that morality has biological roots. He observes that children are born with "a large number of psychological properties that are inherent in their genomes," including the ability for language and the ability to "make moral judgments."[7] Similarly, Churchland connects what she calls "brain-based values" directly to our social life, observing, "At the root of human moral practices are the social desires; most fundamentally, these involve the attachment to family members, care for friends, the need to belong."[8]

It is not enough to say that morality has its origin in biological drives. As responsible adults, we are required to distinguish between good and bad morality—that is, we must select our ethics. For example, the "need to belong," which is cited by Churchland, is not necessarily a positive social ethic, since it can lead to obsessive conformity and to reflexive hostility toward strangers.

Much as I do, Churchland roots the origins of "other-caring" in mammalian nursing of its young and connects that to "the emergence of what eventually flowers into morality."[9] There is a direct line between the nurturing and nursing mother and the Golden Rule of "Do unto others as you would have others do unto you." The common core is the profound physical and emotional closeness between mother and infant and the resultant craving to share intimacy and to be empathic that is built into every human being.

The mother's nurturing, feeding, and protecting of the helpless infant as a separate individual outside her own body provides the initial basis for human social morality. It is the paradigm for placing the lives of others at the center of our own. There is no better example of how evolution builds morality into the brain in the form of socially driven emotions. That little shrewlike mammal huddled with its nurslings beneath dinosaurs was indeed, as suggested in the beginning of this book, the progenitor of our human desire for connection with each other and, ultimately, of our higher values and purposes. Nonetheless, ethical living requires evaluating these primitive, prehistoric drives to determine how we wish to shape and direct them in our own lives.

YEARNING FOR SOMETHING OR SOMEONE GREATER THAN OURSELVES

The instinct for spirituality, much like the instinct for morality, takes an infinite variety of shapes under the influence of cultural evolution and human choice and consciousness. I am using the term *spirituality* to encompass many diverse human experiences that call upon or seek higher values, including a belief that love and empathy can and should prevail over more self-centered and aggressive values.

Humanism tends to see values as derived from and based in the human experience as biological entities. It attaches prime importance to human, rather than divine or supernatural, sources of truth and guidance. It emphasizes rational approaches to solving human problems and rejects faith in something greater than humanity.

However, when humanism addresses "humanity" as a whole, it indulges in a philosophical abstraction that rises above or beyond the individual. In doing so, humanism can be viewed as exploring the edges of spirituality, including the yearning for a connection to something beyond, above, or independent from biological or individual existence. A faith in humanity or in human progress is purely a faith and, therefore, can be viewed as essentially spiritual in nature. Given the contradictory and self-defeating impulses that drive human beings— and the often-destructive outcomes—faith in humanity is certainly not rational.

Many people who reject traditional religious ideas nonetheless believe there is something going on in the universe that is greater than they are. To believe that life has deeper meaning than our personal biological survival and that we should choose and act upon higher purposes is a spiritual outlook.

AN INSTINCT FOR SPIRITUALITY

Why would biological evolution lead to the natural selection of human beings with a relatively well-developed spiritual awareness? We can speculate without coming to a solid conclusion. It is probably important that spirituality builds social cohesiveness, enhancing the strength of the community. People in all cultures are united by myths about their origins and by faith in their particular understanding of spirituality. Spirituality can also encourage self-sacrifice that may enhance group survival. It can lend courage in combat and hunting. It can strengthen the bonds of family life and lend value to procreation and children.

The first archaeological evidence for spirituality in humans, in the form of cave drawings and ritual burials, dates back to twenty-five thousand to fifty thousand years ago. By this time, scientists agree, *Homo sapiens* had become a spiritual and potentially religious creature.[10]

I find it touching and enlightening that twenty-seven thousand or more years ago we seem to have had not only working relationships with our dogs but *spiritual* relationships with them! Research by anthropologist Pat Shipman indicates that dogs enabled humans to hunt large numbers of mammoths during that time. *Science Daily* neatly summarizes, "A fragment of a large bone, probably from a mammoth, Pat Shipman reports, was placed in this dog's mouth shortly after death. This finding suggests the animal was accorded special mortuary treatment, perhaps acknowledging its role in mammoth hunting."[11] Shipman may be right that the dog was honored for its hunting, but I like to think that he was loved like a human and buried with his favorite food or chewy toy for the afterlife.

There is earlier evidence of burial with ritual goods approximately one hundred thousand years ago in Israel.[12] Other scientists push back the possibilities of human spirituality to three hundred thousand years ago.[13] There is debate about whether the Neanderthals displayed aspects of it.[14]

All known human cultures, including the five hundred Native American tribes or nations, have had spiritual beliefs, often involving the importance of their community and one or more gods who favored them.[15] Expressing gratitude for what the gods provided and for living resources, such as deer and vegetables, was a shared feature among many or most Indian nations. In every culture, spiritual beliefs have played a central role in the social life of the group. Like language, spirituality usually centers on social activities and bonding. This, in itself, is a strong argument for its instinctual nature—that spirituality is a built-in receptivity waiting to be elicited by our environment, especially our social interactions.

Evolutionary biologist Richard Dawkins is famous for cutting no slack whatsoever in his criticism of spirituality and religion, including the concept of

God.[16] Even Dawkins sees the universality of the human desire to believe and to have faith, although he does so with frustration and outright enmity:

> Though the details differ across the world, no known culture lacks some version of the time-consuming, wealth-consuming, hostility-provoking rituals, the anti-factual, counter-productive fantasies of religion.[17]

Would Charles Darwin have sided with the Darwinist Richard Dawkins in loathing the ideas of religion and God as absurd, irrational, primitive, and destructive? Darwin was critical of religious oppression, but he referred to "religious feelings" as a healthy modifier of instincts and viewed the idea of God as the highest moral accomplishment in man's intellectual development as a reasoning being.[18] He believed that evolution by itself could not have led to "the ennobling belief in the existence of an Omnipotent God."[19]

SPIRITUALITY AND NEUROSCIENCE

In *The Holy Longing*, Connie Zweig writes, "I suggest that there . . . lies within us a will to transcend, a longing for the eternal."[20] She wants to "acknowledge the pervasiveness and worthiness of our holy longing and to place it in the broader and deeper context of human evolution: you will see that your soul's desire is not separate from the vastness of life, but that it participates as an innate and vital part of it."[21]

Dawkins and Zweig agree that spirituality is built into us. Dawkins uses this insight to discredit spirituality, and Zweig uses it to give us a broader perspective and deeper respect. Atheists claim there is an instinct for God built into us and use that fact to "prove" that God is a myth driven by genetics and biology, but others use the same evidence to argue that God designed human beings to seek and to love their creator. Darwin was too thoughtful and philosophically sophisticated to believe that evolutionary biology or science itself could solve the deepest questions about life, including immortality or the existence of God.[22]

The brain's innate capacity for morality and spirituality cannot be used to prove or disprove the validity of beliefs about morality or spirituality. The actual existence or nonexistence of a nonbiological source for morality, spirituality, or human nature will have to be determined by something other than biological evidence, neuroscience, or any other empirically based approach.

Experience teaches me that most people accept or adopt spiritual beliefs based on sources other than scientific analysis or empirically based conclusions about human nature. Most do not rely exclusively on religious teaching, either, especially in Western culture. Usually, people reach spiritual conclusions about human nature, free will, and God by drawing on their own unique combination of family values and religious education, reason, empiricism, intuition, personal experience, revelation, and faith. Ask many, if not most, people with strong faith why they hold their beliefs, and they will talk about their personal spiritual experiences of a guiding hand in their lives without relying on either science or religious texts for proof.

The yearning for spirituality is so deeply embedded in our human nature that even Dawkins cannot escape it. Beneath the surface of his and most other secular and humanistic belief systems lie tightly held beliefs in something greater than ourselves, such as reason, positivism, skepticism, science, ethics, truth, the deification of humanity, or the deification of the earth (renamed Gaia). The merit of these beliefs lies beyond their biological origin or their propagation by natural selection. Biological evolution has resulted in many capacities, such as our willfulness and violence, that are potentially destructive to human life and personal development.

FREE WILL

A fundamental premise of this book is that the human spirit and free will can triumph over what nature has given us. Another premise is that there is no inherent contradiction between science and spirituality.

I agree with evolutionary biologist Stephen Jay Gould, who criticized sociobiology for its reductive view of humanity. That our social and intellectual capacities have evolved biologically and continue to have an obvious biological basis does not mean that they are fully determined by biological evolution, the structure of our brains, cultural evolution, or environmental factors in childhood. Evolutionary biology cannot tell us whether our thoughts and decisions are predetermined. Free will remains a personal, subjective, philosophic, and theological question that empirical science cannot answer by itself.[23]

Pragmatist and psychologist William James hits the philosophical mark when he points out that the staunchest advocates for determinism conduct their lives as if making choices and exercising free will. When individual human beings stop thinking and acting as if they have free will, they spiral downward into emotional and mental collapse and become dependent on other people. I am in agreement with psychiatrist William Glasser, who places individual choice at the center of psychotherapy, emotional recovery, and successful living.

Most important for this book and for your life, every successful human being I have known has displayed profound faith in his or her ability to make freely chosen decisions, even in the face of threatening circumstances and oppression. Every hero exemplifies for us how a person can surmount real-life obstacles with courage, force of will, and sound values.

Our spirituality is one more reason we have these giant frontal lobes inside our heads. Spirituality requires subtle, complex brain capacities. Because it is a higher human capacity, it is one of the first to go when the frontal lobes and limbic system are damaged by accident or by psychiatric interventions such as lobotomy, electroshock, and psychiatric drugs.[24] When higher brain functions are disrupted, spirituality is crushed, along with the finer social capacities—in particular, empathy and love.

THE LIMITS OF SCIENCE

Although with difficulty and grave limits, the human sciences can attempt, as this book does, to make empirical or fact-based observations upon which to build theories about human nature and human activity. Science, however, has its shortcomings. It is only as good as the people who contribute to it. Scientific conclusions can be distorted or corrupted by culture and politics. These days, what masquerades as the "neuroscience" of psychiatry is little more than an extension of pharmaceutical marketing into research funded by drug companies and their allies. The psychopharmaceutical complex promotes false links between psychiatric disorders and brain disorders in order to convince people that there is a rationale for taking psychiatric drugs.[25] Ironically, when people do have genuine brain disorders, such as Alzheimer's or Parkinson's disease, or even a mild concussion, psychiatric drugs will make them *worse* by adding additional biochemical dysfunctions to the ones already caused by the physical illness or trauma.[26]

Many authors have tried to make reductive and simplistic scientific arguments for a genetic or biological receptivity for spiritual beliefs. For example, according to physician and spirituality researcher Andrew Newberg and psycho-spiritual counselor Mark Waldman, "researchers found evidence that different types of hemispheric interactions in the brain might bias an individual toward embracing or rejecting creationist and evolutionary perspectives."[27] The idea that creationist and evolutionary beliefs involve different parts of the brain is an egregious example of the corruption of neuroscience. The article Newberg and Waldman cite is "The Serotonin System and Spiritual Experiences."[28] This is the same serotonin system that is active in every corner and crevice of the human brain from the frontal lobe to the brain stem, down the spinal cord, in the bloodstream and even in the gut. It is the same serotonin neurotransmitter system that pharmaceutical companies and their minions want us to believe is at the root of many "mental disorders" that require drug treatment.[29] Now, it is the seat of our higher spiritual life? All of the brain, and not merely one of several hundred neurotransmitters, is involved in higher human functions. To point to one or another particular neurotransmitter as key to some specific mental function is a simplification with no scientific basis, but it piques the public interest, *seems* scientific, and encourages the false belief that intervening in one or another of these systems with drugs might somehow have a beneficial effect.

The discovery of mirror neurons in monkeys has caused considerable excitement in neuroscience and the media. These brain cells activate not only when an individual performs an action but also when the individual observes someone else making the same movement. If this turns out to be true in humans, it may shed some minimal light on how we learn from each other on a reflexive level. Unfortunately, neuroscientific euphoria has led to unfounded speculation about how this might explain everything from empathy to how the mind works.[30] Almost certainly, formulating a neuroscientific basis for empathy—let alone the whole mind—will require a much more thorough understanding of how the entire brain functions.

Ignorance of the complexity of brain function and an overestimation of what we know about it lead many people to believe the most simplistic assertions about the relationship between brain function and mental or emotional activity. This is a perverse faith. In reality, we have no idea how the brain participates in the creation of specific emotions or even in emotionality in general. The brain-mind connection remains, at present, cloaked in darkness.

Newberg and Waldman also get caught up in neuromania by trying to link the personal development of spiritual practices to new brain pathways. They observe, "We believe that people who engage in spiritual practices are learning to alter neural patterns of cognition voluntarily, in ways that promote measurable degrees of happiness, compassion, and peace."[31] This is a misleading statement. The same "learning to alter neural patterns" could be said for anything from reading comics to cheering for our favorite team on television. As we have seen, childhood experiences create and also prune neuronal pathways. All mental activity probably has a related process in the brain, so anything we do—and especially anything we do repetitively—is going to alter the brain in some way. To say that any specific activity alters neuronal patterns is a meaningless observation. All human activity alters the brain. Beyond limited kinds of observations such as those made in this book, neuroscience has very little practical information to offer us in dealing with our emotional problems and our lives. The dominant fake neuroscience is doing considerable harm by giving the false impression that your brain is in charge of you and your life. Do not be seduced by the false neuroscience that seeks to convince you that you are the victim of your brain's biochemistry. If anything, our brain biochemistry is the victim of us and our environment. We can improve our brain function by improving ourselves emotionally and spiritually and by making our social and physical environment more conducive to our well-being.

ARE EMOTIONS "HARDWIRED" INTO OUR BRAINS?

Human evolution and neuroscience offer encouragement about our individual capacities to improve our lives. Especially when we are emotionally overwhelmed, our feelings and thoughts can feel as if they must be hardwired into our brains. We seem to be at the mercy of our emotions. At times, our demoralizing, self-defeating inhibitory emotions seem to keep coming at us no matter what we do. This might lead us to think of the brain as a tangle of cement and wire, when, in fact, it is an organ as subtle and complex as our own identities.

From playing video games to starting a new profession, the brain has a great capacity to learn. It should have been no surprise that the brain grows new connections and networks throughout life, and when injured and under stress, it can even grow new neurons (*neurogenesis*).[32] Recent studies have discovered growth factors, such as brain-derived neurotrophic factor (BDNF), that influence the development of new brain cells and new connections among brain cells.[33] Growth factors and neurogenesis become especially active at times of physical trauma and environmental stress.

Even this recent view of the brain's plasticity does not come close to capturing how well our brains can adapt and grow in response to how we choose to live. The human brain is not a bunch of wires. It is not pliable like soft plastic. If the brain looks like anything familiar, it is wet pudding or Jell-O packaged in thin cellophane. How that odd amorphous stuffing inside our skulls can express a human being lies wholly beyond our current understanding. We need to give up the image of hardwiring and instead think of the brain with the same awe as we think of the human as a person, being, or soul.

We are far more likely to prosper if we focus on ourselves, rather than our brains, as both the source of and the solution to our problems and if we work both on our own and with others toward a better life. Empower yourself by realizing that you—like millions have done before you—can improve your psychological and spiritual state. You can do it through the hard work of developing your wisdom and understanding and by practicing better approaches to how you feel, think, and make choices. It is a cornerstone of good psychology and psychotherapy that our individual brains and minds provide us the power to transform our individual lives, much as humankind has transformed our societies over the past 150,000 or more years.

EVEN BRAIN INJURY DOES NOT STOP PEOPLE FROM PROSPERING

The concert of the brain, mind, and spirit has enormous strength and can overcome great impediments and distress. I frequently work with patients who have endured serious brain damage and dysfunction from psychiatric drugs or electroshock and, more occasionally, from illness or accident. This damage is sometimes so severe that it shows up on gross neurological examination in the form of abnormal reflexes and sensory or motor dysfunctions. Sometimes, it shows up on brain scans or in neuropsychological testing, as well as through clinical evaluation. The injuries are to the biological machinery—the brain itself. Yet, time and again, I have seen my patients triumph over persisting injury to their brains to live effective and satisfying lives.

Because the mind and spirit can grow in strength and compensate for physical damage to the brain, many brain-injured patients actually end up living more happy and fulfilled lives than before. They learn to reject their self-defeating legacy emotions and to move forward with the guidance of self-determination, sound ethics, and love. Despite any persisting physical discomforts or problems with memory or concentration, they are no longer mired in emotional distress because their psychological and spiritual liberation makes their lives better than ever.

A BETTER WAY TO THINK ABOUT OURSELVES AND OUR BRAINS

Given the demands of being human, with our social life, language, higher mental processes, creativity, and spirituality, it is no wonder that the human brain is complicated far beyond our current capacity to understand its most rudimentary functions. Beware of anyone who claims to know how your brain biochemistry is influencing your mind or behavior—and beware especially of anyone who wants to do something to your brain in order to improve your mental and emotional functioning.

The basic physiological effect of any physical intervention into your brain is to disrupt and suppress the brain's function, sometimes resulting in detectable physical damage. Although the initial effect of dulling or euphoria may provide some relief for emotional suffering, the ultimate result is harmful to the recipient's brain, mind, and sense of self-efficacy. Drugs cannot change human nature and its built-in problems and conflicts; drugs can only impair the function of our brains.[34]

Rather than imagining the human brain as a simple biochemical machine that develops imbalances that need correction, we will prosper if we think of our brain as complex beyond all current human understanding; highly orchestrated within itself; and built by not only biological evolution but also cultural evolution, our upbringing, and our entire lives to date, including personal choices and values.

Reject the idea that feelings of guilt, shame, or anxiety, or moods of despair and depression, are caused by genetic and biomechanical defects that can be fixed by physical or pharmacological intrusion. Our most painful and destructive emotions are an inevitable part of being human—but we can learn to manage them and even triumph over and transcend them.

The subtle and as-yet unknowable complexity of our brains reflects our complexity as human beings, and our complexity as human beings can help explain why our brains far exceed our current scientific understanding. We need a respectful and treasuring attitude toward the human brain.

Solutions to our mental and emotional problems always require making changes in our mental and emotional processes through understanding and hard work, often with the help of those who care about us and sometimes with the help of professionals. We have to begin with ourselves and find ways to change our emotions, our attitudes, and our choices in order to improve our mental lives and, hence, our overall lives.

Chapter 6

WE ARE BORN HELPLESS AND DEPENDENT

We human beings are born into a state of abject helplessness, and this contributes greatly to our emotional conflicts and suffering as adults. At birth, we cannot hold up our heads, let alone obtain nourishment or protect ourselves. After being born, we enter into a long period of helplessness and corresponding dependence on the people around us. We begin learning to be human—we develop our personalities and our social identities—during a time in our lives when we are relatively helpless and immature and, indeed, when our young brains are still growing at a rapid rate. Our enormous need for human companionship, touch, physical and emotional intimacy, and love cries for attention, and inevitably when there are lapses in any of these, we feel more helpless and dependent.

Although this prolonged helplessness and dependence prepares us to become functioning adults, it also creates psychological problems that can last throughout our lives. In particular, it makes us very susceptible to guilt, shame, and anxiety, as well as excesses of anger and numbness. From infancy into adolescence, and even into young adulthood, we remain dependent while trying to become increasingly independent and social.

Because of this combination of helplessness and dependence, as children, we develop emotional responses, draw conclusions about life, and make decisions for ourselves—all before acquiring adult brains and achieving adult mental maturity. Much of what we experience, learn, and decide in childhood and adolescence will turn out to be self-defeating, sowing the psychological seeds for emotional pain and failure in adulthood. If we are neglected or abused in childhood, then we will be overloaded with these negative emotions.

To help fulfill our potential, we can unlearn the damaging lessons of our first one to twenty years while simultaneously learning more mature ways to manage our emotions and guide our lives. We can become most successful in life when we are most free of childhood helplessness, along with guilt, shame, anxiety, and excessive or chronic anger and numbing, and when, instead, we develop independence in combination with the greater fulfillment of our enormous desire for satisfying social relationships.

HELPLESSNESS THAT IS ALL IN OUR HEADS

In infancy and childhood, our helplessness and dependence is not the result of our emotional or psychological attitudes; it is our real, objective condition. Because we must rely upon siblings, parents, and other older humans for our survival and growth, and because we so desire their love and companionship, we are readily compliant with them and more prone to inhibit our willfulness and aggression toward them.

As we mature, it becomes necessary to distinguish between this *objective* helplessness and psychological or *subjective* helplessness.[1] Subjective helplessness, in contrast to objective helplessness, is an attitude, not a reality. It is emotional or psychological in origin.

As a dramatic and poignant example, an adult can be rendered almost as objectively helpless as an infant after an accident severs his spinal cord and leaves him quadriplegic. Yet many courageous individuals overcome this grievous physical and emotional trauma and loss. Despite their objective helplessness, they refuse to become subjectively helpless. They reject *feeling* helpless or having a helpless attitude and instead focus on rehabilitating themselves. They retake control over their lives in order to remain or to become loving, productive individuals.

A central task throughout our lives is, first, recognizing our helpless feelings in order to reject their influence over us and, second, taking charge of our lives with new and better approaches. Otherwise, we remain at constant risk of being overwhelmed with helplessness or its manifestations in the form of guilt, shame, anxiety, anger, and numbness.

THE CATASTROPHE OF SLIPPING INTO SUBJECTIVE HELPLESSNESS

In childhood, our survival depended on loudly expressing our objective helplessness in order to draw the attention of caregivers. In adulthood, unfortunately, any expression of psychological or subjective helplessness becomes potentially catastrophic. Individuals who appear helpless or vulnerable in public may attract helpful attention, but they are also likely to attract predators, such as con artists, rapists, and robbers. Adults who act helpless within the family generate enormous amounts of fear and self-destructive emotional distress in other family members.

When we act helpless, we broadcast that we are in desperate need of a response from other human beings. This can lead to drastic interventions, including forced psychiatric hospitalization and treatment. In my clinical and forensic experience, when adults persistently act helpless, they are at high risk of being hospitalized against their will, heavily drugged, or electroshocked.

Nothing is more self-defeating in an adult than subjective helplessness. In dealing with the challenges of living, the most serious obstacle to successful living is this self-destructive belief, unconsciously imported from childhood, that nothing we think or do will matter and that our minds and lives are not under our control. This subjective helplessness always leads to bad outcomes in adulthood.

All children express feelings of helplessness, especially when they get frustrated or overwhelmed. If feelings of helplessness have an evolutionary function, it is to gain the attention of adults. Adults are primed to respond with nurturing to an infant or child who expresses helplessness through crying and nonverbal signals. Unfortunately, adults can also respond with resentment and anger, especially if the child's distress stirs up their own feelings of helplessness along with a load of primitive emotions.

Sadly, subjective helplessness is encouraged in children and adults through misguided child rearing and many of our culturally evolved institutions. Modern societies are replete with school environments, religious teachings, and government policies that reinforce childlike subjective helplessness and dependent behavior in adults.

Subjective helplessness is the common denominator of all negative legacy emotion. It, too, is self-defeating and inhibitory. In many ways, it is *the* underlying self-defeating legacy emotion. It guides us toward dependence on others, even when this dependence is unnecessary or harmful, and it encourages us to succumb to feeling inhibited and paralyzed by painful emotions that order us to be compliant. If we delve deeply into these emotions, we will find feelings of helplessness, often associated with a sense that love and satisfying relationships are a lost cause.

Feelings of guilt, shame, and anxiety are inseparable from their underlying feelings of subjective helplessness. Sometimes, the connection is obvious when we use our negative legacy emotions to justify or explain our inaction and helplessness. We say, "I'd feel too guilty to do that," "I'd end up embarrassed if I tried that," or "I'm too anxious to do anything like that." Making us feel helpless fits with these emotions' biological evolutionary function of inhibiting us so that we do not act willfully or aggressively. The evolutionary purpose of negative legacy emotions is to stop us dead in our tracks when our assertive or aggressive emotions cause conflict within our intimate relationships, especially during childhood.

WHAT CAUSES AN EXISTENTIAL CRISIS?

In psychology and psychiatry, an existential movement was very influential several decades ago. Psychiatrist R. D. Laing, in the *Politics of Experience*, placed the origins of human psychological suffering, including that of people diagnosed with schizophrenia, in existential crises typical of the modern age. Laing made a huge contribution by criticizing the assumption that some people are "mentally ill" and, therefore, inherently different from the rest of humanity. He made clear that all of us struggle with the same human issues. However, I believe Laing erred in seeing severe emotional suffering as "existential" in origin—rooted in the search for meaning in life—when, in fact, most such suffering is caused by processes from biological evolution and natural selection that make us susceptible to self-defeating, demoralizing emotions in our personal relationships.

Under the rubric known as terror management theory, there have been numerous attempts to relate psychological attitudes, as well as human society and culture, to our unique awareness of our own mortality.[2] Our need to be with others, for example, is interpreted in part as a defense against the fear of death. I have not found this kind of theoretical thinking particularly useful in my own life or in counseling others. In therapy, such ideas tend to distract the individual from facing difficult choices, seemingly irresolvable conflicts, and tangled primitive emotions.

In my personal and clinical experience, it is not that the reality of death causes guilt, shame, and anxiety. Rather, guilt, shame, and anxiety make people fear death. Adolescents, whose lives are commonly embroiled in negative passions, fear death far more than older, more emotionally secure people who live much nearer to death.

Shame can make us feel small, powerless, and meaningless in relationship to other people, and it can lead to dreary speculation about our place in the universe rather than an enthusiastic engagement with life. Guilt can make us question our own value, and anxiety can shake our confidence in life and cause enormous self-doubt and demoralization. Are these emotional reactions existential in nature? Are they driven by experiencing a spiritual void, a meaninglessness in the universe, or the inevitability of death? No, they result from our biological capacity to become demoralized and emotionally paralyzed by painful emotions, especially when dealing with conflict within the family.

There are, of course, genuine existential issues in life. If we are actively engaged in life, we are likely to confront these issues every day. Is there something more to life than my material existence or mere survival? How do I explain evil? What are my highest values? Can I choose to live by my principles? Should I? What does it mean to live a life based on love? How do I pursue, identify, and act upon the meaning and purpose of life? Am I doing enough for other people? Does it make sense to take on a new risk consistent with my principles and ideals? Do I have the courage?

Those of us who devote much of our lives to dangerous reform work have to decide on a daily basis what sacrifices to make and what risks to take. Although these decisions may seem more dramatic when we are confronting powerful medical interests, huge corporations, and government agencies, the same kinds of challenges arise in everyday living—in each of our efforts to raise children, to maintain an honest and loving adult relationship, and to do work that is honorable and contributes to the community.

ADOLESCENCE, PSYCHOSIS, AND IDENTITY

Adolescents and those who are experiencing an acute psychotic episode are likely to frame emotional pain in existential terms, but they are suffering from guilt, shame, and anxiety imposed on them by prehistoric biological evolution and prehistoric childhood experiences.

When we feel emotionally crushed, disabled, or on the verge of personal extinction—when we no longer feel like we belong to the human family—we are caught in the grip not of existential questions but of primitive, prehistoric emotions. When freed of these emotions, we are much more able to rationally evaluate the meaning and purpose of our lives.

Our prehistoric emotional reactions can destroy our sense of self or identity and even our will to live, producing a "live or die" internal conflict that, in the extreme, can result in suicide. People struggling with psychosis are losing their identity, sanity, or ability to deal with reality, but the causes are closely tied to feelings of abject humiliation, usually with a large component of childhood neglect, rejection, or abuse.

I have worked with people caught in the throes of psychosis who felt they were drowning in shame. Overwhelmed by humiliation, they felt as though they were shrinking into nothing and on the verge of disappearing. Although it is important to acknowledge that the struggle feels like life and death, and can have life-and-death implications, demoralizing emotional reactions are driving the despair.

Individuals in the psychiatric reform movement have reported to me that they have recovered from psychosis by sheer willpower. They realized that their minds, and hence their lives, were coming apart and made a colossal effort to regain control of themselves.

In my experience as a therapist, recovery usually begins when an individual embroiled in psychosis begins to trust that he or she can develop a relationship with another person without being humiliated and emotionally destroyed in the process. The reassurance, comfort, and understanding of loving family members can make all the difference. As I have confirmed in my own private practice, the best therapies for so-called schizophrenia or any emotional "breakdown" involve drug-free or largely drug-free interventions by caring therapists who work with the designated patient and family members.[3]

When an individual becomes strong enough to self-examine, recovery from psychosis can include identifying the humiliation and its sources in evolution, childhood, and adolescence, coupled with the individual's self-determination to overcome and replace disabling passions with more uplifting ones. If the most emotionally battered among us can learn to give up dependence and helplessness, even of psychotic proportions, then there is hope for us all.

Chapter 7

WHY NONE OF US ESCAPE EMOTIONALLY FREE FROM CHILDHOOD

From toddlers to preadolescents, human children display enormous energy that brims over and creates management problems for adults. A robust sixteen-month-old can run an adult into the ground. On top of that, a healthy child, when thwarted, will often ramp up the energy level and become even more self-assertive and aggressive. Violence in the form of throwing objects, scratching, kicking, and hitting is common. Children cannot help but run into emotionally disabling conflicts with adults, many of which will leave lasting effects.

LIKE A DOG STRUCK BY LIGHTNING

The relatively secure lives of well-loved and protected puppies illustrate the impossibility of growing up without developing some irrational emotional responses. My wife, Ginger, and I have always owned Shetland Sheepdogs, or "Shelties." At the time of this story, we owned Blue and Cavie. One day, we were walking the dogs in our neighborhood in broad daylight when a lightning bolt struck a lamppost three feet away from us. The flash and bang were so loud that we reflexively clutched each other while the dogs scattered into a tangle of leashes.

After that incident, we could predict when a storm was coming because Cavie would try to crawl out of sight into a protected corner of the room. It was impossible to explain to her that a lightning strike so near us was a chance event that was not likely to be repeated. We couldn't explore with her the possibility that her anxiety was the result of not only the ear-shattering lightning strike but her owners' reaction of momentary terror. It was also impossible to get across to the frightened dog that being indoors added immeasurably to her safety. During the remaining years of her life, Cavie was imprinted with terror at a rumble of thunder so distant that our human ears could not detect it.

Meanwhile, our other Sheltie, Blue, seemed to get through the experience without noticeable distress. The same differences in emotional reactivity occur in children, who respond in their own ways to similar or the same experiences: one may react with guilt; another, with shame, and anxiety; and yet another, without much concern.

Many dog owners share my unfulfilled fantasy of training dogs to fetch the newspaper, especially on cold, rainy mornings or before we feel like getting dressed. My first Shetland Sheepdog, Ted, was a very swift learner. Without instruction, he learned to cross busy, multilane Wisconsin Avenue in the DC suburbs without a leash and responding to hand signals he had picked up on his own. But he would have nothing to do with retrieving a newspaper. Then, I noticed that he didn't even want *me* to fetch it. He would scurry off in fear as I came back to the house with the newspaper under my arm. It was easy to deduce that he'd been threatened and beaten with a newspaper before I adopted him as a one-year-old. Now, the very sight of a folded newspaper lying on the ground—or, even worse, in my hands—terrified him.

Being a small child is not unlike being a puppy. Frightening but inexplicable things happen all the time and then become embedded in our subjective experience of life. We grow up into adults who harbor a variety of emotional reactions that make no sense in terms of our adult lives. The emotional reactions are self-destructive because they cause emotional suffering and inhibit our choices and actions while having little relevance to the real-life situations we face.

Remember that biological evolution embedded the emotions of guilt, shame, and anxiety in our genes and that childhood triggered them before we could make choices or even fully understand them. Lying mostly outside our capacities to remember and to evaluate, they are nearly as prehistoric as our built-in biological drives. Even if they served some purpose in socializing or training us as children, in adulthood they cause unnecessary suffering, cloud our consciousness, seem to take over our minds, and inhibit or misdirect our choices without regard for reason or ethics.

Like my Shelties who were terrorized by a lightning strike or by being hit with a newspaper, we reexperience negative childhood emotions such as guilt, shame, and anxiety regardless of whether this makes rational sense in terms of our current lives. Fortunately, even if we cannot recall the origins of these self-defeating emotions, we can recognize them for what they are and refuse to let them drive our lives.

Developmental psychologist Jerome Kagan describes these early moral lessons in children and relates them to the experience of puppies:

> A child's suppression of actions that were punished, such as spilling a glass of milk, could be treated as the first sign of morality. It is probably impossible for parents to avoid rebuking children on some occasions. The parent's unexpected command and excited facial expression alert the two-year-old, create a state of uncertainty, and evoke visceral schemata for past unpleasant experiences of cold, pain, and hunger. Children quickly learn that spilling food is followed by a feeling of uncertainty, and they suppress this act. This first stage of morality resembles the conditioning process involved in teaching a puppy not to urinate on a rug.[1]

Kagan's description of the infliction of primitive morality on the child and its similarity to dog training makes clear why prehistoric emotions cannot be used in mature adulthood as the standard for mature ethics and conduct. They are too primitive and potentially irrational in their origin. They are built-in, relatively inflexible responses unsuitable for adult decision making.

When Kagan writes about "a feeling of uncertainty" associated with earlier painful experiences, he is describing anxiety. Kagan's vignette illustrates how anxiety, like guilt and shame, acts as an inhibitory emotion, building prohibitions into the child's mental life.

ACCEPTING DEFEAT AS CHILDREN AND ADOLESCENTS

When a child is one, two, or three years old, or even five or six, he cannot understand abstract concepts, such as, "You can try to get anything you want, as long as you do not bully or exploit people and as long as it won't harm you." When a child bites, hits, or screams in order to have his way, the child rarely, if ever, can make rational sense out of why he is feeling thwarted, threatened or punished.

What seems rational to the adult—punishing a child for screaming indoors, eating off the floor, or running into the street—may make little sense to the child. Instead of "Don't touch the stove," the child will learn, "Dad is scary when he's angry." Instead of "Be careful about strangers," the child may learn, "Mom wants me to be afraid of people."

The child learns, for example, "I cannot do whatever I want to do," "I cannot always trust my own judgment," "I don't know what's good for me," and, "Having fun gets me into trouble." The child learns all this without any self-awareness and often without any memory of the critical events.

Children love to touch things. If a child is hit on the hand, however gently, the child may be seen later on to hit himself to thwart his own desire to touch. Or the child may look at the object he wants to touch and instead tell himself, "No. No."

The child's self-inflicted physical or verbal warnings are outward manifestations of the internalization of guilt, and perhaps of anxiety or shame, depending on how the child has been chided or tends to respond. If the child gets the idea that she is bad or naughty, guilt will be instilled. If the child is teased or ridiculed, then shame is likely to result. If the child is given exaggerated or confusing signals of danger, then anxiety may be instilled. Many times, there will be great disparity between the emotional lessons children draw from their experiences and what they will need to succeed in adulthood.

Unfortunately, parents often feel overwhelmed by the needs and activities of their children and thus find it difficult to be at their best or to maintain consistency in their child-rearing practices and attitudes. Mom and Dad can end up feeling frazzled and frustrated. The child's excitement about life begins to generate negative responses from the adults. Once again, the child learns confusing lessons that contribute to her pattern of emotional reactions.

Even with the best parents and ideal circumstances, children will inevitably undergo experiences that bring about self-defeating emotional reactions. One child may have to endure a series of bad ear infections that cause doctors and parents to inflict painful treatments on him. This may engender anxiety and lead to distrustful attitudes he cannot explain as an adult. Another child may lose the beloved nanny who raised her and cared for her for the first five years of her life. Without ever remembering the nanny, she may, as an adult, experience inexplicable fears of abandonment in close relationships due to this loss.

Because of problems or confusions of their own, parents go astray and end up teaching and enforcing unnecessary inhibitions. For example, they may emphasize that "selfishness" is bad in and of itself rather than teach a balance between self and others and encourage empathy by kindness and by example. The result, again, will be deeply embedded emotional reactions that frequently interfere in the adult's life.

Every child's initially uninhibited zest is reined in, sometimes abruptly, during the first several years of life. This is perhaps necessary and, at any rate, inevitable. It can lead to difficulties being spontaneous in adulthood.

Every child does need psychological or emotional methods for inhibiting anger and thoughtless behavior. Fear of consequences has limited value for a highly social being. When fear of consequences alone inhibits behavior, the child tends to become devious and dishonest. The child's natural sociability becomes twisted into scheming.

To function socially, children internalize the inhibitions, regardless of their rational or ethical basis. Even if these compulsive inhibitions may be useful in childhood before the development of judgment and self-control, they have no place in a rational adult life.

Regardless of how benignly or lovingly adults respond, there are dangerous consequences for being angry as a child. Anger causes the child to feel cut off and to withdraw from his parents or other caregivers. Although self-inflicted, the anger brings about feelings of abandonment and loss. The angry child may even push the adult away, hide, or run away; but, in doing so, the child ultimately experiences the terror of being isolated and alone, utterly separate from the people he needs for emotional and physical survival. From running away to throwing temper tantrums, the means the child adopts for handling anger are often self-defeating, especially as the child grows older and reaches adulthood. These family dramas may seem silly and of little consequence to parents at the time, but the child is learning how to handle fear and helplessness by means other than confrontation and anger.

Without enabling the child by giving in to his demands, parents need to respond in a gentle, kind, and loving fashion that reassures the child that their relationship has not been damaged and that everything will be all right. When the child calms down, parents will rarely need to refer back to the child's out-of-control or manipulative behavior. Life can be resumed in a loving manner. If another outburst seems to be brewing, the child can be gently reminded that he never gets anything he wants when he behaves disrespectfully.

TRYING TO PARENT WITHOUT IMPOSING NEGATIVE EMOTIONS

Every normal child and adolescent will, at times, become extremely self-assertive and aggressive. As children, all of us test the boundaries and the patience of our parents. Our task as parents is to teach our own children which behaviors are and are not allowed, and to do so in a firm and loving manner by instruction and example.

As parents, we want to avoid as much as possible inflaming our children's self-punitive and destructive emotions. Because these emotions are biologically driven and because life is full of stressors and trauma, it is inevitable that all children will develop these feelings on their own, as well as from the effects of other people and life experiences.

Meanwhile, parents should avoid eliciting or reinforcing these painful and ultimately self-defeating emotions. Parents need to work on the premise that they can raise their children with love, guidance, and nonpunitive limit setting. Parents can try to avoid instilling guilt, shame, and anxiety without fear of adverse consequences to a child's behavior. The built-in tendency to experience these emotions, combined with inevitable stimulation of them from other people and the environment, will see to it that our children feel these demoralizing emotions whether we want them to or not. Our job as parents is to do our best to minimize these painful emotions in their lives while encouraging their natural desires for emotional intimacy, empathy, and love.

Bad behavior often grows in proportion to the attention paid to it. What a child does wrong should receive minimal attention compared to what a child does right. Children thrive on unconditional love, reasonable limit setting, and child-parent relationships that are so strong that children want to please their parents.[2]

Chapter 8

NATURE'S ANGER MANAGEMENT

Biological evolution and childhood built guilt, shame, and anxiety into us, and our childhood and adolescence triggered and directed their expression. Although all three of these emotions have the effect of inhibiting willfulness and anger, each does so in a different manner. Often, we can identify which emotion is at work by how it redirects or deflects anger and blaming.

HOW ANGER IS DIRECTED

When we feel *guilty*, we become self-critical, we hold ourselves responsible for doing something wrong, and we take the blame, even when we do not deserve it in the opinion of others or by any recognizable ethical standard. In guilt, the painful emotions seem to come from inside ourselves. We feel like our own worst enemy. As our anger builds up in a conflict, guilt makes us feel inhibited about expressing criticism or anger against anyone but ourselves. We turn our willfulness and aggression inward. If we imagine, instead, standing up for ourselves, we foresee being overwhelmed by even more guilt.

When we feel *ashamed*, we feel put upon, embarrassed, or belittled by others, or we feel lesser when we compare ourselves to others. In shame, the painful emotions seem to emanate from outside us. Shameful feelings seem inflicted upon us by other people or circumstances that make us feel worthless and powerless. As our anger builds up in a conflict, shame inhibits our willfulness and aggression by making us feel too intimidated, powerless, or insignificant to assert ourselves. We fear that if we were to take a stand, we would fail and undergo further humiliation. Shyness and a tendency to withdraw from others are the direct results of shame, and they prevent us from being self-assertive.

When we feel *anxious*, we are feeling frightened, confused, and over-whelmed by life itself, rather than by anyone or anything in particular. Anxiety is a state of fear that destroys rational thought and enforces emotional stupidity. Instead of turning anger inward or making us feel too impotent to express it, anxiety disperses our anger, leaving us with nowhere to direct it. We fear that expressing anger would be futile and only make things worse, since nothing can be done about our situation. If we do get angry, we will direct it at "life" or "bad luck" or "the way everything goes wrong at once" rather than at another person. As a result, our assertiveness is undermined and our anger dispersed.

HOW BLAME IS DIRECTED

When we feel guilty, we direct blame inward at ourselves. It can feel like *us against ourselves*. If we fully embrace the demoralizing self-punitive emotion, we decide that we deserve to feel guilty, and we may even seek punishment or inflict it on ourselves. The whole process feels internal. We are hard on ourselves.

When we feel ashamed, we direct blame outward, and it feels like *them against us*. Feelings of shame are usually attached to what someone else has said or done to us, or how we perceive our standing in relationship to someone else or to other people in general. The whole process feels external. We believe that other people find us unworthy, and we may begin to fear they are right.

In anxiety, blame is directed nowhere in particular, and it feels like *life is overwhelming us*. Instead of us against ourselves, or them against us, we cannot identify a source for our helpless feelings, other than our own inability to do anything about our lives. It may feel like we can't cope with the world or that life is stacked against us. We feel confused, uncertain, and fearful, as if we lack the competence or ability to deal with the challenges ahead of us.

THE UNDERLYING FEELING OF HELPLESSNESS

Although our biologically driven negative emotions render us relatively help-less by stifling our self-assertiveness, we often do not experience ourselves as feeling helpless. When guilt dominates us, we often feel powerful, but in a harmful way. Paralyzed by the thought that we will hurt other people, we stop pursuing our own interests or desires. When we succumb to guilt, it leads to depression and subjective helplessness. As helpless as we feel, we probably will not admit it because that would make us feel guiltier or perhaps ashamed.

When shame dominates us, we never want to admit to feeling helpless. It is too humiliating. Nonetheless, in our hearts, we feel like nothing we can do will ever have the impact or gain the attention we desire. We may act shy and withdraw from others without admitting that we feel overwhelmed. To bolster our sense of worth, we are likely to think critically of other people—as if we are rejecting them when, in reality, we feel rejected.

When anxiety overcomes us, we may feel too ashamed to tell people that we feel utterly helpless, but, unlike people overcome by guilt and shame, we feel the helplessness in its raw and seemingly inescapable form. Out of pride, we may tell ourselves and other people that we are trying as hard as we can, but, inside, we are giving up.

THE DEFINING CHARACTERISTICS OF EACH LEGACY EMOTION

While the following distinctions will be refined and nuanced as research continues, each of the demoralizing legacy emotions has certain defining or nearly defining characteristics:

- Guilt functions as a negative legacy emotion by making us feel bad or punitive toward ourselves. We are inhibited from asserting ourselves for fear of hurting other people and enduring increased guilt.
- Shame functions by making us feel powerless or insignificant and worthless. We are inhibited from asserting ourselves for fear of failing and enduring increased shame and humiliation.
- Anxiety functions by making us feel overwhelmed, confused, or emotionally dispersed. We are inhibited from asserting ourselves because we feel too helpless to try and fearful of making things worse.

Feelings of subjective helplessness lie beneath each of these emotions. When we are sufficiently overwhelmed by guilt, shame, or anxiety, we feel paralyzed, unable to act, or extremely helpless.

Because negative legacy emotions are inflicted on children when they assert themselves, guilt, shame, and anxiety tend to suppress overall self-assertion regardless of the merits or need for it. These inhibitory emotions become a self-defeating damper on the human spirit, inhibiting our choices and, ultimately, our lives.

DRIVEN INTO COMPULSIVE ANGER OR EMOTIONAL REMOTENESS

It's so demoralizing to be tortured endlessly by negative emotions that many people lapse into the basically defensive positions of anger or numbness. Anger can manifest as oversensitivity or defensiveness. We feel irritable and find ourselves easily provoked. Eventually, we decide that our anger can keep us from being disregarded, steamrollered, and exploited. And because we humans have pride, we decide that being angry in itself shows that we are undaunted, bolsters our sense of self, and proves that we have some power left.

If "everything" makes us angry, or if people notice how often we seem angry, we are probably trying to escape underlying feelings of humiliation. Persistent feelings of anger usually come from feeling belittled, misunderstood, or rejected. School shooters, spree shooters, and mass murderers typically have an emotional profile of seeming shy and feeling humiliated. They react against and compensate for feeling ashamed by striking back against real or imagined perpetrators. Withdrawn and feeling rejected and humiliated, they try to prove that they have power over other people by hurting and killing them.[1]

In addition to anger, numbness is the other main response to feeling emotionally tortured and demoralized. We "just don't care" and we "don't want to feel anything." Eventually, we become uncomfortable with feeling so indifferent and out of touch with our emotions, but, by then, we are like a pressure cooker that will explode if we do not continue to clamp down on our emotions.

Compulsive anger and numbing are surface emotions. There is always something more upsetting lurking beneath in the form of guilt, shame, or anxiety—and, ultimately, feelings of childlike helplessness.

Anger and numbness often occur together. After becoming too angry, we often feel numb. In my forensic work, people who commit violence almost always become numb afterward. Sometimes they were already numb leading up to the violence.[2]

Often, we can gain insight into ourselves simply by refusing to luxuriate in anger or retreat into a state of numbness. Only then do we discover how overwhelmed we feel with guilt, shame, anxiety, or some combination. We can then begin to deal with the root emotions and, ultimately, with the helpless feelings that lie at their heart.

If we feel bored, out of touch, numb, or otherwise unresponsive to others, and if nothing seems to enliven or interest us, we are trying to suppress painful feelings. Life is so inherently exhilarating and challenging to human beings that we become numb or seemingly bored only as a last resort. Again, our task is to unearth and deal with the underlying negative legacy emotions of guilt, shame, and anxiety, along with anger and numbness, and, ultimately, to replace them with more life-enhancing feelings, thoughts, and purposes.

Chapter 9

WHEN ABUSE OVERWHELMS THE CHILD

You may not have experienced severe abuse, or it may turn out that you have experienced more abuse than you thought. Regardless of our personal experiences, understanding how people respond to abuse can help us to develop a deeper understanding of negative legacy emotions.

THE BIG PICTURE

Most of what we know about relationships and life, we first learn in childhood, largely from our parents and caregivers. We learn to speak their language. We may go to their church. Often, we adopt their politics and sports teams—at least, for a while. We get many of our interests from them. More subtly, most of what we know about relationships, we learn from watching them as models and experiencing how they treat us. Not surprisingly, childhood has a profound impact on how we relate to other people and think about life in our adulthood. Neglect and abuse can leave lifelong emotional scars.

After childhood, adults who undergo severe stress and trauma for only a limited time can also incur enduring emotional scars. This is how posttraumatic stress strikes down soldiers after exposure to combat (see chapter 10). What is it like when *childhood* is a war zone of child abuse and neglect or of domestic conflict and violence? Children are far more helpless and impressionable than adult soldiers. Their abusers are family members instead of foreign enemies. They have no combat team to rely on. The exposure lasts for years on end, and they can see no end to their tour of duty. They never volunteered for this war zone and can see no higher purpose, such as defending their nation. No wonder abused and neglected children grow into adulthood with suffering that can interfere with successful living and require help for recovery.

PERPETRATORS MANIPULATE VICTIMS
WITH GUILT, SHAME, AND ANXIETY

Unfortunately, child abuse is common. In a random sample of 1,442 people in the United States surveyed by mail, 14.2 percent of men and 32.3 percent of women reported sexual abuse and 22.2 percent of men and 19.5 percent of women reported physical abuse.[1] Child abusers, bullies, and perpetrators of domestic violence manipulate their victims by arousing their negative legacy emotions; keeping them in an emotionally helpless state of submission; and preventing them from fighting back, leaving, or reporting the abuse. An enormous amount has been written about child abuse, bullying and domestic violence.[2] Many recent books and websites focus on how abuse produces guilt and shame. However, until now, no one has developed a unitary concept of all three negative legacy emotions, including how they act as enforcers of abuse by crushing self-assertion and resistance. Guilt, shame, and anxiety are the emotional hammers that pummel people into submitting to abuse, and they are the source of most of the emotional suffering that results.

NEGLECT VERSUS ABUSE

Parents and caregivers can harm infants and children directly with physical, emotional, and sexual abuse. They can also harm infants and children indirectly by neglecting their fundamental needs for companionship, socialization, unconditional love, and rational discipline, as well as for basic necessities such as food, clothing, shelter, safety, education, and medical care.

The term *neglect* can be misleading, since deprivation can be at least as devastating as more obvious abuses. It can also be inflicted intentionally. Depriving children of nurturing love or failing to teach them limits and boundaries can contribute to the ruination of their lives.

Neglect can be subtle. A parent may show preference for one child over another, provide one child with new clothes and another with hand-me-downs, or inflict harsher punishment on one child than the others. When a child feels that it is intentional, neglect can leave her feeling especially worthless, even unworthy of life.

THE RANGE OF ABUSERS

Parents, siblings, other relatives, houseguests, and babysitters abuse infants. Anyone with access to a baby is a potential abuser. As the child grows older, the list of potential abusers expands to include teachers, coaches, religious authorities, neighborhood children, and classmates—once again, anyone with access to the child.

In thinking about your own life and why you feel so much guilt, shame, and anxiety, remember that any number of perpetrators in your infancy and childhood could have abused or neglected you. Avoid being stuck on an idea that nothing happened to you to cause all your upset. Between biological evolution and the hazards of childhood, we have all been primed for and exposed to enough trauma and stress to explain our emotional suffering in adulthood. In short, you did not generate these painful emotions on your own.

"BUT I'M DIFFERENT"

People who have been neglected and abused frequently decide they are different from other people. They understand that others have essential worth, deserve to create good lives, and are able to find happiness, but they put themselves in another category, one reserved for the undeserving and unable. Treat your feeling of unique unworthiness as an emotional signal that perpetrators abused you and then claimed you deserved it. Since you are reading this book, I suspect you are unusual in an admirable way—in the strength of your determination to live an ethical and rational life.

DO PEOPLE "JUST COMPLAIN" AND "MAKE UP STORIES" ABOUT THEIR CHILDHOODS?

During parental conflicts, unscrupulous adults can sometimes induce children to tell false stories of abuse. However, the overwhelming tendency of both children and adults is to minimize or deny the neglect and abuse they have endured. In therapy, patients of all ages resist recalling and talking about painful childhood experiences, especially those imposed on them by their own families.

Most victims do not even view neglect as a form of abuse. They see their childhood deprivation as a natural and accepted part of family life and probably due to circumstances beyond their parents' control. They make excuses for their parents, such as, "Mom and Dad never paid much attention to me, but they both had to work," "Dad never said he loved me, but his whole family was like that," "Dad gambled and sometimes couldn't put food on the table, but he had a hard life," "Mom did have a terrible temper, but she never meant it," or, "Maybe they did all those awful things, but I know they loved me."

People rarely exaggerate abuse and neglect; instead, they repress most or even all memory of it. On several occasions, as a psychiatrist, I have been able to corroborate abuse and neglect through family meetings and police evidence. In each instance, none of the victims could remember the whole spectrum of emotional and physical pain inflicted upon them in the family.

We want to avoid making excuses or blaming our parents, brothers, and sisters. As noted earlier in this chapter, this can leave us confused and make us feel that "there's something wrong with me." Keep in mind that when we are suffering emotionally as adults, we are probably struggling with emotions driven by our biology and childhood experiences. Even when the suffering has been precipitated by recent traumatic events, such as illness, rejection, job loss, or death of a loved one, Stone Age emotional reactions are likely fueling or at least contributing to our suffering.

THE POWER OF EARLY CHILDHOOD STRESS AND TRAUMA

It is now well documented that abuse and neglect of infants and children profoundly impairs their present and future lives.[3] Starting in the 1950s, psychiatrist and psychoanalyst John Bowlby studied the strength of attachment between infants and toddlers and their caregivers. He found that the quality of an infant's or toddler's emotional growth depends on the maintenance of a stable attachment with a sensitive, responsive, and consistently present caregiver. When infants and children are neglected or abruptly deprived of their familiar caregiver, they can lapse into profound states of anxiety, withdrawal, and depression.

Attachment theory continues to emphasize the pivotal importance of physical and emotional closeness between small children and their parents. Jeanne Stolzer, a professor of child development, summarizes the advantages of breastfeeding for infants, including higher IQs and fewer mental and emotional problems. In addition, mothers benefit psychologically and emotionally. Attachment theory correctly sees most psychiatric disorders as originating in dysfunctional nurturing in childhood.

Scientific studies of premature and normal-term infants show that "kangaroo care" with cuddling brings lasting improvements in the infant's physical, intellectual, and emotional health.[4] We are born to be bathed in love and human connection, and, for our entire lives, our emotional well-being will depend upon the quality of our relationships with each other.

The lives of chimpanzees further demonstrate the importance of early attachments. Jane Goodall's sensitive observations of chimpanzee life cycles in the wild demonstrate that the quality of early mother-infant relationships influences the later quality of the chimpanzees' emotional lives and self-care.[5] In *Toxic Psychiatry*, I draw lessons for understanding humans from Goodall's description of how a little chimp named Flint suffered from inadequate child rearing at the hands of his elderly and infirm mother.[6] Flint developed excessive dependence, anxiety, and other emotional problems. After his aging mother passed away, he fell into depression and died. Flint was 8½ years old at his death, by which time chimps have usually become self-sufficient, but his mother's inadequate childcare had left him unprepared to manage after her death.

Unfortunately, modern psychiatry has regressed into arguing that "mental disorders" have little or nothing to do with child rearing and family life, instead focusing on concocted biological theories. In the past, psychiatric journals much more frequently published epidemiologic studies linking childhood trauma to adult emotional disturbances.[7] Now that it has become beholden to the drug companies, psychiatry makes believe that the emotional distress traceable to childhood is actually caused by genetic and biochemical aberrations. Tragically, Jane Goodall shows more empathic understanding for chimpanzees than modern psychiatrists show for their human patients.

CHILDHOOD STRESSORS THAT FALL SHORT OF ABUSE

Here are examples of less traumatic aspects of childhood that nonetheless could have caused you or family members considerable guilt, shame, and anxiety:

- divorced parents
- aloof, emotionally unavailable, or poorly engaged parents
- parents who unleashed angry outbursts at each other or the children
- coming home to an empty or indifferent household after school
- losing the center of attention to a new baby
- feeling unable to keep up with an older or more successful sibling
- feeling nothing you ever did was good enough for your mother or father
- parents who abused alcohol or generally took poor care of themselves
- parents who were depressed and anxious
- parents who did not support you at school and showed little interest in your accomplishments
- parents who lived vicariously through your accomplishments
- being hospitalized and feeling lost, alone, and abandoned
- being ill more than other children
- a father who clearly favored boys over girls, making his sons feel unrealistically superior and his daughters inferior
- a mother who confided too much in you, especially about her disappointments with your father
- being frequently teased or bullied by peers or siblings
- a mother who hinted that you should remain home to take care of her in her old age
- parents who made their own lives much more important than yours by being unavailable for or inattentive to your needs

Such relatively commonplace childhood experiences can lead to heavy loads of negative legacy emotions.

CHILD-NEGLECT MEMORIES GET BURIED

Neglect is by far the most common abuse reported to child-protection agencies, and most of these reports occur in the first year of life.[8] Neglected infants do not receive sufficient medical care. They go hungry or live in squalor. They are left alone for sustained periods. Often, their endless crying draws the attention of concerned neighbors. The frequency of child neglect suggests that our emotional reactions may have been shaped by such events in our first few years of life, leaving us with no memory of what happened and driving us with emotions that have no relationship to adult values or needs.

MORE GROSS CHILD ABUSE

We can learn a great deal about the development of negative legacy emotions by looking at the impact of more severe forms of child abuse. Here are examples of abuse that lie outside the ordinary but are representative of the childhoods of people who are heavily burdened by guilt, shame, anxiety, chronic anger, and numbness:

- A mother believes her daughter's birth caused her to give up all her dreams and repeatedly reminds her daughter, "I could have had a life if you hadn't been born."
- A big brother repeatedly humiliates his little sister, digs his knuckles into her flesh until she screams, and shames her about her body, while the family dismisses this behavior as, "Boys will be boys."
- A toddler is hit with wooden spoons, belts, or hairbrushes.
- An eleven-year-old girl is forced by an uncle to commit sexual acts.
- A mother threatens to put her four-year-old son in an oven and to carve him up like a turkey.
- A seven-year-old child is told that she should have been aborted and will be sent away to an orphanage.
- A mother burns her son's hand on a stove for "talking back."
- A father tells his preadolescent son that he is a "fag" and a "sissy" and will never be a man.
- A child endures "spankings" by a furious and out-of-control father.

- A mother, when upset in the kitchen, regularly chases and hits her children with spoons, spatulas, and anything else she can grab.
- A father shoots his son's pet dog to show the boy "what you're in for if you don't shape up."
- A mother locks her scantily clothed nine-year-old outside to huddle in the snow on the back porch.
- A father routinely comes home drunk while the children tremble in terror that he will lose his temper and hit them.
- A child is repeatedly excoriated by her parents with hateful statements like, "You're not worth the garbage we feed to the pigs" and "No one else will ever want you."
- A mother drives her car into a creek, screaming, "We all need to die!" with her three children huddled in terror in the backseat.
- A father towers over his little son, smashes him across the face, and throws him against the wall for refusing to say, "Yes, sir."
- A mother says she will kill herself to shut up her three small children and starts cutting her wrists in front of them until they beg her to stop and promise to be good.
- A big brother tries to stop his little brother from crying in bed at night by crushing his toes with pliers. Amid bloodcurdling screams, the parents listen from the next room, hoping it will "teach the brat" to stop keeping them up at night.
- A four-year-old is locked in a closet for a day without food or water by her stepmother.
- A father turns his daughter into a sex slave from ages nine to twelve, while her mother warns her and her older sister not to tell anyone or it will "destroy the family" and cause both girls to be "taken away to some awful place."

Beneath every severe psychiatric diagnosis or emotional disability, there is a personal story of trauma and abuse. It would be better to dispense entirely with psychiatric diagnoses and the medical model. We are much more likely to achieve emotional freedom by understanding and triumphing over our individual life stories of abuse and neglect.[9]

WITHDRAWING INTO FANTASIES,
THEN NIGHTMARES AND HALLUCINATIONS

When living amid terror and humiliation, children often withdraw further and further into a private world as their only means of escape. Beginning at age three or four, a child may withdraw by escaping into pleasant fantasies, such as stepping into a movie or storybook or being with a seemingly caring celebrity.

Eventually, the reign of terror destroys any hope for escape into happiness, and the child's imagination deteriorates into a waking nightmare. The obliteration of trust and shattering of ties to other people creates a collapse or fragmentation of mental processes and hampers the child's willingness or ability to distinguish between fantasy and reality.

We are such social beings that our brains are literally made of our relationships with each other. Children's sense of reality is based on relationships with their parents, caregivers, and siblings. When fear and distrust take over, they shred the fabric of the child's reality. Emotionally wounded children can be driven into a nightmarish world where trauma rules their imaginations and fantasy life. The horror of being physically, emotionally, or sexually tortured and humiliated takes over their impressionable brains and minds. Healthcare professionals diagnose them with depression, anxiety, bipolar disorder, or schizophrenia and prescribe toxic medications, but what they need is psychological, social, and educational help.[10]

Many abused children are brainwashed by their parents with warnings like, "I can read your mind" and "I can see your thoughts," so that there is no safety and no escape, not even within the inner sanctum of their personal feelings and thoughts. As adults, they harbor fears that their parents, even when dead, are continuing to monitor everything they think and say. Their venomous voices can be heard as hallucinations.

In therapy, I have worked with successful and highly educated men and women whose parents' voices inside or outside their heads were so terrifying that they were afraid to even *imagine* saying, "I want you to leave me alone."

VOICES CLEARER THAN REALITY

Hallucinated voices can seem "realer than real." They usually say the same nasty things that the abuse victims heard in childhood: "You're a piece of crap," "Nobody will listen to you," "Nobody cares what happens to you," "I'm all you've got," "You will die if you tell anybody." The terrorized child, now grown, complies with the voices and avoids disclosing the abuse to anyone.

Until they find an able therapist, victims of auditory hallucinations may not realize that the voices sound like their abusive parents or grandparents or older siblings. They may not realize that the voices are actually repeating nasty accusations and threats they heard in childhood. Often, they are saying mean things to themselves in unison with the voices.

Visual hallucinations can be even more terrorizing than voices and, again, more vivid than ordinary reality. Like auditory hallucinations, visual ones usually involve fragments of experiences from childhood. Faces peer in through the windows. Shadows turn into lurking monsters. A threatening figure stands over the bed.

A man in his thirties periodically hallucinated witches entering through the walls of his locked apartment, driving him to cower beneath his bed. Although the man did not remember it, the police later confirmed that he and another child were the victims of abuse involving parents who sometimes dressed as witches.

SEEKING INVISIBILITY

Abused children surreptitiously study the faces of other people to detect any threatening hint of disappointment or irritability. They do so while trying to avoid any direct eye contact that might bring down a rain of insults or blows for "insolence." They carry these habits into adulthood, always afraid that something dreadful is about to befall them.

Because their abusers are unpredictable and because even a hint of resentment, let alone fighting back, can result in catastrophic punishments, these children learn to restrain any behavior that will draw attention to them. They try to become invisible. Partly as a result, abused children can develop a robotlike demeanor. As adults, they continue to avoid being noticed. Fear of their own overwhelming feelings drives them to robotic emotional numbness. They suffer from indescribable onslaughts of guilt, shame, and anxiety.

OVERCOMING SEVERE ABUSE

Adult victims of severe child abuse and neglect can overcome their emotional terrors by the same means as everyone else: the three steps to emotional freedom described in Part 2 of this book. They have a more difficult path than most, but they can learn from their vulnerability and from the evil they have endured and become unusually empathic and helpful to others. Some become psychological and artistic trailblazers.

For some abuse victims, the nagging and terrifying voices gradually dim and eventually play little or no role in their lives. Others learn to manage or control the voices, sometimes turning them into friendly companions. Many continue to struggle with the voices while living worthwhile lives.

For several decades, there have been groups of "voice hearers" in Europe and North America, most of whom seek self-empowerment by rejecting psychiatric diagnosis and drugs and insisting that they are normal.[11] The movement of voice hearers is a tribute to the human spirit and to how people find the strength and courage to make the most of their lives.[12]

ADULT VICTIMS OF CHILD ABUSE BLAME THEMSELVES, NOT THEIR ABUSERS

One might expect that children subjected to horrific emotional, physical, and sexual abuse would be especially prone to blame their parents for their problems, but, as we have seen, it is not necessarily so. Instead, the greater the mistreatment the child endures, the more likely the child is to self-blame and to feel overwhelmed with self-defeating negative legacy emotions. Even after learning that they were abused in childhood, most adults continue to blame themselves while remaining unable to express anger against the perpetrators. In childhood, they were warned that speaking to anyone would have severe consequences, even torture and death—and that no one would believe them anyway. They cannot shake that brainwashing.

Why do the most abused individuals heap the most blame upon themselves? Children face horrific reactions from their abusers if they stand up to them. As a result, bouts of seemingly inexplicable anxiety, along with shame and guilt, can overcome adults when they first start to think or talk about their childhoods.

Even after they have grown old enough to leave home, some abuse victims continue to live with their perpetrator family members. Newspaper reports describe older children or young adults killing their abusive parents instead of walking away from them. Many victims of severe abuse feel too helpless, powerless, and trapped to escape or to report their parents to authorities. Instead of going free, in a helpless rage, they kill the people who have tormented them.

The great majority of abuse victims do not become abusive adults. Many consciously decide as children never to be cruel like their parents, and they find the strength to leave home and construct independent lives. Nonetheless, they wrestle mightily with the combined results of biologically built-in self-destructive passions and severe childhood abuse.

"BUT I KNOW MY PARENTS LOVED ME"

If adults can convince themselves that they were loved as children, anything seems forgivable to them. With few exceptions, people who reveal childhood abuse at the hands of their parents will add, "But I know they loved me." Most adults seem unable to bear the thought that they were unloved as children. Not being loved is the most devastating aspect of neglect and abuse. In addition, the excuses adults make for their abusive parents are, in part, to protect themselves from facing how much they suffered and how much they were betrayed. Excuses may also allow them to perpetrate against their own children without feeling so guilty. After all, if their parents can be forgiven for not controlling their behavior, they can also be exonerated. The sad truth is that not all parents love their children. Even worse, some parents gain a sense of power and take twisted gratification from systematically hurting and demeaning their children.

Some acts of abuse are seemingly hateful and even sadistic. The perpetrator purposefully violates the victim's sense of security and worth.

Victims of severe abuse can help their emotional liberation by acknowledging that the perpetrators were acting hatefully and certainly did not love them at the time. Seeing the source of their painful emotions as inflicted upon them from the outside by a hateful abuser can help victims in rejecting the self-defeating impact of these feelings. In cases of severe child abuse, criminal prosecution can bring some closure to the victim and at least temporarily prevent the perpetrators from inflicting themselves on new innocents.

DO WE FORGIVE OUR ABUSIVE PARENTS?

Individual circumstances, personal ethics, and spiritual and religious beliefs go into deciding whether to forgive our parents, older siblings, or other caregivers and people in authority who abused us. Whether we forgive or not, a preoccupation with emotional injuries from childhood can lead to persistent feelings of victimization and helplessness in adulthood. The goal is to understand, as much as we can, the childhood origins of our self-defeating legacy emotions in order to identify them and impose reason and sound ethics upon them.

We can best take care of ourselves by not allowing our childhood abusers to continue harming or upsetting us in adulthood. Often, this means overcoming guilt, shame, and anxiety in order to completely separate from the perpetrators and, when appropriate, to report them to the police.

GENERATION RX[13]

It is particularly tragic to prescribe psychiatric drugs to suppress the normal or natural responses of children to stress, trauma, neglect, and abuse. Not only are these drugs abusive in themselves, they lead to neglect of the children by school personnel, families, and therapists who no longer think they need to make an all-out effort to help them.[14]

Children who have suffered neglect and abuse, such as those in foster care, are the most vulnerable to further neglect and abuse caused by psychiatric drugs.[15] Unfortunately, all of America's children are now at risk. The Centers for Disease Control and Prevention (CDC) found that, according to parent reports, 11 percent of all children and 20 percent of high school boys were diagnosed with attention-deficit hyperactivity disorder (ADHD) by a health-care provider. Nearly all of them are likely taking psychiatric drugs.[16] Many more children are being drugged for more serious diagnoses, including bipolar disorder, autism spectrum disorders, oppositional defiant disorder, conduct disorder, and various anxiety and depressive disorders.

Long-term outcomes for children started on stimulant drugs for ADHD are tragic. The drugs have no proven positive effects, but they have proven harmful effects that worsen over the years. Multiple studies, including a recent multicenter study, have failed to show that stimulants for ADHD have any positive effect after a few weeks or months. The only demonstration of any effect at thirty-six months of use was confirmation that the drugs inhibit the growth of children.[17] In the long term, the drugs have not been shown to improve behavior, social skills, feelings of well-being, or academic performance.[18]

Individuals started on these drugs, compared to a control group, more often become lifetime mental patients. They experience shrinkage of their brains, lower IQs, higher suicide rates, higher death rates, more drug addiction, more hospitalization and incarceration, lower socioeconomic status, and overall decreased quality of life. These negative outcomes are documented in a series of studies lasting several decades that followed boys originally diagnosed with nothing more than mild hyperactivity.[19] The authors want to blame these tragic outcomes on the mild hyperactivity the men supposedly displayed several decades earlier as children. But it was the diagnosing and drugging of these essentially normal children that put them on a disastrous path to lifelong dependence on brain-damaging drugs.

Diagnosing children stigmatizes them and robs them of their confidence in learning to manage themselves. It makes teachers, parents, and other caregivers stop thinking about better approaches.[20] It too often leads to lifelong diagnoses and drugs with severe adverse consequences. All this should be no surprise. Drugs cannot raise children. Based on a review of current scientific information, I have recently called for professionals to work toward an eventual ban on giving psychiatric drugs to children.[21]

Psychiatric drugs cannot correct the causative stressors and trauma in children's families, schools and communities. Rather, they start a child on a potentially disastrous trajectory of drug–induced disability.[22] Unwitting parents and teachers are not the villains. The pharmaceutical industry, the psychopharmaceutical complex, and their collaborators (so-called experts) who promote these drugs are responsible for this tragedy. They are massive child abusers.

HEROIC CHILDREN

How does a small child, in the midst of horrific betrayal and suffering, decide never to harm anyone else? It is not simply guilt; the children are making conscious decisions about the right way to behave. For me, the mystery remains how some children manage to find such remarkable moral strength while enduring unimaginable abuse.

When I find that people have remained true to their higher ethics despite horrific childhoods, I view them as heroes. Without minimizing the physical courage for which we often award medals, I am sure it takes far more courage for children to keep alive their inherent loving tendencies through years of torment. I work with these heroes on a daily basis in my practice and meet them through our Center for the Study of Empathic Therapy.[23]

We can be heroes in our own lives by overcoming our negative inheritance from biological evolution and childhood and becoming the persons we have always wanted to be.

Chapter 10

BULLYING, DOMESTIC VIOLENCE, AND POSTTRAUMATIC STRESS

Human violence sullies every arena of human life. This chapter examines the harmful effects of bullying in the schools, domestic violence, and posttraumatic stress in general. You may find that it applies to you or the lives of your family and loved ones more than you first imagined.

Much like child abuse in the home, abuse in the wider society and in adulthood relies on rendering the victims helpless by triggering guilt, shame, and anxiety in them. If abusers could not overwhelm victims with the helplessness induced by these emotions, many more would fight back and free themselves from oppressive people and situations.

BULLYING INFLICTS NEGATIVE EMOTIONS AND SUBJECTIVE HELPLESSNESS

The Centers for Disease Control and Prevention (CDC) conduct surveys of school bullying, defined as "any unwanted aggressive behaviors."[1] Students from the ninth through twelfth grades were asked to report any bullying during the previous twelve-month period. Twenty percent of girls and boys (girls slightly more than boys) reported being bullied on school property.[2] In the same survey, 22 percent of girls and 11 percent of boys reported experiencing electronic bullying by e-mail, chat room, website, or text message. These are self-reports, and many youngsters probably felt too ashamed to admit, even to themselves, how often or how much they had been bullied.

There are now many books and websites aimed at understanding and preventing bullying. What is largely missing is an understanding that bullies victimize children, adolescents, and adults by demoralizing and controlling them with negative legacy emotions. The power of bullying and domestic violence, much like the power of child abuse, requires subduing the victim with guilt, shame, and anxiety—and, ultimately, overwhelming feelings of helplessness.

Bullying can occur almost anywhere during childhood, including at home, school, church, and sports activities. Often, it takes place on school buses or when youngsters are walking home. In recent years, bullying has taken on new dimensions and ferocity through cell phones and social media. A few hateful words spread on the Internet can humiliate a child to the point of suicide.

Children of all ages are susceptible to shaming by their peers and by authorities, including parents and teachers. In the teenage years, shaming can be devastating, and even through college, bullying remains a major cause of suffering.

Well-meaning adults often turn a blind eye on bullying because thinking about it triggers their own emotional suffering and helplessness as bullied children. Instead of dismissing bullying as normal or inevitable, we owe it to ourselves and any victims we know to reexamine our thinking, consistent with the three steps to emotional freedom in Part 2. Then, we can rationally decide how best to protect our loved ones from outsiders or each other.

Whether in school, in the workplace, on the sports field, or at home, those in charge must create an atmosphere of zero tolerance for bullying. Adults are central to stopping bullying by exerting moral authority and enforcing a policy of quick and decisive intervention.

A LIFETIME OF TORMENT

Being bullied as a child can lead to a lifetime of torment from guilt, shame, and anxiety. In therapy, most men and women report painful experiences of bullying in school that still afflict them emotionally. Here are some representative examples:

- A twelve-year-old girl was followed home from school by a neighborhood bully who so frightened her that she developed stomachaches and headaches every day before school. She frequently came home late because she had to skirt the bully's neighborhood on her walk.

- A five-year-old girl was already shy when she entered the first grade, where she was teased, pushed, and groped by boys in her class. This never let up, and her childhood and youth were marked by fear and humiliation until she graduated from high school.
- A girl in high school had some quirky habits that marked her as a target in the eyes of the most popular clique of girls. They made her life miserable for three years, until she was practically friendless. She attempted suicide.
- A little boy was much taller than his classmates and yet a little younger, which made him seem immature and awkward. This led other boys to ridicule and bully him, often by hitting him on the arm, twisting his arm, or punching him in the stomach. By the fourth grade, he was convinced that he must avoid other boys.
- A fourteen-year-old boy was effeminate, and other boys heaped ridicule upon his sexual identity until he grew suicidal.
- A boy in elementary school who was shorter than his classmates was called "dwarf." His parents could not understand why he never wanted to go to school.
- Two older boys held a high school freshman down and tormented him with spit and dirt in his face and mouth. The next time they started up with him, he cracked one on the side of the head with a rock. He was suspended and mislabeled in the system as a potential violent delinquent.

In *Medication Madness* and other books and articles, I describe the important role that exposure to psychiatric drugs has played in many school shootings. But the single most consistent contributing factor, present in nearly every case, has been bullying. Almost all the attackers were shy loners, some of them seemingly psychotic and some not. In almost all cases, an awkward, quirky, isolated youngster decides at last to fight back and "show them." He gets the "last word" by unleashing violence on his classmates and often escapes by killing himself.

TEENAGE GANGS AND CLIQUES

Most people can recall being teased, ridiculed, and shamed by their teenage peers. In describing the experiences of an adolescent named Alyson, Maia Szalavitz and Bruce Perry observe, "Even the kindest, most sensitive person may behave ruthlessly under the influence of peers; again and again, history has shown that in-group pressures can erase empathy for outsiders."[3] That adolescent girls and boys can attack each other with extraordinary emotional and sometimes physical ruthlessness confirms how potent these years can be in stimulating negative legacy emotions. The aggressiveness of teens toward each other demonstrates the constant conflict between humanity's violent and social aspects, which both reach new peaks in adolescence.

When teenagers gang up on a vulnerable peer, it is not far-fetched to see in their actions the same impulses that motivated our prehistoric ancestors to band together to assault strangers and large animal prey. Teenage cliques and gangs usually justify their emotional and physical assaults by identifying themselves as somehow "special" and their victim as somehow "different." Thus, in effect, they identify the victim as not belonging to the family or clan. Teenagers' coexisting drives for intense relationships and intense aggression exemplify this inherent conflict in human nature—the conflict that led to the natural selection of people genetically endowed with guilt, shame, and anxiety to inhibit their willfulness and violence.

The long perspective on shame can be very helpful. Remember that your feelings of shame are not really *your* feelings at all. They have nothing to do with you. They are your heritage from biological evolution and from childhood and youth, including contributions from those who bullied you.

DOMESTIC-VIOLENCE VICTIMS ARE
CONTROLLED BY NEGATIVE LEGACY EMOTIONS

Many men and women remain in abusive relationships because they feel too guilty, ashamed, or anxious to leave them. Because of abuse in childhood, they may not clearly recognize abuse in adulthood, they may feel abuse is inevitable, or they may compulsively try to at last get love from or "fix" abusers who resemble their parents.

Domestic violence usually refers to oppressive adult relationships in the home. It includes shoving, hitting, and physically restraining partners; raping or sexually abusing them; and threatening or intimidating them. It can also include keeping partners isolated from family and friends, controlling their access to money, preventing them from obtaining or holding a job, and stalking them. Perpetrators in the home try to demoralize, manipulate, and control their victims.

Many women report that although they were physically assaulted, cruel words are what they most painfully remember. It is impossible to exaggerate the power of hateful words in stirring up demoralizing legacy emotions.

An abusive domestic relationship reinforces childhood experiences of abuse and can, over the years, transform an otherwise-competent adult into someone who feels dependent, helpless, and unable to leave the oppressive partner. Realistic limitations and fears can also trap women in abusive relationships. Men tend to have greater financial resources than their wives do. Since they have cut their wives off from other people, they also have greater social resources and more people who will side with them. The women have often been taking care of children instead of working outside the home, and often their husbands have prevented them from getting jobs. As a result, their lack of financial and social support thwarts their desire to escape.

Such imbalances of power make women afraid to go to court in defense of themselves and their children. They fear reporting husbands who will retaliate by further abusing them or their children. If they want to separate or seek divorce, they fear having to share unsupervised custody with an abusive father—or, even worse, losing custody to him. Abusive male partners will often threaten to harm them and the children if they try to leave, and so attempts to separate become the most dangerous time for women.

Despite the practical barriers to women escaping from abusive relationships, negative legacy emotions remain probably the biggest impediment, especially the feeling of subjective helplessness engendered by years of bullying. Regardless of our situations, the more that we can overcome our guilt, shame, and anxiety, the more able we are to make realistic assessments and to free ourselves from abuse.

OUR INALIENABLE RIGHT TO EMOTIONAL SELF-DEFENSE

The Declaration of Independence speaks of our inalienable right to life, liberty, and the pursuit of happiness. We cannot fully achieve this right without also exercising an ironclad right to protect ourselves from emotional torment and aggression. For example, many people have trouble standing up against abuse from their families or in-laws. They submit because standing up for themselves brings up tormenting emotions from childhood. Instead, they try to get used to the emotional punishment. Here is a key to life: none of us grows so strong that submitting to emotional abuse will not tarnish or even ruin our enjoyment of life and our ability to love.

In some situations, we may choose not to exert the right to emotional self-defense. If physically ill patients in a hospital behave abusively to their doctors and nurses, the staff cannot simply walk away from them. We are obligated to protect their lives. If our dependent young children abuse us, we cannot abandon them. We are obligated as their parents to teach them respect, which will increase their emotional safety and ours, eventually allowing love to prosper.

Adults commonly continue to accept abuse from their aging parents. They speak of their obligations and the desire to avoid upsetting an elderly mother or father. However, they could insist on being treated respectfully at last. In doing so, they would give their abusive parents the chance for an improved relationship and a measure of redemption before the end comes. If an abusive parent rejects this generously offered opportunity, it may be wise for their child to exercise the unconditional right of emotional self-defense and stop or reduce spending time with them.

Another common situation occurs when men or women in an abusive domestic situation are reluctant to break up the relationship because of children or on ethical and religious grounds. Similarly, students or employees may find themselves at the mercy of an emotionally abusive teacher or boss but believe it is in their best interest to endure the situation, at least for a limited period. These are complex and difficult decisions, and we will do best when we strive to make them without the influence of self-destructive emotions.

POSTTRAUMATIC STRESS FROM WAR

Like child abuse, domestic violence, and bullying, posttraumatic stress from combat—often called "posttraumatic stress disorder," or PTSD—is not a disease or mental disorder and, to emphasize this, I am dropping the word "disorder." When we are already traumatized, we should not be subjected to stigmatizing psychiatric diagnoses. Our suffering is the normal reaction of a normal person with a normal brain to unusual stress, trauma, or abuse.[4]

The concept of posttraumatic stress has much wider application than its standard uses. Most so-called mental disorders result from stress, trauma, or abuse in childhood, often with additional triggers or stressors in adulthood.[5] The emotional suffering caused by child abuse, bullying, and domestic violence is an expression of posttraumatic stress. As a result, victims of these acts often resemble soldiers traumatized by war.

Combat stress and trauma can amplify all three negative legacy emotions. Most obviously, anxiety plagues many returning soldiers. They can be hyperalert, highly reactive to loud noises, unable to relax or sleep, and generally anxious. Many suffer from terrifying nightmares and flashbacks. Their psychological and spiritual well-being can become grossly impaired, requiring a flexible and varied approach from those helping with recovery.[6]

Guilt also afflicts many returning combat soldiers. They may have survivor guilt. Some may have unintentionally injured or killed noncombatants. Others may feel guilty about violent acts they performed as soldiers, whether they were within the rules of combat or not. Witnessing the overall carnage of war can burden soldiers with guilt, leaving them depressed and even suicidal.

Shame can also overwhelm returning soldiers. They may feel they let their comrades down or acted cowardly. They may be embarrassed about being "mentally ill" and feel powerless in the face of their uncontrollable emotional reactions. Many struggle with irritability and must work hard to contain their anger.

Posttraumatic stress can be very persistent, lasting and sometimes worsening over a period of years. I have seen cases erupt years after the wartime stress. Posttraumatic stress often leads to persistent anger and emotional numbing. Soldiers' varying degrees of guilt, shame, or anxiety may reflect their prewar emotional profiles, but the war is the reason they become so overwhelmed.

Can human beings overcome the horrors of child abuse, domestic violence, bullying, and combat? The answer is yes. What do they need in order to heal? To begin with, they do *not* need the cocktails of psychiatric drugs routinely imposed upon them. Psychiatric drugs, especially in combination, almost inevitably worsen the sufferer's condition.[7] Instead of psychoactive substances that dull and disorganize the brain and mind, people recovering from trauma need exactly what everyone needs in life—thoughtful, caring, and nurturing human relationships to rebuild their trust and sense of security. Understanding and overcoming guilt, shame, and anxiety can greatly help in the process of finding the emotional freedom to reestablish healthy self-assertion, autonomy, and love.

Chapter 11

DON'T PEOPLE NEED SOME GUILT AND SHAME?

When I talk about negative legacy emotions with my friends, patients, graduate students, and conference audiences, one question keeps coming up: "Don't we *need* some guilt and shame?" The answer can transform our lives. When we fully grasp that we can live honorable and happy lives without clouding our minds with negative emotions, we begin our emotional liberation.

WHY DO WE NEED AN ABSOLUTE RULE?

Why do we need an uncompromising rule that guilt, shame, and anxiety have no place whatsoever in our lives? Because, like cocaine or alcohol to an addict, negative legacy emotions will seize any opportunity we give them and take over. Having gotten a piece of us, they will try to swallow us whole. We need absolute determination and all our strength to reject their influence.

Because the capacity for these emotions was built in by biological evolution and natural selection and then stimulated and amplified through childhood, we are programmed to believe we are supposed to feel these primitive, prehistoric emotions. As described earlier, when we feel guilty, we believe we are guilty—even in the absence of any rational explanation for the guilt. When we feel ashamed, we believe on some level that we deserve to feel rejected or worthless. When we feel anxious, we find reasons to justify our helpless feelings.

To flourish emotionally, we need to question and reject the idea that there is any justification for taking orders from guilt, shame, and anxiety. These negative emotions are imperfect remnants of evolution and child development that impede mature, rational, and loving conduct in adults.

THE ULTIMATE IRRATIONALITY

Those of us who know and work with victims of extreme physical, emotional, and sexual abuse can bear witness to how overwhelming feelings of guilt, shame, and anxiety have no basis in reality, sound ethics, or any other objective measure. As documented in chapter 10, they are the direct result of abuse.

Even after a court of law has found their abusers guilty and sent them to jail, adult victims of child abuse may continue to struggle with demoralizing feelings of guilt and shame. It seemingly makes no difference that they were only three, four, or five years old when they were physically, sexually, and mentally tortured. They blame themselves in ways that reason cannot rectify. Their negative legacy emotions are too deep to be uprooted by reality. These adults will need years of hard psychological work and affirming relationships to gain emotional freedom.

WHY IT IS FUTILE TO HOPE FOR PERPETRATORS TO FEEL GUILT OR SHAME

Intuitively, we imagine that perpetrators feel guilty and ashamed and only need a bigger dose of these negative emotions to stop abusing other people. Unfortunately, perpetrators typically have justifications for their behavior. They feel entitled to do what they did—that is why they did it! If confronted, instead of feeling remorse, they are likely to deny any memory of their actions. The truth is that they felt empowered by abusing helpless victims, and they have no inclination to feel bad about it.

Here is another key to life: People who seriously or persistently abuse other people almost never feel bad about it; instead, it is the victims who suffer emotionally. If you feel a great deal of guilt and shame, you almost certainly do not deserve it.

Emotional liberation thrives on a full awareness that these painful emotions do us no good and have no connection to our real value. They are always self-defeating when we act upon them. We will thrive to the degree that we are able to eradicate them from our emotional life.

Perpetrators may feel guilty, ashamed, or anxious about something else, such as being abused by their own parents. They may feel humiliated by the smallest sign of disrespect from a child, and they may feel guilty when someone in authority chides them. Nonetheless, they almost never feel guilty or ashamed about their abusive actions toward other people, including their own spouses, children, or employees.

It bears repeating: Perpetrators do not feel guilty, ashamed, or anxious about their vile actions; they feel justified, entitled, and empowered. Their innocent victims are the ones who end up with a lifetime legacy of self-defeating, negative emotions. If we are going through life feeling awful about ourselves, the odds are that our feelings do not reflect anything we have done wrong. Our internal misery is not about what we did to someone else. It is about our innate self-defeating emotions triggered in childhood, usually when someone did something harmful to us.

Are there any exceptions to these observations? Yes: People who do terrible things under circumstances that are *not* under their control commonly feel bad about it. Many soldiers return from combat with feelings of guilt and shame, but, when they committed violence, they were almost invariably acting under enormous duress and carrying out orders consistent with military ethics and tactics.

Individuals who become violent while taking psychiatric drugs often feel terrible about themselves afterward. As I describe in *Medication Madness*, psychiatric drugs can drive people to take actions that are wholly out of character.[1] They suffer from what I call *medication spellbinding (intoxication anosognosia)*—a drug-induced brain disorder that renders them unable to control themselves, to appreciate what they are doing, or to recognize that they are under the influence of psychoactive substances.[2] Afterward, they cannot believe they could do something so harmful to another person.

Why should victims feel bad about themselves while perpetrators do not? It only makes sense in light of the origins of negative legacy emotions in biological evolution and childhood rather than in sound ethics.

REMORSE AND REGRET

It is important to recognize our mistakes, including how our bad judgment, selfishness, or self-absorption may have harmed people we love. When we recognize what we have done wrong, we should make amends, when possible, and change our conduct. Then, it is time to forgive ourselves and find the courage and strength to live and love again.

If, instead, we continue to feel guilt and shame about our conduct and anxiety about our future relationships, this will only hold us back and deprive others of our contributions to life. We need to recognize our mistakes. We need to feel regret and remorse, to make amends, to change our behavior, and to forgive ourselves. If, instead, we persist in feeling guilty, ashamed, and anxious, we need to look further into why. We need especially to look for causes in our childhood, as well as in our current relationships with anyone who is continuing to make us feel bad about ourselves, including a parent or other family members.

SHOULDN'T A MAN FEEL GUILTY FOR HITTING HIS WIFE?

A man has hit his wife. Shouldn't he feel guilt? Partly, we want him to feel guilty as a punishment. Unfortunately, it rarely, if ever, works that way. When he struck his wife, he was probably feeling, "She deserves it," or, "I'm not going to let her talk to me like that." That is why he hit her—because he felt justified in doing so.

Let us suppose, for argument's sake, that the violent husband simply lost his temper and, afterward, realizes he behaved badly and begins to feel guilty. First, it rarely happens this way. Second, feeling guilty is not really going to make him a better or more reliable husband. It might end up making him even angrier and more violent. People resent feeling guilty and often respond by getting angrier at the person they perceive to be causing their painful emotions.

Furthermore, many people respond to feeling guilty by refusing to think about what they have done. To avoid their guilt or shame, they deny how much they have hurt or offended others. Yes, feeling guilty would punish them emotionally after the fact, but it would probably not make them better, more respectful, or less dangerous.

It would be best for a man who has hit his wife to feel empathy for her and to recognize that he has done something dreadfully wrong. Ideally, he would cry with sadness over hurting and frightening her, betraying her trust, and failing to be a loving partner. He would then reassess his conduct, make amends for his brutality, and promise himself and his wife that he would never again threaten or harm her. However, if he were feeling guilty, he would more likely fake feeling remorseful and apologetic and, ultimately, get even angrier or sullenly withdraw. Guilt is not likely to encourage a positive or loving response, but empathy almost certainly will.

GUILT MAKES US LESS RESPONSIBLE

Feeling guilty and ashamed does not make us better people. It is not likely to improve our self-understanding or correct our misdeeds. Instead, it discourages us from thinking about ourselves in a constructive fashion. Guilt, shame, and anxiety are never our friends; people who encourage us to feel them are not being friendly.

These self-defeating emotions are potentially antilife, too often leading to suicide and violence. They are also antilife in a more subtle fashion: Commonly, they are hammered home to children to suppress their attempts to be self-assertive, self-determined, and independent. In adulthood, these negative emotions can rob individuals of free will by miring them in painful and even paralyzing feelings.

In adult life, our self-defeating primitive emotions actively oppose our best aspects, such as empathy, love, and creativity. They can inhibit positive psychological values such as resilience, independence, freedom, and self-development, as well as empathy and love. Emotional freedom requires liberation from our antilife, inhibitory legacy emotions.

A man who neglects to keep track of his finances, for example, may feel so guilty when he thinks about it that he continues to ignore the subject. If he does get himself to examine the numbers, he may then feel so guilty, ashamed, or anxious in response to the bad news that he again stops looking at the financial facts. A woman may feel so bad about slapping her daughter that she cannot discuss it with anyone or figure out how to prevent it in the future. She may even grow angrier with her daughter, blaming her child for "making Mommy feel so bad."

Feeling guilty, ashamed, or anxious does not make us better people; it makes us less rational and less effective. If we have committed misdeeds in adulthood, our negative legacy emotions can become so painful that we cannot face what we did to stimulate them. Their demoralizing impact ends up impeding our efforts toward personal responsibility and personal growth.

NEGATIVE EMOTIONS IMPAIR OUR SAFETY

Guilt, shame, and anxiety can suppress healthy and effective responses when individuals need to face real threats. In clinical practice, it is common to work with men and women who are emotionally inhibited from defending themselves against other people. As a result, they also have difficulty defending their spouses or children. When a teacher, for example, humiliates one of their children, these parents want to stand up for their child, but defending the child seems so much like defending themselves that negative legacy emotions prevent them.

Because prehistoric emotions were stimulated before we can remember and before we understood what was happening, they are not flexible and adaptable to successful adult life. They can utterly fail to alert the individual to actual moral problems or harmful personal behavior. A man who feels ashamed and paralyzed when another adult threatens him physically may not feel at all ashamed of hitting his children. Perhaps he was bullied and humiliated by his own father, so he fears grown men but has learned from his father that children can and should be hit. Another man feels guilty about failing to earn enough money for his family, but he may feel even guiltier about refusing to lend money to a manipulative friend, thus depriving his family of his wages.

A woman reacts with so much anxiety to the outdoors and to meeting people that she cannot leave home, but she feels so unrealistically safe alone in the house that she neglects to lock the doors. Another woman overreacts with violent anger toward her children but remains passive when her husband abuses her.

DO *YOU* NEED TO FEEL GUILT?

Even if you believe that other people need to feel guilty or ashamed in order to behave well, *you* can nonetheless decide for yourself that you do not need these emotions to make you a better person. You can decide to govern your life based on reason and love. In living your own life, you no longer need to remain compliant with inhibitory relics from evolution and childhood. You can decide for yourself that you will become more loving as you become as free as possible from demoralizing emotional restraints.

I have never known a person who was happily taking charge of life and then, out of the blue, committed violence. I have never known anyone who was loving while nonetheless plotting harm to another human. I have never known anyone who felt empathy for another person and then purposely abused the individual.

From the outside, it might seem that some people feel good while abusing other human beings. However, whenever we delve into the minds of perpetrators, their destructive acts are thinly veiled attempts to overcome their own calamitous lack of self-worth. Typically, they have felt beaten down by shame and humiliation, often at the hands of earlier abusers, and are now inflicting their pain on others in the hope of achieving some modicum of power and self-respect.

If you look into your own heart, I believe you will find that at your best as a human being, you are relatively free of painful emotions and instead indeed guiding yourself via reason, ethics, and love. Therefore, regardless of what you think about unspecified *other* people needing to feel powerful oppressive emotions to keep them in line, you certainly do not need them. You have the ability to bring out the best in yourself by throwing off the emotional thrall of our prehistoric past.

Anyone motivated and able to read this book will have nothing to lose by letting go of prehistoric emotions and by choosing instead to live by higher principles such as justice, empathy, and love. If you are a parent, friend, teacher, minister, coach, or healthcare provider, the same is undoubtedly true for those in your care. You will do far more good if you triumph over and transcend disabling negative emotions and find the emotional freedom to love, to be loved, and to enjoy life.

DON'T WE NEED MORE SHAME IN PUBLIC LIFE?

Sexual escapades and abuses by famous politicians and other public figures have given rise to well-intended calls for a revival of public shaming of perpetrators. Similarly, the proliferation of reality television shows and outrageous YouTube videos has led people to want more emphasis on shame in our culture. In effect, it is said, "These people should be ashamed of themselves. We will shame them on the radio, the Internet, and anywhere we can." Yet these same well-meaning critics often admit that the perpetrators do not feel shame. That is why politicians can commit acts that seem utterly shameful and yet thrust themselves right back into the limelight: they do not feel the degree of disabling shame that most people would if such behavior were made public. Nor do they feel the genuine remorse of someone who rationally understands that they have done wrong. If they do start to feel shame, they are likely to turn it into anger at the people who exposed and criticized them. The reactions of politicians and others who feel unashamed in public, or who defy their feelings of shame and blame others, confirm that the shame we learn to feel, or not to feel, often has little to do with mature, adult ethics. What is needed is rational ethics. When political leaders chose to take honorable stands against abuses or misconduct that are widely accepted, they may have to endure and overcome the shame heaped upon them by those who wish to enforce conformity to these bad practices that they oppose.

Sometimes, largely by chance, our shame reactions may result from bad conduct, but, at other times, they will be caused by built-in reactions to admirable behavior on our part that we imagine other people will disapprove of or that were disapproved of in our childhood. For example, we may wish to stand up at a school board meeting or at a conference to defend someone who is being mistreated by the chairperson, but we are too afraid of being humiliated. Or we may have learned in childhood to feel shameful at the very thought of standing up to authority. When feeling shame, it is always necessary to use reason and sound ethics to determine our course of action.

Many religious and political leaders promote guilt to make people toe their particular line, but a guilt-ridden society will not function on as high a level as an empathic society bonded together by caring and generosity.

WHACKING US AT THE MOMENT WE WANT TO BETTER OURSELVES

Remember that the relationships we most care about are the most likely to be disabled by feelings of guilt, shame, and anxiety, as well as anger and emotional numbing. Because these emotions biologically evolved to suppress our self-assertive and aggressive impulses within the family and clan, these feelings erupt most destructively in our intimate familylike relationships in adulthood. They are likely to strike us in regard to those we love most, such as our own partners in life and our children.

In my clinical practice, I witness people who become stymied by guilt, shame, or anxiety when someone else shows them love, admiration, or respect. Exposure to someone who seems to love them stirs up first their hopes, then their fears, and finally every kind of self-defeating emotion. They end up rejecting the kind of people who could bring them happiness.

These self-defeating emotional reactions prevent many people from finding and keeping a loved one. Guilt-provoking childhood and youthful experiences have made them feel bad about wanting someone to love and be loved by. Shaming in childhood has made them feel unlovable and afraid of being demeaned and used. Anxiety-inducing experiences have convinced them that anyone they love will die or abandon them.

We are also likely to experience overwhelming self-defeating emotional reactions at exactly the moment that we are contemplating or doing anything new that matters to us. These reactions can overcome us when we are engaging in a hobby or recreational activity that we love. They can overcome us when we merely think about doing something we have always wanted to do, from finding a better job to improving our marriage to simply enjoying a vacation or a few quiet moments beside a lake.

Our primeval legacy emotions can hinder us in the most important and productive activities on Earth, including raising our children with discipline and love. Guilt-driven parents feel bad about exerting the authority necessary to set limits. Shame-driven parents may feel too powerless to discipline their children or too embarrassed to love them openly. Anxiety-ridden parents may overcontrol their children or undermine their feelings of security.

Overall, our primitive emotions drive us compulsively in the wrong direction while inhibiting us from determining the right direction. They hobble us by taking us out of the present moment and thrusting us back into childlike helplessness and dependence.

SUMMARY: HOW NEGATIVE LEGACY EMOTIONS HARM US

It is so important to understand how and why guilt, shame, and anxiety are always destructive in our adult lives that it is worth recapping the main reasons:

- Guilt, shame, and anxiety are prehistoric products of biological evolution and natural selection that were then triggered and molded in childhood and adolescence, often in a random or irrational fashion and before we could reason or can even remember. Therefore, they are not reliable as guidelines for adult choices and decisions.
- They can drive both anger and emotional numbing.
- They are so emotionally suppressive that bottled-up resentment and anger stay unresolved and can build up to the bursting point.
- To avoid feeling them, we end up avoiding self-examination, which makes us less able to feel empathy for those we have harmed and to make amends and corrections in our conduct.
- As adults, we irrationally continue to believe that our feelings of guilt, shame, and anxiety are legitimate signals that we really are bad and shameful or that our anxiety is justified or realistic.
- These emotions were inflicted on us when we were being willful or self-assertive as children. As a result, they self-defeat us by suppressing our adult self-assertiveness even when it is rational, ethical, or needed for self-defense and the promotion of our higher ideals.
- Stimulated in our most emotionally and physically intimate relationships as infants and children, these emotions are especially likely to be reactivated in our adult romantic and family relationships. They cause most failures in love and family life.
- Having been imposed on us as infants and children when we were exploring and trying something new, these emotions are likely to strike

us in adulthood at those moments we are contemplating important new choices that could improve our lives and the lives of those we care about.

- Negative legacy emotions rip us out of the present moment and instead thrust us back into a primitive, prehistoric place before we could guide our lives by reason, principles, and love.

As a great step toward achieving emotional freedom and living fulfilling lives, we can tell ourselves that feelings of guilt, shame, or anxiety have nothing to do with our true identity or worth and should be replaced by reason and love in guiding our adult lives. We need to throw off these prehistoric emotions—forced on us by biological evolution and childhood—like the horrendous bullies they are. Treat your most painful emotions as primordial or alien intruders into your mind and life. Regard them as entities in no way friendly or useful to you.

We now turn to Part 2 and the three steps to emotional freedom from guilt, shame, and anxiety, as well as chronic anger and numbness.

PART 2.

ACHIEVING EMOTIONAL FREEDOM

INTRODUCTION TO PART 2

Born within a maelstrom of conflicting impulses, both loving and willfully aggressive; driven by instincts embedded in us by millions of years of biological evolution; and inhibited by a primitive legacy of guilt, shame, and anxiety— how can we take charge of our lives and become the people we want to be?

For better and for worse, evolution has done its work. We have thus far survived as a species. If you are reading this, you have been born and survived as an individual representative of this species. Now, we face the task of making the most of the best of what nature has given us.

The steps to emotional freedom are not difficult to understand, but their implementation takes hard work, determination, and courage. Along the way, you will be tempted with shortcuts. You may want to turn to anger and resentment for false empowerment. You may start to become emotionally numb as an escape. You may be tempted to turn to alcohol, marijuana, and other drugs, or health professionals may try to seduce you with psychiatric diagnoses and prescription medication, but there are no shortcuts to emotional freedom.

Chapter 12

TAKING THE THREE STEPS TO EMOTIONAL FREEDOM

Anyone who has tried to grow even a small garden knows a simple lesson: if you do not regularly tend your garden, invasive weeds and vines will strangle and snuff out your beautiful flowers and your nutritious vegetables. Guilt, shame, and anxiety act like invasive weeds and vines in our minds. Like weeds, we must not allow them to take over, and, if they do, they require ruthless weeding out and replacement with more valuable emotions and attitudes.

Continuing with the gardening metaphor, here are the three steps to emotional freedom.

First, learn to *identify* the weeds in your mental and spiritual garden—those primitive wilderness emotions and their underlying childlike feelings of helplessness and dependence.

Second, *reject* and pull out your emotional weeds, going after them with determination to remove them as quickly and fully as possible from your emotional landscape.

Third, regularly *replenish* your mental and spiritual garden with new emotional flowers that will flourish to your benefit and that of everyone you influence. As you become less confused and inhibited, you will be more able to select and cultivate your new emotions based on reason, sound ethics, and love.

In summary, the three steps to emotional freedom are to

1. *identify* your negative legacy emotions;
2. *reject* any compliance with these emotions; and
3. *triumph over* and *transcend* these emotions.

Use reason, ethics, and love as your guidelines. Ultimately, *learn to identify, embrace, and live by higher ideals and purposes and love.*

To *triumph* means to win a great victory over passions that can destroy us. It means to defeat those aspects of biological evolution and childhood that stymie our full development. It is literally an internal battle that we must win by mounting our own determination and strength against the primitive forces within us.

Our triumph is not merely personal. We are confronting and correcting the failures of human evolution and child development, then going on to create new and better alternatives. We humans confront this challenge daily, usually with little or no conscious awareness. We can succeed far better by facing the challenge on a conscious, informed, and determined basis.

To *transcend* means to rise above what we have been given biologically and in childhood and youth in order to live by higher values and purposes, including love, and, ultimately, to exceed our own initial expectations for a principled and satisfying life.

INVADED BY SQUIRRELS

More than a decade ago, when my office was in the suburbs of Bethesda, Maryland, I used to enjoy feeding the squirrels in the yard through which my patients walked to reach the waiting room. The little critters—certainly nothing to be afraid of—grew increasingly tame, until some were taking the peanuts from my outstretched hand. I left a can of raw peanuts in my office waiting room to remind me to give them a few handouts each day.

One day, I was sitting with one of my patients in the office when we heard a startling clatter coming from the waiting room. I got up somewhat fearfully to investigate. The door from outdoors into the waiting area was ajar and the can of peanuts knocked to the floor. Encouraged and empowered by my generous freebies, squirrels had invaded the inner sanctum of my office.

That invasion seemed humorous and harmless enough until a few days later, when I heard one of my patients shriek as she came through the pathway to the office. A squirrel had climbed up her pants leg, seeking a peanut handout.

I stopped feeding the squirrels.

Obeying negative legacy emotions is like feeding wild critters. They will take over and grow in power until we have unmanageable beasts trying to overwhelm us from inside our heads. We need to stop feeding the squirrels in our heads. We can start by refusing to listen or respond to them.

TAKING STEP ONE

Many people live amid so much guilt, shame, or anxiety that they become like a fish that has been swimming in polluted water since escaping its egg. The poor fish may have no idea that it is living under abnormal environmental conditions. Yet it will feel the equivalent of fish joyfulness when it finally experiences fresh, clean water. This will be the same for you.

Guilt, shame, and anxiety are so painful that we will do almost anything to ward them off. To avoid feeling guilt, we make no choices that seem remotely bad, selfish, or self-serving. To avoid feeling shame, we hold back our opinions at work or in our marriage, and we never try anything creative, like writing, artwork, or dancing. To avoid feeling anxiety, we give up taking risks or trying anything new or different.

If your life seems constricted, boring, or meaningless, your primitive emotions are probably sapping your vitality. To test this possibility, try imagining doing something different, and monitor your feelings for negative emotions. Imagine indulging yourself in some mildly selfish fashion. Imagine speaking your opinion to friends or taking a small risk to add excitement to your life.

When you experiment with imagining something new and daring, do you experience guilt, shame, anxiety, or some combination? Practice identifying your negative emotions, and you will take your first step toward emotional freedom and a better life for you and the people whose lives you touch.

TAKING STEP TWO

Do you want to redecorate your home, build furniture, play music, draw, or paint? Do you want to go to the theater or travel? Do you want to start a small business or volunteer to help others? Pursue a career you will love? Get a degree? Find a person to share your life? Improve your marriage or your relationships with your children? Make a difference in the world? If you have failed to act on these desires, your demoralizing negative legacy emotions are probably stopping you. They probably kick in whenever you consider or imagine asserting yourself toward fulfilling your wishes or dreams.

Instead of obediently complying or caving in to these painful emotions, recognize and name them like enemies you plan to confront and overcome: "You are guilt! You are shame! You are anxiety! You are chronic anger or numbness!"

Take the second step toward emotional freedom by rejecting your painful, self-defeating emotions. Tell your negative emotions, "I will not be paralyzed by you. I will not let you misdirect me. I refuse to be controlled or compelled by you."

Guilt, shame, and anxiety behave like unwanted houseguests who repeatedly come back until we start saying no to them. They are like friends who have grown accustomed to taking advantage of us. They are emotional bullies who feel entitled to intimidate us. They are like children given no limits. They push us harder and harder and take over our lives. They are like bad dreams that we allow to continue even after awakening.

We need to remind ourselves that our most painful emotions have nothing to do with reality, with who we really are, or with how we should act. Instead of consulting your negative legacy emotions, ask yourself what you want to do when you succeed in rejecting them. Then, begin to make decisions based on reason, mature ethics, and love.

Our wretched feelings toward our lives and ourselves do not make us better people. Instead, they build anger and resentment and can drive some of our worst behaviors. They can blind us to our real misdeeds and make us unable to work toward becoming better people. Even if you believe that other people need these emotional inhibitions to make them behave, you can decide that you do not need them because you can use your emotional freedom to become more rational, ethical, and loving.

TAKING STEP THREE

The third step toward emotional freedom requires fulfilling your potential to become a source of love. For several decades now, this has been my working definition of love:

Love is joyful awareness.

When your awareness of someone or something brings you happiness or joy, you are probably experiencing love. It can be your dog or cat, a person or place, nature, creativity, your chosen ideals, or your concept of a higher power. If your awareness of this aspect of life makes you feel wonderfully glad to be alive, then you are experiencing love. This is what flowers, sunny days, starlit nights, streams and lakes, pets, music and art, marvelous ideas, and higher purposes have in common: they can inspire us with joyful awareness, or love.

This is a simple, straightforward concept—that love is joyful awareness. It contrasts sharply with all the disappointing, self-defeating unhappy feelings and experiences in our lives.

Take a moment and imagine this for yourself: No more guilt, no more anxiety, no more shame, no more chronic anger, and no more emotional numbness—or, at least, a lot less than you currently endure. Now, imagine filling your mind, heart, and spirit with more love than you ever dreamed of. Imagine feeling joyful in the presence of others and of life itself. Imagine being happy.

These three steps to emotional freedom can change your life forever: Learn to *identify* guilt, shame, and anxiety; learn to *reject* them; and learn to fill yourself with *love* for other people, life in its many aspects, and your greater purposes.

Keep in mind that love is joyful awareness. If you are thinking about something or someone, and it makes you feel miserable, then it is probably not love. If you think about something or someone, and you light up inside with joy or happiness, that is almost surely love.

You may have had so many negative experiences surrounding "love" that the very thought of it makes you succumb to painful emotions. Love may have initially attracted you to someone, and then it went sour. This may have happened a number of times, leading you to feel frustrated and angry as well as numb. Reexamine what happened, and you will find the problem was not with love. Your relationships were held back, distorted, or corrupted by negative legacy emotions afflicting you and your partners.

How does this apply when one partner simply feels more love than the other, or when the two partners have differing views of what the relationship should be? Often, people suffer in relationships from feeling unloved or from irresolvable conflicts. Although rational compromises are made, one or both partners may feel disappointed, frustrated, or bereaved. What matters is how each partner handles his or her inevitable painful feelings. If guilt, shame, and anxiety, or chronic anger and numbing, complicate their responses, they will become mired down with increasing feelings of helplessness. If these negative legacy emotions can be held off and helplessness rejected, then effective decision making and emotional recovery are enhanced rather than impeded.

Your misguided or abusive parents or spouse may have told you they loved you at the same time they were making you miserable and trying to control your life. That was not love. Love motivates us to nurture, respect, and protect whomever and whatever we love, from a special person to our spiritual relationship with life. If your experiences are not making you feel wonderful and happy, either they are not imbued with love, or you are not yet ready to recognize, give, and receive love.

MANY WAYS TO LEARN AND GROW

The three steps to emotional freedom are laid out very simply here in order to clarify the necessary components. In therapy and life, these steps can be explored and adapted in a variety of ways, many of them less easily categorized.

In therapy, for example, patients or clients learn a great deal, if not the most, from the empathic relationship. If therapists are nonjudgmental, their clients become more able to explore and accept their confusing and frightening hodgepodge of emotions. If therapists are confident and steady in demeanor and in spirit, they provide a model for clients in learning to overcome anxiety and to approach life with more self-control. If therapists feel confident in handling potential emotional emergencies, such as suicidal or violent feelings, without resorting to psychiatric drugs, then clients learn they have the resources within themselves to handle anything that comes up. If therapists emanate what I describe as a "healing presence" in the *Heart of Being Helpful*, they help the client replace feelings of guilt and shame with loving attitudes.

These relationship benefits are not unique to therapy. Anyone pursuing the three steps to emotional freedom will find the journey enhanced by personal relationships that are relatively free of negative legacy emotions and based on ethics, reason, and love. *I hope that individuals will share their journey with others who are seeking emotional freedom and will perhaps develop self-help groups to encourage one another in the three steps.*

Many other life-enhancing activities, such as nutrition, exercise, massage, yoga, relaxation techniques, mindfulness, meditation, prayer, visualization, dance, art, and music, can help people release negative emotions in favor of more joyful ones. Later in the book, I will suggest a simple exercise for getting in touch with yourself as a source of love.

For me, nature brings me close to my spiritual center and to God. When I open my heart to spiritual feelings in response to nature, it banishes primitive inhibitory reactions and brings peace, confidence, and a connection to what is good and important in life. These experiences refresh me spiritually and remind me that I want to remain optimally in touch with myself in my everyday life and my personal understanding of God. Walking along Lake Cayuga near my home in the Finger Lakes region of New York State combines three of my most life-enhancing experiences: exercise, immersion in nature, and spirituality.

Nothing in my life, however, compares to sharing my work and leisure time with my wife, Ginger. My love for her has been a great motivation for overcoming my own self-punishing emotions. Any time either one of us feels guilt, shame, or anxiety, let alone anger or numbness, it creates a disturbance in our personal universe. It makes it harder for us to relate in the peaceful and loving manner we desire. I believe that implementing the three steps to emotional freedom within a loving relationship is the most effective way to reach toward emotional freedom—in this case, *mutual* emotional liberation to share as much love as possible.

WHAT LOVE IS NOT

Jealousy, envy, possessiveness, neediness, and desperation can all seem to come along with love, but that is a mistaken notion. These destructive feelings come from lack of genuine love.[1] When we love, we gain in our sense of security, respect for our loved ones, and mutual independence. When we feel loved, we grow even stronger. The negative feelings we associate with love, such as jealousy and desperate neediness, come from our early bad experiences with love and from our inability to allow love to flow from within us toward those we want to love.

Often, when I talk with my patients about their most loving childhood relationships, they gratefully remember their dog. The dog, and not their parents, joyfully greeted their return home from school every day. Their dog alone took unbounded pleasure from playing with them. Their dog, and no one else, seemed genuinely happy about their existence and offered unconditional love. One of the best books ever written about love is Jeffrey Masson's *The Dog Who Couldn't Stop Loving.* For dogs, unconditional love flows freely, unimpeded by guilt, shame, or anxiety. In contrast, we humans have to fight our way through these stifling emotions to express unconditional love. Probably for tens of thousands of years, dogs have taught us about love.

Believe in love, keep love in your heart as much as you can, and, whenever possible, base your actions on love—and you will one day discover that you are amazingly free from self-defeating emotions and living on a higher, happier plane than you ever imagined possible.

Chapter 13

IDENTIFYING FEELINGS OF GUILT, SHAME, AND ANXIETY

You can self-assess your personal profile of primitive emotions by looking down the list of characteristics associated with each emotional reaction. The checklists in this and the next chapter cannot and should not be used as diagnostic tools. The whole idea of psychological and psychiatric diagnosis is flawed and subject to increasing criticism.[1]

The checklists are for your personal enlightenment—to help you continue the process of looking inside yourself at your personal pattern of self-defeating emotions. They can be especially helpful with the first step toward emotional freedom, which is to recognize and identify your more stifling and self-defeating emotions.

People vary in how they combine guilt, shame, and anxiety within their emotional profiles. Some of us suffer predominantly from one of the three negative legacy emotions, while others have a roughly equal measure. Shame is the most difficult emotion to identify within ourselves because we feel ashamed to do so.

Some items in the checklists in this and the next chapter may seem inappropriate or even offensive, or seem wrong in their implication. Keep in mind that the questions aim to discover your irrational beliefs. After answering the questions, you can then evaluate the merit of any one particular thought or attitude. The goal is to find a pattern.

To preserve your privacy, you may want to avoid checking off your answers on the pages of the book.

RECOGNIZING SELF-DEFEATING GUILT FEELINGS

Experiencing any of the following in excess or beyond what you wish or can handle may indicate that you have self-defeating guilt reactions:

- Feeling guilty or bad about yourself
- Making sacrifices that, at times, seem excessive
- Feeling undeserving
- Being worried
- Having too many duties and obligations
- Thinking that good people often lose out or get the worst of it
- Finding it difficult to relax and to enjoy yourself
- Being concerned about doing something bad rather than about failing
- Getting upset if someone thinks you have bad intentions
- Working hard to get rid of bad thoughts
- Wanting never to be selfish or even to seem selfish
- Being preoccupied to your detriment about the suffering in the world
- Doubting your right to feel happy when so many others are suffering
- Wishing others would take as much responsibility as you do
- Finding it harder to do things for yourself than for others
- Taking on responsibilities you really don't want
- Treating yourself worse than you would treat anyone else
- Being unable to say no
- Fearing punishment when good things happen to you
- Treating yourself badly
- Having other people tell you not to be so hard on yourself
- Having other people reassure you that you are a good person

RECOGNIZING SELF-DEFEATING SHAME FEELINGS

Experiencing any of the following in excess or beyond what you wish or can handle may indicate that you have self-defeating shame reactions:

- Being quiet and shy
- Feeling sensitive
- Feeling unappreciated
- Blushing uncontrollably
- Feeling used
- Feeling rejected
- Feeling you are small or have little impact on people
- Being concerned about what other people think of you
- Worrying that people don't treat you with enough respect
- Feeling taken advantage of
- Wishing you could have had the last word
- Keeping your thoughts and feelings to yourself to avoid embarrassment
- Not wanting to seem stupid or inappropriate
- Being concerned about failing rather than about doing something bad
- Being a perfectionist
- Feeling left out, different, or like an outsider
- Being distrustful or suspicious
- Avoiding being the center of attention
- Feeling like a "shrinking violet" or "wallflower"
- Feeling like withdrawing or shutting people out

RECOGNIZING SELF-DEFEATING ANXIETY FEELINGS

Experiencing any of the following in excess or beyond what you wish or can handle may indicate that you have self-defeating anxiety reactions:

- Feeling cautious
- Feeling nervous or anxious
- Avoiding the unfamiliar
- Avoiding taking risks
- Worrying about life getting out of control
- Worrying about the unexpected
- Having trouble keeping up

- Wishing you had better luck
- Worrying about being left alone or abandoned
- Fearing that everything will go wrong at once
- Feeling vaguely apprehensive
- Finding it hard to focus your thoughts or to stay calm under stress
- Wishing people knew how hard you are trying
- Feeling scared for no apparent reason
- Feeling physical arousal for no apparent reason: your heart beating fast, or your hands shaking, or your body sweating, or your breathing becoming irregular, or your mouth drying out
- Wanting more security
- Having rituals or obsessions
- Being surprised by how easily other people cope
- Getting the wrong kind of help
- Feeling tempted to find an easy way out or a quick fix for your problems

These checklists are aimed at helping you recognize which negative legacy emotions play the strongest or most disabling roles in your life. The next chapter will help you recognize self-defeating anger and emotional numbing.

Chapter 14

RECOGNIZING FEELINGS OF ANGER AND EMOTIONAL NUMBNESS

After experiencing guilt, shame, and anxiety for long periods, we can end up seeking refuge in anger or numbness. Without realizing it, we lapse into being chronically irritable and defensive or into feeling emotionally dulled or bored. These checklists will help to familiarize you with the manifestations of anger and numbness.

As in the previous chapter, try to read down these lists without making a judgment. The goal is simply to identify emotions. It is not about what kind of person you really are or what you really believe. It is to help you identify emotions built in by natural selection and reinforced in your childhood. After taking the test, you can evaluate which of your answers provide useful information. Remember, you are looking for a pattern of personal self-defeating tendencies.

To preserve your privacy, you may want to avoid checking off your answers on the pages of the book.

RECOGNIZING SELF-DEFEATING ANGER FEELINGS

- Feeling frustrated or having a low frustration threshold
- Feeling irritable
- Feeling defensive
- Snapping at people
- Teasing people until they protest
- Complaining or feeling resentful
- Being cynical about other people, politics, humanity, or life
- Feeling angry at other drivers
- Imagining getting even

- Playing or having sex so roughly that someone has protested
- Becoming especially irritable or difficult when tired, ill, or drunk
- Losing your temper
- Slapping or hitting someone, even once, since becoming an adult
- Using alcohol, drugs, or psychiatric medications to suppress your anger
- Having other people say that you seem defensive or oversensitive
- Having other people seem afraid of your anger
- Telling other people, "I'm not angry, I'm just frustrated"

To find additional ways of exploring anger, review the discussions of shame in the earlier chapters. In the meantime, if you have used force or threats to get your way with anyone, you probably have an anger problem that needs your attention.

RECOGNIZING SELF-DEFEATING EMOTIONAL NUMBNESS

- Feeling bored
- Feeling like you don't care
- Losing interest in the people around you
- Believing it is too dangerous to have feelings
- Feeling so numb it scares you
- Feeling so little emotion you want to pinch or cut yourself
- Feeling indifferent or apathetic
- Wishing you could get rid of all your feelings
- Taking alcohol, drugs, or psychiatric medications to further numb yourself
- Feeling alienated or remote
- Feeling you might burst like a pressure cooker if you don't keep your feelings pushed down
- Pinching, cutting, or otherwise hurting yourself in order to "feel something"

It is entirely possible to triumph over and transcend both anger and numbness. Although anger will continue to arise at times as a signal that you are feeling threatened or harmed, you can learn not to act on it (chapter 20). Letting go of these two emotions will enable you to have better relationships and to accomplish much more.

The following chapter presents a comparative table of things we tell ourselves that are driven by our self-defeating emotional attitudes.

Chapter 15

NEGATIVE THINGS WE TELL OURSELVES

The three-column table below, "Negative Emotional Things We Tell Ourselves," compares the self-defeating things we say to ourselves when under the influence of guilt, shame, and anxiety, respectively. In addition to the two previous chapters, this will further help you to identify and compare the emotions that haunt you.

Although carefully thought out over many years, this table could seem oversimplified and lacking in nuance. This is partly because it is a table. Beyond that, negative legacy emotions in themselves are simplistic. As noted earlier, if they were complex and subtle, biological evolution would not have been able to select them as human traits, and childhood would not so easily trigger them. There is very little creativity in how we experience these Stone Age emotions. It bears repeating that our creativity lies in what we generate through reason and love.

NEGATIVE EMOTIONAL THINGS WE TELL OURSELVES

Guilt-inspired things we tell ourselves	Shame-inspired things we tell ourselves	Anxiety-inspired things we tell ourselves
"The worst thing in the world is to feel guilty or bad about yourself."	"The worst thing in the world is to feel embarrassed or ashamed of yourself."	"The worst thing in the world is to feel anxious and scared all the time."
"I will do anything to stop feeling guilty."	"I will do anything to stop feeling ashamed."	"I will do anything to stop feeling anxious."
"If I try to have a good time, I will end up feeling like I'm bad and don't deserve it."	"If I try to have a good time, I will end up feeling like I've made myself look silly or foolish."	"If I try to have a good time, I wouldn't know where to begin or how to find someone to do it with."

"I hate it when people make me feel guilty and bad for not doing what they want."	"I hate it when people make me feel small or unimportant just to puff up themselves."	"I hate it when people make me so anxious that I can't figure out what to do or say."
"If I got together with someone new, he or she might want more of me than I can give."	"If I got together with someone new, he or she might not like me or appreciate me."	"If I got together with someone new, I'm not sure I could handle the situation."
"I have to accept getting a little depressed and having trouble enjoying myself."	"I have to accept feeling shy sometimes and wanting to pull away from people for a while."	"I have to accept getting nervous around people, even though I don't know why."
"I always end up taking on too much because there's so much to do."	"I always end up taking on too much because other people won't do their share."	"I always end up taking on too much because life just keeps coming at you."
"I'm not really a good person."	"I'm not really a special person."	"I'm not really a capable person."
"People are not grateful for all that I do for them."	"People want me to feel indebted to them."	"I'm not sure I have enough going for me to give to anyone else."
"What do I have to do for people to see that I'm a good person or at least not a bad one?"	"What do I have to do for people to see me as worthwhile person or even to notice me at all?"	"What do I need to do for people to see the kind of help that I need—or at least that I'm really in need of help?"
"I will always judge myself; it's just the way I am."	"People will always be judging me; it's just the way life is."	"I don't really have the best of judgment."
"Love can become a burden requiring too much sacrifice."	"Love can require trusting someone too much."	"Love is too uncertain and too risky."
"I can't relax, or I'll be overwhelmed by all my obligations."	"I can't relax, or I'll let down my guard."	"I can't relax, or the world will fall apart around me."

"I wish someone would listen to how burdened I feel."	"I wish people would stop talking about sharing feelings."	"I would share my feelings with someone if I knew they would help."
"I would like to believe that I'm a good person who works for the benefit of others."	"I would like to believe that I'm a strong person with great accomplishments."	"I would like to believe that I'm someone who is competent to handle whatever life brings on."
"I would most hate for someone to find out that I was hiding something selfish and bad that I had done."	"I would most hate for someone to find out that I was hiding something shameful like a big mistake or failure."	"I would most hate for someone to find out that I was never really trying to take responsibility for myself."
"I should get over feeling that my parents made me feel I was never good enough for them."	"I should get over feeling that my parents made me feel like I never counted for much in the family."	"I should get over feeling that my parents made me feel so scared, alone, and insecure."
"I wish I didn't do and say so many bad things to hurt my parents' feelings."	"I wish I didn't feel so mad about feeling teased and left out of the family circle."	"I wish I didn't feel insecure and afraid of change the way I did as a kid."
"I will never get free of feeling weighed down and unable to fully enjoy life."	"I will never get free of thinking about what other people think of me."	"I will never get free of feeling fearful and finding life difficult and hard to cope with."
"It is hard to live happily in a world where so many other good people are suffering."	"It is hard to live happily in a world where people won't leave other people alone."	"It is hard to live happily in a world that's so out of control and unpredictable."
"I can't stop feeling angry, or I'll end up taking on even more stuff that I can't handle."	"I can't stop feeling angry, or people will walk all over me."	"I can't stop feeling angry until life stops coming at me all the time."
"If I stop feeling numb, then I won't be able to stop crying, or I'll feel so bad that I will become immobilized and stop doing anything for anyone."	"If I stop feeling numb, I'll have to avoid people, stay by myself, or finally fight back and end up saying or doing hurtful things."	"If I stop feeling numb, I'll be wiped out by anxiety, or do something desperate to get help, and probably fall apart."

Some people may wonder, "What's wrong with thinking that I will do anything to stop feeling guilty, ashamed, or anxious?" When we say something like that to ourselves, it indicates that we are being controlled by these emotions—driven to do things we do not freely choose to do. Our goal should be to stop responding to primitive emotions and instead to guide ourselves with sound ethics.

Similarly, many people wonder why we should not feel guilty when there is so much suffering in the world. Others may think we should feel threatened when there are so many encroachments on us. Still others may feel that we have to feel anxious when there is so much chaos in the world. However, we will do far better and contribute much more to the world when we are able to maintain our inner competence and determination, and even happiness, while we recognize that the world has always been full of desperation and injustice. Then, we can make rational decisions about how much of our lives we want to devote more specifically to the relief of suffering and the increase of prosperity in the world.

Guilt, shame, and anxiety do not motivate positive reform. At best, they exhaust us; at worst, they drive us toward negative feelings and actions that harm and alienate other people. Reason, sound ethics, and love motivate actions that genuinely improve our own lives and the lives of others.

Chapter 16

HOW OUR BODIES TELL US ABOUT GUILT, SHAME, AND ANXIETY

Recognizing and understanding the physical manifestations of our primordial emotions can enhance our ability to identify these emotions. Many of us experience negative legacy emotions in our bodies before they enter our consciousness. As we become more aware of these signals, they can alert us in advance.

If we have any remaining doubt that biological evolution and natural selection have genetically programmed us to feel Stone Age emotions, we need only consider that shame and anxiety instantly activate innate and largely predetermined physiological responses that are very similar from person to person. Biological evolution developed these emotions to stop us from dangerous willfulness and aggression in our personal relationships. It did this by inflicting painful, demoralizing emotions upon us in association with self-assertion and then hammered the lesson home by making sure that our bodies feel the impact. Negative legacy emotions deliver body blows!

BEWARE OF THINKING "IT'S ALL IN MY HEAD"

Strong emotions commonly make us feel ill, and sometimes they can cause psychosomatic disorders—that is, physical problems induced by painful emotions. Nonetheless, it can be a tragic mistake to dismiss physical discomforts or symptoms on the basis that they are "just emotional." In every case where physical symptoms are of concern, a medical evaluation is required to rule out an underlying physical disorder.

As a psychiatrist, I frequently evaluate patients who have been told by their medical doctor or previous psychiatrist that their physical symptoms are "all in their head." On a number of occasions, my own evaluation has led me to suspect a serious physical disorder. During my career as a psychiatrist, cases that other doctors have thought to be psychological in origin have turned out to be brain tumors; severe infections; multiple sclerosis; inner ear disorders; various hormonal disorders; and, most commonly, serious adverse reactions to psychoactive substances, such as alcohol, marijuana, and, especially, psychiatric drugs.

Too often, patients are prescribed psychiatric drugs when they really need a thorough medical evaluation to evaluate underlying physical diseases, such as neurological disorders, endocrine system disorders, diabetes, chronic infection, and heart disease. Any medications, supplements, or herbal remedies the patient takes should also be evaluated. You and your doctor should suspect an underlying physical cause, including adverse medication effects, for any unexpected mental or emotional distress, especially when it is recent onset, severe, or unusual.

As a medical expert, I recently evaluated a legal case in which an emergency room failed to perform an electrocardiogram or any specific heart tests on a man who arrived in a state of "anxiety" and complained that it "felt like a heart attack." The ER treated him like a psychiatric case, and his primary care doctor placed him on an antidepressant. Shortly after starting the antidepressant, he committed suicide, most probably induced by the drug. The coroner's report reported that, on autopsy, he had chronic heart disease. Instead of being treated with an antidepressant, he should have been evaluated and then treated for heart disease.

To avoid having their physical symptoms dismissed as psychiatric, some patients understandably avoid telling their doctors about anything that sounds like an emotional problem. If you wish to tell your medical doctor about feeling emotionally distressed, it may be best to wait until the medical history, physical examination, and laboratory tests are completed to your satisfaction.

NATURE'S LIE DETECTOR

Biological evolution has built a kind of lie detector into our bodies. When we experience shame, our skin lights up with a blush that announces, "You got me! I'm embarrassed, ashamed, and maybe even humiliated." When we experience anxiety, our tremor or sweaty palms may also give us away. It is as if nature intended these emotions to be signaled to others as an open admission that we are inhibiting ourselves in response to them.

Part of shame's unique power derives from the fact that it is so difficult to hide our feelings. When we blush or look sheepish, other people can see that they are having a strong impact on us.

As mentioned above, anxiety can also give off signals, such as paleness, sweaty palms, or nervous tremors, that alert other people we are feeling stressed or upset.

Guilt has no specific physiological effect, but, when feeling guilty, people will often give away their emotion by looking down or slouching, as if expecting punishment.

Physiological responses to our primitive emotions involve the autonomic nervous system, over which we usually have only limited control. However, people can learn to control the autonomic nervous system through mental exercises and practice, including consciously replacing upsetting feelings with a meditative or calm state of mind. People can even learn to fool a lie detector by hiding any physical manifestations of their emotions.

Our potential for controlling our feelings and their associated physical responses can be used for positive purposes. Almost any time we are under stress, we are likely to perform better and to work better with other people if we do not display signs of guilt, shame, or anxiety. Ultimately, we will do best if we actually stop feeling these emotions, but keeping them to ourselves is a good beginning and can diminish their power over us.

THE PHYSIOLOGY OF SHAME

Science has yet to determine whether natural selection favored human faces with blood vessels specifically suited to dilating to produce a blush.[1] Whether it is natural selection or happenstance, the blush response makes clear that there is a specific connection between the feeling of shame and the physiological dilation of the blood vessels of the cheeks and sometimes the face, neck, and shoulders. The increased blood flow can produce a sensation of warmth or heat. Many people also experience creepy, crawly, or prickly feelings in their skin during shame, indicating a direct biological connection from the emotion to the peripheral nervous system.

Feeling ashamed is most often associated with blushing and, sometimes, that hot and prickly sensation. Sometimes embarrassment leads to "funny feelings" in our skin. People call them the "creepy crawlies" or the "udgies."[2] These are signs of social discomfort related to shame, sometimes mixed with anxiety about being around other people.

Shame induces people to try to make themselves inconspicuous. As one of my patients put it, "I've been shrinking since I was a child." People who are ashamed of themselves often feel smaller than they are in relation to others. They may hunch their posture in order to look smaller. Conversely, when compensating for shame, people may puff themselves up and attempt to appear larger or menacing.

On many occasions in my clinical practice, I have worked with men who were sufficiently large to be intimidating, but who thought of themselves as average or small in stature. On occasion, to demonstrate my point, I have stood next to them so they could look down on the top of my now-balding head. I have also held my hand up against theirs to show the difference in size. My patients may have found my efforts endearing, but these demonstrations did not do much for their sense that they lacked stature. These shameful feelings of being small and vulnerable become so deeply embedded that it takes time and effort to overcome them.

Brené Brown poignantly observes about shame:

> Somewhat paradoxically, our bodies often react to shame even before our conscious minds do. People always think it's strange when I ask them where and how they physically feel shame. But for most of us, shame has a feeling— it's physical as well as emotional. This is why I often refer to shame as a full-contact emotion. Women have described various physical reactions to shame, including stomach tightening, nausea, shaking, waves of heat in their faces and chests, wincing and twinges of smallness. If we can recognize our physical responses, sometimes we can limit the powerlessness that we feel when we are in shame.[3]

The above is a good description for identifying shame in order to conquer it.

THE PHYSIOLOGY OF ANXIETY

When we experience anxiety, we may sweat, our breathing may accelerate, hair may stand up on our arms or the back of our head, our hands may tremble, and our pupils may dilate. All these signs allow the acute observer to see that we are indeed reacting anxiously. Out of view, our heart rate, blood pressure, blood flow to the muscles, and other cardiovascular functions rev up during anxiety.

The physiological signs of anxiety are associated with the increased secretion of adrenaline from the adrenal glands into the bloodstream. The heart beats faster, and respirations become more rapid. The mouth gets dry. Blood pressure may go up. Some people breathe so fast they blow off too much carbon dioxide and become dizzy or faint from hyperventilation.

During anxiety, people may experience distortions in relationship to their body or the world around them, which can make them feel remote from themselves (*depersonalization*) or remote from others and reality (*derealization*). To a person lying in bed, alone and anxious, at night, hands and feet can seem small and far away, or the walls can seem to be receding or moving. A person can feel separate from her body. While these experiences can be frightening, they are surprisingly common. They routinely happen to children and teenagers, and they afflict adults during stress or after trauma. They are normal, and sometimes inevitable, responses to trauma and stress, and they can become more disabling following extreme abuse.

It is common for an acute anxiety attack to feel like a heart attack. These physical manifestations of anxiety are labeled *psychophysiological* because the stress in the mind (*psycho-*) leads directly to changes in the body (*-physiological*). The adrenaline rush that causes increased heart rate, respirations, blood pressure, and sweating is a classic example of a psychophysiological reaction.

The great physiologist Walter B. Cannon named this adrenaline outpouring the "fight-or-flight" response. There is no solid physiological distinction between fear and anxiety. The difference between fear and anxiety is mostly in our attitude. Fear is a reaction to something that is recognized or understood, and that we can respond to, such as a train barreling down on us. Anxiety is a response to insecurities and feelings of being overwhelmed, usually without a recognizable cause. When we respond with anxiety to something that should inspire fear, such as the train barreling down on us, the anxiety is more primitive in nature than the fear and will interfere with our taking rational actions to escape. All self-defeating legacy emotions derive from long-lasting patterns of response that have no intrinsic connection to the events that stimulate them in adult life.

Some of my first scientific papers examine the effect of adrenaline on rats and human beings.[4] In the early 1960s, it struck me that anxious people could misread these normal signs of stress or exertion and then fear they were having an anxiety attack, ultimately escalating their anxiety. It turned out that this is true and that the perception of adrenaline-induced symptoms can, in itself, increase anxiety.

THE PHYSIOLOGY OF GUILT

Unlike shame and anxiety, guilt has no direct physiological links to bodily signs or symptoms. However, people do experience guilt in their bodies in various uncomfortable ways, often involving gastrointestinal discomfort, headaches, and exhaustion. Guilt commonly drives people into feelings of depression, which cause a wide variety of uncomfortable and even disabling physical symptoms.

When people feel depressed, everything about their minds and bodies can seem to slow down—except, perhaps, for obsessive worrying or agitation. Some people find that their digestion is sluggish or their stomach aches. Food can become tasteless or unpleasant, so appetite diminishes. Or eating may become compulsive in an attempt to dull the painful emotions and fill the "hole" inside.

As many psychiatrists have observed:

> Physical symptoms are common in depression, and, in fact, vague aches and pain are often the presenting symptoms of depression. These symptoms include chronic joint pain, limb pain, back pain, gastrointestinal problems, tiredness, sleep disturbances, psychomotor activity changes, and appetite changes. A high percentage of patients with depression who seek treatment in a primary care setting report only physical symptoms, which can make depression very difficult to diagnose.[5]

Many of my psychiatric colleagues unscrupulously use this well-known relationship between feeling emotionally depressed and feeling physically distressed to claim that depression is a physical disease. They do this to empower themselves as physicians and to justify giving psychiatric drugs. In reality, however, depression is an emotion or mood that then drives physical responses. Avoid being misled by the fact that emotions are felt in the body; they are generated by mind and spirit. In addition, these same symptoms can reflect a variety of genuine physical disorders from chronic viral infections and autoimmune disorders to drug toxicity. Focusing on them as symptoms of depression can interfere with adequate medical evaluations and interventions, including withdrawal from psychiatric drugs.

When we have bad news to give, we often ask the recipients to sit down. We are afraid they will faint and hurt themselves when they hit the ground. Fainting occurs because bad news can shock the cardiovascular system, leading to a sudden loss of blood pressure, lack of blood flow to the brain, and collapse. Does this mean that bad news is a physical disorder?

Prescribers of psychiatric drugs often confuse the issue by telling patients their emotional distress has a "physical component" because of changes in their eating and sleeping habits or because their cardiovascular or gastrointestinal functions are stressed. Our negative emotions do have physical manifestations, but, when the emotion is handled, the physical manifestations subside.

Depressed people often have a vague feeling of, "There's something wrong with my body." Some feel there is, specifically, "something wrong inside my head." The suspicion that there is something "wrong" inside oneself is often the result of guilt and self-blame. Guilt and depression are no more physical diseases or disorders than are shame and anxiety, or bad news, for that matter. Strong emotions cause strong bodily reactions. That in no way suggests the presence of a disease process, biological abnormality, or biochemical imbalance, none of which has been demonstrated in psychiatric or mental "disorders."[6]

Because sufferers feel that something is wrong inside their heads or bodies, depression makes people easily convinced that taking psychiatric medications will fix them. Some of these unfortunate individuals end up submitting to electroshock treatment (ECT), sometimes seeking punishment to relieve the feelings of badness inside them.[7] If you are feeling depressed, do not let your doctor convince you there is something biochemically or genetically wrong with you. The evidence for biochemical and genetic causes of emotional problems, including serious diagnoses like schizophrenia, is slim to nothing.[8] You are almost certainly suffering from a spiritually crushing amount of guilt, often combined with other stifling negative legacy emotions.

THE PHYSIOLOGY OF EMOTIONAL NUMBNESS

Being out of touch and numb to their own feelings can lead people to neglect themselves. When not paying attention to their emotional signals, people are likely to shut down physical sensations as well and fail to notice when something is amiss with their bodies. If they do notice a pain in the chest, stomach, or kidney region, they may dismiss or suppress it, exactly as they are doing with their emotions. Emotional numbness is a hazard to health.

Being emotionally numb can feel like being physically cold, or like losing touch with your hands, thus becoming more awkward in using them. Some people become so emotionally numb that they stub a finger or toe and do not realize they have fractured it.

Emotional numbness is an indescribable pain of its own. Put another way, being emotionally numb feels horrible. Many people end up cutting themselves, or inflicting pain on themselves in other ways, just to feel something. They may also take these self-injurious actions to punish themselves in response to guilt and shame from childhood neglect, rejection, and physical or sexual abuse.

WHERE DO YOU FEEL YOUR PAINFUL EMOTIONS?

Many people feel their emotions in specific parts of their bodies, often in a way that is characteristic for them. After the loss of love, we speak of a broken heart. Grief, which is a life-affirming response to loss and not a negative legacy emotion, can feel like a hole in our stomach or chest. Anxiety, too, can be felt in the heart, causing palpitations, or in the head, causing headache, ringing in the ears, or blurring of vision. Guilt can be felt in the shoulders and back as an expression of burdens. Shame, of course, frequently makes itself known with a blush. Almost any emotion can stir up or shut down our very sensitive stomach or gut. Locating and remembering where you feel your emotions can help with the first step toward emotional freedom.

LEGACY EMOTIONS CAUSE MOST INSOMNIA

Nighttime is a psychological and spiritual challenge for many people. There are many good books about relaxation techniques and other approaches for enhancing sleep. Here, I want to emphasize that insomnia presents an opportunity for identifying and understanding our emotional profile. Staying awake worrying or reliving the day can be driven by guilt, shame, or anxiety, as well as anger and numbness, depending on what the individual is focused on.

Guilt can make people stay awake ruminating over something bad they have done. They can lie in bed, compulsively reviewing their burdens and duties, resenting them, and worrying about how to get them all done. Lying awake, the guilt-ridden person may imagine being judged by other people or God. Guilt can exhaust people and make them want to hide from their burdens, causing them to sleep excessively. Sometimes, people manage to fall asleep, only to be awakened a few hours later by depressing feelings of guilt.

In anxiety, people are usually worrying about something vague but threatening happening to them. They may obsess over what they can do to prevent some terrible event, like an car accident during an upcoming trip with the family.

In shame, people worry over having been embarrassed or disrespected. They can stay awake thinking of things they should have said to someone who offended them, or they may contemplate ways to get even. They may go over conversations from the past few days, wishing they had said something to fight back against real or imagined slights.

Chronic anger, usually driven by shame, can cause insomnia as people struggle over what to do about the circumstances about which they are angry. Numbness can make people languish in bed, feeling out of touch with themselves and their environment.

Sleep difficulties often go straight back to emotional suffering from childhood and adolescence. Many children overhear their parents fighting at night, so night makes them anxious. Others are sexually abused in bed, so bed stirs up the whole range of intolerable emotions. If you prefer sleeping on the floor or on a couch, or anywhere except in bed, your childhood bed and bedroom may, at times, have become a chamber of abusive horrors.

Nighttime can become a time for emotional or spiritual growth. This growth can begin with identifying the primitive emotions that keep us awake, enabling us to start taking the three steps to emotional freedom. We can introduce new psychological practices at night. We can think about the people we love. We can imagine how to make the coming day into a good one. We can count our blessings, feel gratitude, think about the beauty of nature, and pray or meditate on our relationship to what is good in the universe.

Keep in mind that difficulty sleeping can provide a productive opportunity to identify self-defeating emotions that may be subtly afflicting you out of awareness during daytime. Identifying the guilt, shame, and anxiety behind insomnia can open the way for understanding these emotions when they crop up during the day and enable you to replace them with better feelings, thoughts, and ideas, including plans for a better life.

"EATING DISORDERS"

Anorexic youngsters are usually, if not always, driven by complicated primitive emotions. Girls can feel so ashamed of their bodies, especially as they approach or enter puberty, that they starve themselves in order to look less like biological females and stop their menstrual periods. Obsessive perfectionism, another manifestation of shame, can push them to extremes in trying to look as thin as a model. Many feel tormented by anxieties over what will happen to them if they become fat. They may experience self-defeating guilt at the thought of enjoying food. Girls and young women are also prone to binge and purge (bulimia) in order to control negative feelings, often instilled by subtle attitudes within the family and more grossly apparent images within the culture where excessive thinness is promoted in advertisements, modeling shows, among celebrities and elsewhere.

People with anorexia and bulimia hold out the vain hope that they can control their tortured feelings by developing a fatless body. Instead, what will fuel their emotional recovery is gaining a sense of worth beyond how they look.

That sense of worth can be remarkably facilitated when their whole family works toward reducing negative communications and increasing unconditional love. This can be a difficult but emotionally liberating effort for everyone involved.

Telling these youngsters that they are wonderful, marvelous, perfect, or otherwise deserving of esteem misses the mark. They are already overinvested in wanting to feel self-esteem, which is approval based on accomplishments. They need to feel something far more basic: unconditional parental love. Parents who are reading this, I urge you to practice communication free of negativity with an emphasis on unconditional love and to set reasonable limits on younger children.[9]

As a parent, you may not have caused your child's eating problem. Peer pressures, distorted cultural values about women and their bodies, and other societal conflicts imposed on women and youth contribute to eating problems. On the other hand, your own perfectionist attitudes or anxieties may have played a role. All of us parents contribute to our children's emotional difficulties. More encouraging, as parents, regardless of the source of our child's problem, we are in the best position to aid in the healing process through positive communication and unconditional love, along with reasonable limit setting.

Overeating and obesity are also driven by our prehistoric emotions, and, once again, in a complicated fashion. People often overeat to handle their painful emotions. Food can soothe anxiety and loneliness, make us forget our feelings of guilt, and allow us to ignore our sense of being shameful.

OVERLY FOCUSED ON YOUR BODY

Painful emotions that we do not understand and cannot seem to control can make us preoccupied with our bodies instead of our mental and spiritual lives. Through the three steps to emotional freedom, we can begin the process of becoming free from obsessing over our anatomy and physiology.

Physical manifestations of anxiety, such as increased heart rate and sweating, can get people compulsively focused on their bodies. Fears of a heart attack or cancer often mask anxieties about living that are traceable to childhood and adolescence. If people are distressed about the way they live and not dealing with it, it is easy for them to become preoccupied with their bodies or physical health. Although it is distressing to suffer from these physical obsessions and fears, they may unconsciously seem less frightening than dealing with the underlying painful emotions and feelings of helplessness.

Any one of the self-defeating legacy emotional reactions can cause people to become preoccupied with bodily symptoms. Shame tends to make people overly concerned about their physical appearance rather than the function of their bodies. A shame-ridden person, for example, may become very self-conscious about looking overweight, bald, or older. Adolescents are extremely susceptible to shame about their bodies. Due to the nature of shame, the focus is on how they look to others, not on how they really are or want to be. The emphasis on physical appearance and on the opinion of others further negates the importance of the individual's inherent worth and unique qualities.

Guilt can focus people on how tired and exhausted they feel from taking care of others instead of taking care of themselves and their loved ones.

EMOTIONS CAN AGGRAVATE PHYSICAL DISORDERS

Many different physical disorders are aggravated by emotional distress, including neurological disorders such as multiple sclerosis (MS) or Parkinson's disease, any of a variety of gastrointestinal disorders such as gastric ulcers or ulcerative colitis, cardiovascular problems such as arrhythmias or hypertension, and skin problems. Stress and emotional problems may not cause any of these problems, but they can make the symptoms temporarily worse.

Tardive dyskinesia is a movement disorder caused by a number of psychiatric drugs, especially all antipsychotic drugs, such as Haldol, Risperdal, Invega, Seroquel, Zyprexa, Saphris, and Abilify.[10] It can also be caused by Compazine, which is used to treat nausea, and by Reglan, which is also prescribed for nausea as well as stomach problems associated with diabetes. Patients can develop bizarre-looking movements of any of their voluntary muscles, including their face, eyes, tongue, mouth, neck, arms, hands, legs, feet, and torso.[11] Breathing, speech, and swallowing can be impaired. Neurologists and psychiatrists who are loath to recognize disorders caused by psychiatric treatment often fail to make this diagnosis. They may label the symptoms emotional because they often calm down when the patient is relaxing and worsen when the patient is upset, stressed, or tired. However, this waxing and waning, especially in response to stress, is a characteristic of tardive dyskinesia.

PHYSICAL DISORDERS CAN AGGRAVATE EMOTIONS

Physical problems, in turn, can make emotional problems worse—and, less commonly, become the major cause of them. Exhaustion, with or without insomnia, will always increase an individual's difficulty in handling emotions. For a hard-driving person who works to the limit most of the time, becoming fatigued can bring out vulnerabilities such as feeling guilty, ashamed, or anxious about not getting work done. Chronic physical pain can become very discouraging and lead to depression, anger, and emotional numbness. Of course, the fear or reality of having a serious illness can amplify negative legacy emotions.

Many physical disorders can also cause emotional crises by reducing the oxygen or nutrient supply to the brain or by directly harming the brain. The common cold and the flu can make people feel depressed, perhaps through direct compromise of brain function and certainly from exhaustion or discouragement. Endocrine disorders that impair thyroid or adrenal functioning can sometimes cause depression and psychosis. Nonetheless, there are no known underlying biochemical or physical causes for any psychiatric diagnosis, including attention-deficit hyperactivity disorder (ADHD), major depressive disorder (MDD), bipolar disorder, schizophrenia, posttraumatic stress disorder (PTSD), or any behavioral or anxiety "disorders."[12]

TRIUMPH OVER PHYSICAL ILLNESS

A healthy, positive attitude will improve health and speed recovery from many physical disorders. In addition, people can maintain their emotional stability in the face of dreadful diseases if they can overcome their self-defeating emotions. I have seen patients develop cancer and become depressed and suicidal in response, and I have seen others lift themselves out of lifelong negativity to improve their spiritual state with the determination to give as much love to their family and friends as they can in their remaining days on Earth.

Chapter 17

REJECTING GUILT AND SELF-DESTRUCTIVE FEELINGS

People have the most difficulty believing that guilt is an unnecessary and wholly self-defeating emotion. Because shame feels imposed on us, shame is easier to reject as unwanted and unnecessary. By contrast, guilt seems to emanate from within and to express sound moral values. Unfortunately, if you harbor the belief that you are morally obligated to feel guilty when you have done something wrong, it will impede your emotional freedom, and so you may want to review chapter 11 before going further. It is critically important to understand and to remind ourselves that guilt feelings are unlikely to have any redeeming features in our personal lives. On the other hand, if you are ready to see guilt as a useless remnant of Stone Age emotions that you can replace with reason and love, you will make better use of this chapter.

BEREAVEMENT

Loss of a loved one—especially when sudden, unexpected, or involving a child—can be devastating. Because we are social beings, a severe loss can feel like an irreparable tear in the fabric of our brains, minds, and souls. Joanne Cacciatore, who works empathically with traumatically bereaved people, warns against assuming that bereavement has a time limit and opposes viewing it as a mental disorder suitable for psychiatric treatment. The bereaved need acceptance and understanding, as well as companionship when they desire it. I find it can also be helpful for anyone suffering from grave loss to identify and overcome the negative legacy emotions of guilt, shame, and anxiety that loss inevitably triggers.

ACTIVE EXPRESSIONS OF GUILT: DUTY BOUND AND OVERBURDENED

Guilt, shame, and anxiety each have active and passive expressions. The active style of handling guilt involves taking on duties, obligations, and burdens. We tell ourselves, "Don't forget all the things you have to do!" We feel pressured to get things done and never have enough personal time. It gets worse and worse as things pile up. There are not enough hours in the day to do everything. We do not realize we are doing it to ourselves by assuming increasing burdens in order to deflect or suppress our guilt feelings. Instead, we feel as if the duties and obligations have a power of their own to demand our attention.

In the later stages, we feel like we are "coming apart" or "breaking down" from overwork and worry. We keep thinking of the proverbial camel—one more straw will break our back. We worry over what will befall us and our families if we become ill or disabled. Yet, sometimes, we wish for illness as a way to get a precious few minutes of relief. We certainly cannot vacation—at least, not without taking along a mountain of work. Our friends begin to wonder if we will collapse under the strain.

We feel like a "good person" when we are working so hard, but we are fighting against fears of being selfish that will not let us rest. Yet, despite our compulsive taking on of responsibilities, we often fail to fulfill them. Probably, our resentment gets in the way. Having worked so hard to suppress our anger, we end up becoming angrier and angrier.

When driven by guilt, we often let down the people who matter to us most. Just as we have no time for ourselves, we have no time for them. We feel so driven to take care of other people, even if we don't like them, that we neglect those we love. Because our families miss our attention, we end up resenting them as burdens and obligations, whether they are at fault or not. These are the unintended consequences of natural selection favoring a genetic vulnerability to feeling guilt.

If we do not feel guilty, it is because we are so busy collecting burdens, each one aimed at warding off additional unbearable feelings of guilt. The active and seemingly aggressive approach to appeasing our guilt seems more socially acceptable than lapsing into helpless depression. It seems better than passively giving up and disappointing other people. Eventually, though, we run ourselves into the ground and fall into a more passive state of overwhelming depression. The way out of this process begins with identifying guilt and deciding we want to reject it.

PASSIVE EXPRESSIONS OF GUILT: DEPRESSION AND SELF-HATE

Depression and emotional immobility are passive expressions of emotional depletion due to our efforts to stay ahead of guilt. When we begin passively reacting to guilt, we can end up believing that people would be better off without us. No longer able to keep trying to be a "good person," we conclude, "I do not deserve anything."

The earliest signs of passive expressions of guilt are the "blahs," frequently experienced as trouble getting out of bed in the morning or a lack of energy. Nothing looks inspiring or exciting, and we feel we need a change, with no inkling of what it might be. We feel achy and tired and generally low in energy. We wonder if we are physically ill, but there is no evidence for it. As we become more apathetic, other people begin to say we look "poorly" and "depressed."

If we seek help from a mental health professional, we will be told that we have a biochemical disorder called "clinical depression." We feel so physically bad that we are ready to believe there *is* something wrong in our brain. But taking psychiatric drugs will further suppress our genuine feelings—our natural self-assertive and aggressive impulses and desires. The drugs will muddle our emotions and stifle recovery, especially in the long run.

GUILT LEADS TO FEELINGS OF HELPLESSNESS

Remember that underlying guilt, shame, and anxiety are feelings of helplessness from childhood, when we were utterly dependent on the goodwill of people around us. Blaming ourselves and feeling angry toward ourselves are the expressions of helplessness that we call guilt.

As described earlier in this book, guilt differs from genuine remorse. Remorse requires holding ourselves responsible for a destructive action, making amends, forgiving ourselves, and going on to live a more principled life. Guilt is blaming ourselves without doing anything effective about it—more akin to futile self-punishment than to self-help. We inflict pain on ourselves to no avail. As described in chapter 15, we have endless bad things to say to ourselves.

The self-defeating attitudes tied up with our legacy emotions are often so much a part of ourselves that we hardly notice their existence. If someone could get our attention in the midst of our guilt and say, "Hey, you don't have to carry those heavy, self-destructive principles around with you," we might retort, "What principles? I'm just doing what I'm supposed to do." We might also be shocked and resentful that other people do not act according to our guilt-ridden ideas and feelings. We might even get angry with them and accuse them of being selfish and self-centered—an accusation we have been mercilessly leveling against ourselves. Instead of getting angry at others who refuse to live by guilt, we are best served by no longer letting our own guilt drive us. Remember, guilt is inhibitory and self-defeating, and it does not lead to our taking beneficial actions. The underlying helplessness and dependence of guilt guarantee personal failure and continued emotional suffering.

Depression may last only a few minutes or a few hours. For some, it lasts a lifetime. However, at any time, we can begin the process of finding our way out of this emotional morass through the three steps to emotional freedom.

FEELING *GUILTY-IN-ADVANCE*

Your feelings of guilt may not enter your conscious awareness because you anticipate it and quickly take on new burdens and responsibilities in order to avoid feeling it. You notice that your wife is not happy, so without her even wanting it, you use the family savings to renovate the kitchen. Your husband is working too hard to make ends meet, so without discussing it with him, you fire your housekeeper. You know the ungrateful company you work for is heading for trouble, so you take on additional duties without compensation. You realize that Mom is all alone, so you use up your only vacation time to visit her, even though she shows no joy about seeing you and your family. You end up tired and resentful. You are aware that there is no time left for the kids, so you send them to an overly expensive summer camp.

Guilt can make us feel so ugly toward ourselves that we never let ourselves do anything that might stir up our guilt. We go through life being so "good" that that we hardly realize how bad we feel about our hidden desires for personal happiness.

You work hard but find little satisfaction in it. You want to take steps toward a much more exciting but less remunerative career. Then, you remind yourself how your parents sacrificed so much to prepare you for the job you have. Guilt is inhibiting your choices because you are so alert to any potential feelings of guilt that you never take action that could allow them entry. You never let your imagination delve into finding a happier career.

Feeling guilty-in-advance can express itself subtly in your life. You have a sixth sense that enables you to guess other people's needs even before they know them. You offer to help Joe move his furniture, even before he asks. You insist on lending Jim money, even though he shows every sign of not wanting to take it from you. Your relatives all know you will invite them to stay with you whenever they hint they might be passing through. You avoid guilt by becoming masterful at anticipating and providing for the needs of others.

Meanwhile, you almost never ask anyone for favors. You would wreck your back carrying your furniture before asking Joe to help you move; you would go bankrupt before asking Jim for money; and, as for your relatives, you would rather die than impose upon their hospitality. Guilt keeps your relationships with others out of balance in the returning of favors.

You end up feeling like a martyr to your job, spouse, children, friends, parents, or anyone who asks anything of you. You may not even be able to say goodbye to, let alone hang up on, an unwanted telephone caller. You are likely to end up feeling resentful or angry toward those people to whom you feel obligated, including your family and friends, and even toward the world in general.

You may never feel the underlying guilt until you decide you have had enough: you do not want to be bugged by your relatives anymore, you cannot stand your job, you need more help raising the children, or you want more love in your life. Once your wishes for a better life begin to surface, then your underlying guilt will blare out that you do not deserve anything better, that it is wrong to want happiness, that you are bad for having such aspirations, and that you will be punished like a criminal for wanting more for yourself. You will find you have been carrying a ton of guilt. If you do not become aware of what is happening, or do not have the support of a loved one or therapist, you may become mired in depression without knowing why.

We can become most guilty at the very moment that we are drawing closest to choosing something good for ourselves. At exactly the time when we are fed up with our way of life and getting a glimmer of a better one, our feelings of guilt are likely to slam us the hardest. Instead of breaking through to a more joyful vision of life, we break down into depression.

YOU ARE AS PASSIONATE AS YOU ARE DEPRESSED

The intensity of our guilt and depression is proportional to our passionate desire for more joy and excitement. This is another reason not to think of ourselves as "clinically depressed" or "mentally ill" and not to turn to psychiatric medications, alcohol, or other drugs. The moment we feel lowest is the moment of our greatest challenge. Feeling down and out, or lost, presents the opportunity to at last recognize and confront our disabling and debilitating feelings of guilt. It can inspire us to begin the work of overcoming our negative legacy emotions and replacing them with a better viewpoint on life.

NO MORE PREEMPTIVE GUILT STRIKES

In military jargon, a preemptive strike is an attempt to defeat the enemy before they attack. In effect, we hit them before they can hit us. The ethics of this are undoubtedly questionable in many cases, but when we do it to ourselves—when we hit ourselves before someone else does—it is unquestionably self-destructive and unethical toward ourselves.

Earlier, we saw how young children sometimes internalize guilt by hitting their own hands when tempted to touch something forbidden. That behavior illustrates what goes on inside our own heads. We punish ourselves to keep our behavior in line, but in line with what? With the same Stone Age emotions we are using to punish ourselves.

We learned as children to take preemptive strikes in order to avoid the guilt that we perceived our parents or other authorities intended to inflict on us. By our facial expressions and posture, if not by words, we communicated, "I feel guilty already, so please don't hurt me or make me feel worse." We learned to look guilty in order to show that we were already suffering—in effect, begging, "Please don't make me feel worse. Look how terrible I feel already." Again, we attacked ourselves in order to avoid being attacked.

TRYING TO BE A GOOD PERSON

By focusing our attention on being good, we drive ourselves toward depression and failing relationships. The underlying feeling that we are bad compels us to present ourselves as supergood. Instead of catering to these bad-person feelings, we can identify and refuse to act on them, gradually eroding their power over us.

Guilt actually interferes with our becoming better people. The guiltier we feel, the more angry and resentful we tend to be, and, therefore, the less loving. As already described, if we have truly behaved badly, it does no good to feel bad about ourselves. We need to improve ourselves, to make amends or apologize when feasible, and to change our conduct for the better. We are most likely to examine and change our conduct when we feel positive enough about ourselves and loving enough toward others to face our human vulnerabilities.

Guilt does not encourage the pursuit of higher ideals. The lives of people who lived by higher ideals, from Christ and Buddha to Sojourner Truth, Gandhi, Rosa Parks, Martin Luther King Jr., and Nelson Mandela, show that guilt was not their dominant motivation. They found inspiration in love for others and love for principles, ideals, humankind, and the divine.

THE MASQUERADE OF RIGHTEOUSNESS AND GOODNESS

When we insist that we are "good," it is often because we are trying to escape a feeling that we are very bad. Taught by family, friends, school, or religion that we are not inherently good, we try to fake it. We act very righteous. Inside ourselves, we have accepted the self-defeating idea that we are unworthy, even evil, and so we feel driven to create a superficial, unreal exterior. We feel compelled to work so hard to feel good because, deep inside, we feel so selfish and so bad. We suffer from guilt masquerading as righteousness. In that masquerade, we demand of others, "Why aren't you doing more for others?"

As a person who has devoted much of his life to reform work, I strongly believe that we prosper to the extent that we give to others, but guilt-driven actions based on prehistoric emotions undermine our ability to bring forth good results.

HOW WANTING TO DIE MEANS YOU REALLY WANT TO LIVE

Guilt and depression can drive us to feel suicidal, but there is good news hidden beneath these unbearable feelings. The strength of our wish to die is a hopeful sign. It corresponds with the strength of our wish to live. If we were truly indifferent about life, we would not feel driven to kill ourselves.

Our vision and hope for a better life can make us react despairingly to what our life has become. If we did not have this underlying drive to passionately love life, we would have no energy to misdirect into self-hate. Decide that your wish to die or to harm yourself is a frustrated response to how much you want to live. Then, determine to reject your negative legacy emotions and to work on the three steps to emotional freedom.

Remind yourself as often as necessary that feeling guilty, ashamed, or anxious has nothing whatsoever to do with our real value. After all, these self-defeating emotions originated prehistorically in biological evolution and in childhood experiences we often cannot recall. None of us deserve these emotions. They do not reflect on our real value. We must not allow them to ruin our lives and the lives of people who need and love us.

Take heart from how negative you feel about yourself and your life. It indicates the strength of your spiritual energy. Now, turn that marvelous energy in the positive direction of making a wonderful life for yourself and everyone you touch.

Chapter 18

OVERCOMING SHAME AND DEFENSIVE FEELINGS

In the words of Brené Brown, a well-known speaker and professor of social work, "We have to talk about shame." As she reminds us, talking about shame makes us feel vulnerable. In fact, the word "vulnerable" hardly captures how vulnerable shame makes us feel. Crawling away to hide in a bottomless hole— that is what shame makes us want to do. The root word for "shame" probably comes from ancient words meaning "to cover." This dramatically conveys that when we feel ashamed, we want to hide ourselves from view.

Keep in mind that all of us are ashamed to admit we feel ashamed—so please do not think shame is not one of your problems. Shame is an inescapable part of the human experience, but it is so painful that many people who struggle with it on a daily basis have little or no awareness of it.

We need to remind ourselves that shame is a primeval emotional response that has no place in a good life. It is not merely our personal experience of being rejected or belittled; it is the universal human experience, a prehistoric drive or instinct built into us by natural selection and triggered in early childhood beginning before we can remember. Shame is the great enforcer of negative legacy emotions, an emotional slap in the face to keep us in line.

Feeling ashamed makes us feel excluded from our own family or group. When severe enough, shame makes us feel that we are excluded from humanity—that we are fundamentally different, and the difference amounts to an irredeemable flaw.

Psychologists have long recognized that shame crushes our very identity.[1] This is because shame makes us feel excluded from our family and society, from the very source of our childhood identity. Shame shreds the fabric of our social relationships and leaves us in emotional tatters. At times, it can make us want to crawl away and die.

PASSIVE EXPRESSIONS OF SHAME: SHY AND WITHDRAWN

When passively reacting to shame by becoming shy or by trying to be perfect, we may not realize we are trying to avoid feelings of shame. We tell ourselves that we are withdrawing because we do not like other people when, really, we are afraid that no one will like us. We may focus on being perfect, but we feel worse than imperfect. We feel nearly worthless. We withdraw or try to be flawless in a last-ditch attempt to avoid criticism and embarrassment.

At times, we may mutter to ourselves about being worthless, foolish, or stupid. We may wonder if we have anything in common with other human beings. Despite this, our deepest conviction is that *other people* do not respect us, care about us, or give us any credit. That is why we want to avoid them or to act defensively.

When feeling shy, we think of ourselves as "too sensitive." Without realizing that we are angry with people, we feel defensive about what they think or say about us. We can become dreadfully mired in loneliness.

SHAME DRIVES SHYNESS AS A PASSIVE RESPONSE

When we are shy, we are afraid. What do we fear? Other people. Shyness is easily misperceived as harmless and even endearing. As children, and too often as adults, we succeed in making our fearful withdrawal look appealing, innocent, or cute.

Men commonly find shyness appealing and even alluring in women. Women who are afraid of strong men can feel drawn to shyness in men as well. Nearly all adults seem to prize some degree of shyness in children. Yet shyness is nothing more than a built-in self-defeating reaction to the fear of being shamed or humiliated. We are shy because we are afraid of the consequences of being more open, forthright, or assertive. We are shy because we have experienced too much humiliation in the form of being belittled, ridiculed, ignored, or just plain unloved or unappreciated.

You may have thoughts such as, "I wouldn't hurt a flea," "I never take center stage," "I value my privacy and can make it on my own," or "It's so hard to be perfect, but I keep trying." Ideas like this will not lead to an effective life. Perfectionism is not a positive goal; it is an attempt to avoid criticism for being imperfect.

Shame often corrodes our most precious and important aspirations. A little girl wants love from her parents, but they reject her when she reaches out. A little boy wants his father's attention and is ignored or laughed at when he lets his need show. A youngster in an impoverished and dysfunctional family wants to become an artist, teacher, or doctor, but his parents, siblings, peers, and teachers put down his aspirations. Most people who succeed in life have had to find the strength to fight through a tangle of humiliating circumstances along the way.

People who seem shy may seem harmless while harboring a great deal of anger. This may show itself as irritability and resentment with other people. It can lead to chronic hostility.

It is impossible to grow up without some shyness. Many of us who are very shy feel too ashamed to allow ourselves to realize it or to use the word "shy." We can become quite withdrawn from others before anyone realizes our shyness has become a crippling problem.

ACTIVE EXPRESSIONS OF SHAME: FROM TOUCHY TO VIGILANT

When feeling guilty, we feel powerful. We know we are bad and can do harmful things to the people we care about. We matter, but in a bad way. When we feel shameful, we feel powerless, unable to have any impact. We feel we do not matter at all to anyone. That is what motivates our anger at other people— we believe they are making us feel impotent and inconsequential. If we react actively to the shame, we want to show everyone that we will not take their mistreatment anymore.

Most domestic violence, even when perpetrated by seemingly powerful and arrogant men, is driven by underlying feelings of inferiority and weakness (see chapter 10). The man who towers in a rage over his diminutive wife or girlfriend feels at her mercy. Anything from a perceived slight to a refusal to remain obedient to him stimulates his unconscious feelings of powerlessness from childhood.

Shame is the strongest emotional force for social conformity. Shame crushes our individuality, creativity, and willingness to love. It rules relationships between children on the playground and in school and keeps adults in line with social norms. Fearful of what others think of us, we avoid being noticed, inhibit ourselves, or overreact angrily and defensively.

Nearly everyone is ashamed to admit having feelings of shame, but few things are more important in life than identifying these feelings in order to reject their effects on us. Appreciating the universal power of shame allows us to feel more sympathetic toward ourselves as vulnerable human beings who, like everyone else, are afflicted by Stone Age emotion.

ENVY

Probably every human being alive has experienced envy. When other people accomplish things we have been afraid to try, we are likely to feel envious toward them. They have indirectly shamed us by what they have accomplished. Instead of admitting that they have been braver, more persistent, or more able than we have been, we become spiteful and hateful. Instead of accepting that they may have worked hard, we think that we have somehow been cheated of our opportunities. We tell ourselves, "They didn't earn it; they got it by cheating, stealing, being lucky, or having the right connections." When we become envious, the very existence of successful people seems to be aimed at humiliating us.

When we feel envious, we need to take it as a signal that we are being held back by primitive, self-defeating emotions that keep us from advancing our lives. Instead of indulging in envy, we can emulate people who are more successful and use them as inspiration. We can say to ourselves, "Joanne managed to go to law school; so can I," or, "Sidney got a promotion; I should ask for one, too," or, "Bill and Mary have such a lovely home; I'd like to aim at having one someday," or, "Paul has the courage to stand up for what he believes; I'm going to take inspiration from that and live by my real principles."

It is true, of course, that life is not fair. Some people are born into much more fortunate circumstances than others. Undeserving people sometimes prosper, and good people can fail to achieve their goals. Many people cheat to get ahead, and others miss opportunities for wealth or power because they refuse to lie or steal. If we focus on these injustices in order to complain, to feel sorry for ourselves, or to stop trying to pursue our interests, then we doom ourselves to a shame-driven life. Even if we look successful from the outside, we will know within ourselves that we are being corrupted and made unhappy by envy.

Envy is much more destructive than jealousy. When jealous, we want something that someone else has. We might try to earn something similar for ourselves. When envious, we focus on how much we resent or even hate the other person. In the extreme, we seek to harm the people we envy. Compulsively driven by envy, we may become so destructive or violent that we end up ruining our own lives as we try to harm the other person.[2] Whenever we feel envious, we can take it as a signal that someone is making us aware of our failure to pursue the kind of life we want. By example, they are showing us what we aspire to, whether it is fame, fortune, romantic love, artistic achievement, popularity, or the courage to pursue important principles. Recognizing this, we can let go of our envy and instead strive to get what we want out of life.

FEELING *ASHAMED-IN-ADVANCE*

Just as we may constrict and control our lives to avoid experiencing feelings of guilt, we behave the same way in response to feelings of shame. Being ashamed-in-advance is a guiding force in almost every life. Growing up, we learned to do almost anything to avoid being rejected or slighted. We became experts at anticipating and avoiding situations in which we might be embarrassed.

Being ashamed-in-advance is probably the single most important mechanism of social control. We are trapped in conformity by the perceived or presumed expectations of others and by our anticipation of being shamed if we dare step out of line. Being ashamed in-advance operates so automatically in us that we hardly recognize its dominant role in our lives.

Our introduction to shaming comes early in childhood. Throughout childhood, our social antennae stick up high into the social stratosphere to pick up incoming signals of potential shame. Many people carry around a painful awareness of the chronic shame they felt throughout adolescence as they tried to deal with social standards, their changing bodies, and their peers and families.

By feeling ashamed-in-advance, we end up constricting our lives in a devastating manner. Our existence may appear orderly and rational, but it becomes too narrow and rigidly controlled. We avoid potentially embarrassing experiences, such as love and authentic encounters with other people, and intense emotions of any kind. We may also stop taking risks associated with trying to be more creative. We may never consciously feel ashamed, but our shyness and withdrawal can land us in boredom.

Shame particularly affects us in our social relationships as we compare ourselves to others. Because of our anticipation of shame, we may avoid innumerable activities:

- speaking or performing in public
- showing creative work to other people
- entering into athletics or other forms of competition
- deciding we want to be loved
- speaking our mind in front of other people
- making jokes or telling stories in groups
- taking an unusual or unpopular stand based on principle
- admitting we *really* want to love and be loved
- reaching out to do something good in the community
- reaching out to a friend in need
- making a determined effort to find someone to love

Life is infinitely enhanced when we put all shame aside in order to bring out the best in ourselves and everyone we touch.

NO MORE PREEMPTIVE SHAME STRIKES

As described in the previous chapter, people can make themselves feel guilty in order to ward off being made to feel guilty by others. They make a preemptive guilt strike against themselves before someone else can do it. In the same fashion, people carry out preemptive shame strikes against themselves. At the slightest hint that a situation or person might make them feel embarrassed or humiliated, they do it to themselves.

When we carry out preemptive shame strikes against ourselves, we no longer need enemies to keep us in line. We have become our own enemy.

Early in therapy, people often make negative comments about themselves in anticipation of criticism from the therapist. A client will declare, "I know I've botched up my life," "I know I should have gotten over this long ago," "I know I have no excuse for feeling this bad," or, "I know I'm boring." The client, expecting to be shamed, is, in effect, telling the therapist, "You don't have to criticize me; I'm doing it to myself." There is also an element of saying, "I'm not so stupid that I don't know I'm stupid."

Children frequently do the same thing to themselves, especially when they expect to be made ashamed by an adult. They will say, "I'm stupid." In part, this is a counterattack, aimed at pointing out the parent's meanness. In part, it is a preemptive strike aimed at warding off further assaults.

At times like this, a parent, life partner, or therapist has an opportunity to point out the harmfulness of these reactions and to talk about the importance of giving up self-assault in favor of a more kindly attitude toward oneself.

THE MASQUERADES OF PRIDE AND PERFECTION

See that beautiful woman across the room? She is perfectly dressed and statuesque. She radiates confidence in the restraint with which she greets everyone. The man on her arm is equally impressive with his fine-tuned demeanor. They carry themselves like royalty.

If you get to know them, you may be surprised to discover they are very shy. They feel lonely in the crowd and were relieved when you came over to say hello. They were not feigning humility when they looked uncomfortable in response to your compliments. Their flawless appearance has been cultivated to hide their feelings of being flawed.

When we masquerade as aloof, sweet and cute, demure, or harmless, we are living our lives in response to shame. As innocent as we look, we may harbor resentment over feeling so intimidated.

Shame is an especially potent motivation for creating masquerades. Shame demands a masquerade by making us feel that our real self is worthless or of no account. A woman may act aloof, as if she is more pleased with herself than with the people around her, but she is covering up shame and shyness. A man may bluster about himself and his accomplishments, but he does not really believe in himself. We try to tell the world, "See how proud I am of myself?" but we feel easily hurt. We try to communicate, "Nobody gets away with anything with me," when, in reality, we feel taken advantage of by everyone.

Many thoughtful people make a distinction between justifiable or healthy pride and arrogance, shallow self-promotion, and hubris. Sociologist Thomas Scheff, who has extensively researched shame, distinguishes between false pride and justified pride and points to the classic concept of pride as a high virtue. I suspect that any kind of pride makes us vulnerable to demoralizing humiliation, even from unjustified criticism, and distracts us from focusing on our own reason and ethics as the ultimate arbiter of meritorious conduct. We can feel personal satisfaction from principled living without having to embellish it with pride.

NEEDING TO BE PERFECT

Perfectionism is so common and yet so debilitating that it is worth returning to the subject in more detail. To be perfect means to be preoccupied with never making mistakes. We feel mortified by criticism, regardless of its intent or value.

Perfectionism stifles innovation, exciting new ideas, personal touches of creativity, and other such potentially imperfect self-expressions. To be perfect, or to attempt to be perfect, we must avoid mistakes at any cost. To avoid mistakes at any cost, we must constrict our imaginations, desires, and activities.

Young girls are especially subject to withering humiliation. Early signs of their sexual development draw attention from boys, other girls, and parents, often with an edge that makes them feel uncomfortable. Their attempts at autonomy and independence can make their parents feel anxious and tease them. Many otherwise strong women struggle with a self-protective shyness that prevents them from fully enjoying their lives.

Rediscover your self-assertive core, and assert yourself with reason and love.

Perhaps you will always be somewhat shy—perhaps not—but determine to overcome the inhibitions that keep you from being fully and happily engaged in life.

IN THE GRIP OF SHAME AND HUMILIATION

We all have experiences that make us wary of trusting other people, and it is true that people can take advantage of us. For those of us dealt an especially heavy dose of shame in childhood and adolescence, these feelings can come to dominate our lives and to inflict great harm on ourselves and others. We readily feel that our back is against the wall—that we have to defend pride or dignity—and this can make us dangerous.

Extreme feelings of shame are usually rooted in emotional, physical, and sexual abuse in childhood and adolescence (discussed in chapter 10). Many parents and older siblings try to hammer children into submissiveness by shaming them. Too many family members will take sexual and physical advantage of smaller or weaker relatives, making them feel vulnerable to humiliation for the rest of their lives.

What happens when our feelings of shame become overwhelming—when we are drowning in feelings of worthlessness and humiliation? If we react by quitting, we feel compelled to shrivel up and disappear. If we react by fighting back, we feel driven to strike back so violently that no one will ever slight us again.

Being in the grip of shame is a horrific state, filled with conflicting emotions of extreme pride and humiliation. When we compensate for extreme shame by acting superior, grandiose, and invulnerable like a superhero, we become psychiatrically diagnosed as manic and bipolar. We are really trying to make up for how insignificant and powerless we feel.

If we express our feelings of suspicion and distrust, others will label or diagnose us paranoid. We are really trying to figure out what is going on that makes us feel so intimidated. Young people who become overwhelmed by extreme humiliation end up diagnosed schizophrenic because they withdraw deeply into themselves and begin to live in a world so private that it becomes a waking nightmare. They are really trying to escape from a world that has imposed abject humiliation upon them.

Psychiatric diagnoses can add to anyone's feelings of humiliation. Psychiatric hospitalization commonly amplifies feelings of powerlessness and humiliation. So-called antipsychotic drugs clog the patients' heads with mental and spiritual cement, making them feel even more powerless and vulnerable.

When emotionally wounded people withdraw into themselves and into those intensely personal, fragmented, nightmarish worlds we call "schizophrenia," "mania," or "psychosis," they are usually suffering from overwhelming shame reactions. Unbearably burned by inflictions of shame, as described in chapter 10, they no longer dare to be with people.

By telling these distressed people they have "biochemical imbalances," "genetic disorders," and "mental illnesses," psychiatry not only misleads them, it worsens their stigmatization, humiliation, and feelings of exclusion. They are not suffering from biochemical imbalances; they are suffering from unbearable humiliation.

As a psychiatrist and therapist, some of my most poignant, moving experiences have involved sharing the feelings of people who are undergoing overwhelming psychotic experiences with hallucinations and delusions. When these individuals have trusted me enough to allow me into their emotional world, what they have shared with me is the experience of drowning in shame. I have sat with them while their faces physically swelled as if bursting and turned blood red with humiliation.

What I have tried to offer them in return for their courageous sharing is a professional companion who listens and cares. Through my words and presence, I have welcomed them back into a relationship with another human being who sees their fragility and treasures them. When this miracle occurs, the hallucinations and delusions fade—for moments, at least—and two people sit together with a shared feeling of trust. The recovery has begun.

If people scourged by humiliation can endure and return to us as they do, then surely we can deal with our own measures of shame. The rewards of facing and overcoming shame are enormous. Triumphing over and transcending shame reactions can open the door to a life in which we choose the kinds of social relationships we desire and the social risks we want to take toward becoming more creative, social, or self-determined. Overcoming shame allows us to regain aspects of ourselves thwarted or suppressed during childhood and adolescence.

It allows us to reshape our identities into the emotionally free people we have always wanted to be. Overcoming shame enables us to reach toward our highest ideals.

HOW VIOLENT FEELINGS MEAN YOU REALLY WANT TO HAVE A POSITIVE INFLUENCE

Any negative legacy emotion can breed resentment and lead to violent feelings, but, most often, the culprit is shame. The intensity of violent feelings reflects on how much we cannot stand to feel so vulnerable and how much we wish for positive results in our relationships. Similar to how suicidal feelings indicate a thwarted vision of a better life, violent feelings often indicate a thwarted vision of a life in which we are treated with respect and dignity.

The deepest shame of all is being unloved. It is so painful that most of us do not want to contemplate the possibility. When we become able to accept that we want to be loved, we become more able to seek love. In the process, we learn to both give and accept love, and we learn that, in mature adult relationships, these actions go together.

Shame is a great inhibitor of love. To dare to love, we must feel that we have worth and deserve to immerse ourselves in a life filled with love. Be especially alert to shame when focusing on becoming a source of love. The desire to love and be loved is not shameful—it is the highest human aspiration and lies within every person's ability to achieve.

Sharing love washes shame away.

Chapter 19

CONQUERING ANXIETY AND HELPLESS FEELINGS

It is easy to confuse fear with anxiety. Fear is not a self-defeating emotion. Fear gets our attention, alerts us, and prepares us physiologically and mentally to react.

All of us have had sudden frights, for example, on seeing a child run into a busy street or hearing a friend scream in pain from another room in the house. When we confront the danger by rescuing the child or running to the aid of our friend, the fright begins to subside, sometimes leaving us with a pounding heart, rapid breathing, and sweaty palms. We gradually calm down as we realize that the emergency is over.

Anxiety is very different. Like guilt and shame, anxiety encourages us to be helpless. It gives messages such as, "That's too much to face," "Don't try to think about that," "You can't handle that," "You're going to be overwhelmed," "Something threatening beyond belief is starting to happen to you, and there's nothing you can do to stop it," or simply, "You're doomed." Unlike fear or a fright, it can strike without warning or cause, and, unlike fear or fright, it can persist long after any real threat is gone.

Anxiety is a very raw and primitive feeling, closely related to abject, subjective helplessness. The subjective helplessness that lies at the root of all negative legacy emotions is particularly obvious and dominating during anxiety.

HOW ANXIETY MAKES US HELPLESS

While you are driving on a country road at night, a deer suddenly appears in the headlights. Fear! Your heart starts pumping, blood flows to your muscles, and your brain charges up to focus on the danger. In a split second, you remember what to do. You carefully brake the car without swerving and bring it safely to a stop. Meanwhile, the deer meanders across the road a few feet ahead of your car.

Instead, suppose you react with anxiety. Overcome with helplessness, you let your foot freeze on the accelerator, and you crash; or you overreact, slam on the brakes, and skid into a tree; or you panic, start screaming, and fail to do anything to prevent crashing into the animal. These responses are typical of anxiety. Unlike fear, anxiety is, by its very nature, demoralizing and self-defeating. As an inhibitory legacy reaction, anxiety disrupts our capacity to be in charge and assert ourselves effectively.

Anxiety creates cognitive stupidity that renders us dumb about what is happening to us in the moment it strikes. The emotional turmoil renders us unable to act, and we become childlike and helpless. Anxiety can strike unexpectedly, overwhelming us with feelings of impending doom, or it can linger in the background as a constant nervousness and fearfulness.

The paralyzing impact of anxiety can temporarily deprive us of our ability to reason and to make rational choices. Whether or not this suppressive effect served some use in biological evolution or childhood, it wholly disrupts and can ruin a mature adult life. Be prepared never to allow anxiety to render you mindless, overwhelmed, and helpless.

When reacting actively to anxiety, we can become frantic in our efforts to dispel it. We may struggle endlessly over a task without accomplishing anything. We may demand help from others but find ourselves too confused and upset to make any use of their guidance.

If we go to a doctor, we will be prescribed tranquilizers and sedatives that can temporarily suppress our anxiety by suppressing our overall brain function, making it even harder for us to take charge of our lives and assert ourselves in productive ways.[1]

Once again, it is critical to remember that negative legacy emotions have nothing to do with reality or with real fears and dangers. They are inhibitory emotions built in by biological evolution and further inflicted on us in childhood to stop us from asserting ourselves or acting aggressively in our relationships within the family.

Anxiety may well up when real-life emergencies are at low ebb. In the absence of external threats to preoccupy us, our internal ones can grow more loud and demanding. We fearfully anticipate an unnamed catastrophe.

Anxiety does not prepare us to react; it discourages us from reacting. It does not focus our attention; it confuses, befuddles, and distracts us. It does not prepare us for a real danger; it makes us less able to focus on real and present threats. Like guilt and shame, anxiety should not be given influence over adult decision making.

In recent years, the term "panic disorder" has gained acceptance in psychiatry and among the public. By definition, panic disorder consists of a few or more episodes of anxiety, or what we used to call "anxiety attacks." To understand anxiety is to understand panic attacks. The most remarkable thing about panic disorder is how the pharmaceutical company Upjohn literally made up and promoted the diagnosis in order to create a new market for its old drug Xanax (alprazolam). The drug company covered up that Xanax actually increased the frequency of anxiety attacks and created addiction in many patients after only six to eight weeks.[2]

Anxiety usually has prehistoric causes in childhood and adolescence. The child was made anxious by separations from the parents, an alcoholic and hence unpredictable parent, a broken family, repeated moves in childhood and adolescence, a serious childhood illness, repeated surgeries, bullying, child abuse, or foster care. Anxiety can also come from more difficult-to-detect factors, such as an anxious parent who induces anxiety in the child or traumatic events unknown to the family and unrecalled by the child.

ACTIVE EXPRESSIONS OF ANXIETY: FRANTIC AND FRENZIED

When we succumb to anxiety in active ways, we can get very busy doing things in a chaotic and confused fashion and accomplishing much too little. We pour energy into a project, but the anxiety creates utter confusion. We do this and do that, and we get nowhere. We may even break a few things or frighten a few people along the way.

The active style of anxiety can drive us into frantic, frenzied, or frenetic activity, like a squirrel that dashes madly across the road into an oncoming car.

The amount of energy may even seem aggressive, but rarely is it directed at anyone in particular.

As if someone is screaming, "Emergency! Emergency!" in our ears, we want to hurry to do something without knowing what it is. We want to do it now, without thinking, but cannot decide what it is we're supposed to do. We feel as if we will fall apart or die on the spot if something or someone does not intervene. Everything feels completely out of our control.

Anxious people may protest that they are trying as hard as they can. They may go from one doctor, therapist, friend, or family member to another, seeking help, but they never find it useful. They may try one psychiatric drug after another, or many in combination, and never get the results they want. Underneath all the activity, they feel helpless and confused.

PASSIVE EXPRESSIONS OF ANXIETY: IMMOBILIZED AND PARALYZED

Feeling that nothing can be done to control a situation signals self-defeating anxiety that can readily become invasive. When under the influence of anxiety, we find unlimited justifications for why we cannot find workable solutions. Here are some examples:

- We feel frustrated and confused trying to learn to use the new office computer or our cell phone because we are "not smart enough" or "too old." We get to the point that we do not even want to think about trying.
- We want a new job but decide it is futile to try because we do not even know what kind of work we want. When someone reminds us that we do have well-defined, specific interests, we are not sure what they are talking about. The "whole thing about job hunting" seems overwhelming.
- We are planning that vacation we have always dreamed about; another expense comes along, and we feel compelled to cancel our plans. Yet the expense is a rather routine, predictable one that we can easily handle. Our spouse wants to go over the financial figures with us, but we just do not feel like it.
- The children are out of control, and we cannot think of anything else we can do. We ask for advice from a friend, who recommends a book that

was helpful to her, but we lose the note with the name of the book and never call her back.

Obeying anxiety ultimately leads to helpless dependence, insecurity, slavishness to our fears, chronic tiredness, and resentment of work. In the extreme, we will want to give up.

HOW ANXIETY FUNCTIONS

During biological evolution and childhood, how did anxiety act as an inhibiting negative legacy emotion?[3] As children, when we were faced with threatening communications or actions from family members, anxiety blocked our perception, recognition, or memory of what was happening, thereby making it impossible for us to assert ourselves or to express aggression. Here are some examples:

- A little sister began to be tormented by her big brother when she reached age ten. He often threatened to "do something even worse" if she fought back. Anxiety rendered her unable to feel anger and stopped any potentially dangerous attempt to stand up to the bully. When she grew up and became a mother, something she could not explain stopped her from standing up to her own son when he reached his preteens.
- A five-year-old boy was sexually abused by a babysitter who then threatened to kill his parents if he told. In an instant, the boy felt terrorized. The abuse continued for several months, and the boy began to look anxious and depressed. His parents took him to a pediatrician, who put him on psychiatric drugs.
- When a child tried to assert herself, her mother repeatedly threatened to send her away. Those threats snuffed out any further attempts to stand up to her mother. Even after her mother became elderly and dependent, the grown child continued to take abuse. The mere thought of standing up to her mother brought on paralyzing anxiety she could not explain.
- A nine-year-old boy witnessed his father hitting his mother. When he tried to get in between them, his father threw him against the wall and

swore he would bash his head in the next time. Sitting stunned on the floor, the boy looked to his mother for help, but she was cowering and crying. After that, whenever his father raised his voice, the boy began to panic. As a grown adult, he experienced a panic attack any time he thought of standing up to an authority figure.

ANXIETY RARELY SIGNALS A REAL THREAT

When we feel anxiety, there is usually no real threat. Anxiety has been restimulated from the past. However, at other times, we may be facing very difficult circumstances when the anxiety sets in. Nonetheless, the event itself is not the cause of the demoralizing emotion. Our mind has made an unconscious connection between the recent event and prehistoric stimulations of anxiety in childhood. After the anxiety is identified, rejected, and replaced with self-determination and confidence, the more recent event can be dealt with effectively.

For example, a woman named Georgia who came to see me about frequent panic attacks explained that the episodes did not relate to anything in her life. Her previous psychiatrist had told her they were biochemical in origin and that therapy would be a waste of time. With further gentle questioning, she recalled that they mostly occurred when she was traveling somewhere and that they had become so bad that she no longer took the subway and had begun to further constrict her life.

Halfway through our first session, Georgia recalled that her first panic attack had occurred four years earlier on the subway when she was going to see her lawyer to sign her divorce papers. What had seemed to be a mysterious "mental disorder" suddenly could be understood as her unconscious mind fighting to avoid unbearable emotions related to her divorce. Later in the therapy, she was able to identify how the divorce stirred up feelings of rejection and abandonment from her childhood. She was able to identify and to reject her next anxiety attack and, eventually, to rid herself of the attacks. In the process, she became an overall stronger person.

We can reverse the effects of childhood and adolescence and learn to assert ourselves effectively at home, work, and elsewhere in our lives. Initially, the mere thought of self-assertion will cause anxiety, but we can learn to identify the anxiety, reject it, and instead choose reasonable ways to make ourselves more effective in dealing with people.

FEELING *ANXIOUS-IN-ADVANCE*

In the same way that many people feel so guilty-in-advance that they do everything they can to avoid guilt-provoking actions, and that many shame-driven people will do anything to avoid feeling humiliated, so, too, anxiety-ridden people may do anything to avoid being confronted with their anxieties. Compulsively but unwittingly seeking to avoid anxiety, they avoid anything that seems at all threatening. They do such a good job avoiding stressors that they do not usually feel much anxiety, but anxiety is driving them, constricting their lives by limiting what they dare to do.

Many people never take long trips away from home because of their fears about being away from what seems secure and familiar, including their family and friends. Many never try to go anywhere alone for fear they will not be able to cope with social situations. Taking care of the car, handling the budget, home repairs, and the like are avoided out of anxiety. More and more areas may become restricted, until the individual begins to feel overwhelmed by life.

Feeling needy or dependent are frequent signals of underlying anxiety. Anxiety is closer than guilt or shame to the raw childhood experience of feeling helpless and in need of support by parents or caregivers.

NO MORE PREEMPTIVE ANXIETY STRIKES

Just as we make ourselves guilty or ashamed to ward off someone else making us feel bad, we can make ourselves anxious to avoid even worse anxiety befalling us. When the smallest threat to our security rears up, we well up in advance with so much anxiety that we never approach the seemingly dangerous situation. In this way, people end up living in psychological or social paralysis. To avoid being struck down by an attack of panic in public, a woman lives a reclusive, chronically anxious life as a housebound person. In order to avoid his anxieties about asking for a raise, a man remains stuck in the same salary slot for endless years.

As in guilt and in shame, preemptive anxiety strikes against ourselves are learned in childhood and adolescence. We wrap ourselves in so much anxiety that we cannot tell if anything or anyone else is contributing to it. In effect, we burn ourselves to avoid being burned by others and by life.

THE MASQUERADE OF DETERMINATION AND TRYING HARD

The masquerade of guilt is, "I'm not bad; I am supergood." The masquerade of shame is, "I'm not inferior; I am perfect." The masquerade of anxiety is, "I haven't given up; I am trying as hard as I can."

In my psychiatric practice, I have seen people immobilized by paralyzing fear who nonetheless scream out, "I'm doing everything I can." They believe they are trying as hard as possible against a storm of disabling anxiety or a world that never stops coming at them. In reality, bit by bit, they have become so overwhelmed that they are no longer bringing their intelligence to bear on controlling their emotions and thinking rationally.

Why do people work so hard to look as if they are trying when they are not? We asked the same question about those beset by guilt. Why do they strive to look and act so good? Because they are trying to overcome how bad they feel about themselves. Similarly, the ashamed person strives to look powerful and in control to compensate for feeling powerless and inferior. The anxious person shouts aloud, "I'm trying as hard as I can," while, in fact, feeling too anxious to do what is needed.

Every human being is vulnerable to anxiety. We share the experience of a prolonged period of dependence and helplessness in childhood and adolescence. When we admit to being vulnerable to anxiety, we can renew our genuine determination to work hard toward mastering our emotions and our lives.

Avoid being harsh on yourself for masquerading as exactly what you are not but wish to be—filled with determination and confidence. Everyone, at times, has to put on a front about feeling competent. Masquerading is a self-defeating way of life, but, sometimes, it is necessary and helpful to hide our anxiety from others while we learn to manage our feelings in the face of new situations and challenges. As long as our masquerade does not aim at fooling ourselves, we can put up a good front while we gather our wits and gain self-control over our emotions.

FACING REAL THREATS

When in the grip of anxiety and panic, we feel utterly helpless. Dread can overwhelm us. As already described, if we experience a few episodes of anxiety, we will be diagnosed with panic disorder. If we feel compelled to develop rituals and habits to ward off the anxiety, we will be diagnosed with obsessive-compulsive disorder. If the anxious feelings lurk around most of the time, we will be diagnosed with generalized anxiety disorder. A doctor will prescribe drugs to suppress the anxiety, but this can only work by simultaneously suppressing our overall mental acuity and emotional self-awareness. Taking drugs almost guarantees our anxiety will worsen over time.[4]

It is far better to face the real threats in our lives while rejecting and overcoming the primitive, prehistoric anxiety they have stirred up. Many people who suffer from disabling or fatal disorders go on to live the remainder of their lives on a higher spiritual level. People who have been rejected and abandoned by family, friends, or loved ones can find the strength to create new and better relationships. Even as the deck of the ship begins to slip beneath the waves, some people will marshal their resources to the very end to act rationally, bravely, and with love. People can and do react with reason and courage in the face of all kinds of threats. In anxiety, the actual threat is an emotional one—that anxiety will drive us to give up being in charge of ourselves, our minds, and our spirits.

Anxiety has nothing to do with reality! It is a reemergence of childhood feelings of helplessness and dependence. It can be overcome by taking the three steps to emotional freedom: *identify* your negative emotion, *reject* it, and *triumph* over and *transcend* it.

Two of my patients and the wife of one of my friends held such deeply embedded attitudes of anxiousness, irritability, and rejection toward their children and spouses that I wondered if they could ever change. Each one was eventually diagnosed with a potentially fatal cancer and then, *within days*, decided to give up being bitter and to become kind, gentle, and loving toward their families. My friend's wife died of her cancer but remained a loving mother and wife for the remainder of her several years, and my two patients maintained their new attitudes for as long as I knew them.

It is never too late to reverse our descent into anxiety by identifying and then rejecting it—and by replacing it with stronger and more self-determined principles. Remember, especially, that you can reject the viewpoint that life is inherently threatening, unstable, or unpredictable. It is objectively true that life sometimes hangs by a thread, but we do not have to let that reality generate feelings of overwhelming anxiety in us. Under the most catastrophic stresses, many individuals mobilize themselves to achieve peak physical and spiritual performances. Instead of caving in, they behave more rationally and with more love than ever.

HOW WANTING TO GIVE UP REALLY MEANS YOU WANT TO TAKE CHARGE

Objectively, life can be very threatening, unstable, or unpredictable, but, subjectively, we do not have to let that reality overwhelm us. Even in wartime and in natural disasters, when life becomes especially uprooted, chaotic, and terrifying, we can reject anxiety. Many people respond to disaster by mobilizing themselves to take positive and even heroic actions. In fact, the more genuinely dangerous the present moment, the more important it becomes for us to focus rationally on the immediate threat, unencumbered by blinding, disabling emotions.

When anxiety strikes, it has little to do with reality and a great deal to do with the reactivation of childhood feelings of helplessness. We can change our attitude toward reality. Instead of clinging to security and safety in a seemingly unmanageable world, we can, in every moment of our lives, take reasonable and necessary risks in a world full of opportunities to learn to live and love.

Chapter 20

MASTERING ANGER

Persistent anger and emotional numbness are so closely related to each other, we can easily and rapidly swing from one to another. We may be harboring feelings of rage that frighten us, leading us to become emotionally flat or numb. Both the anger and the numbness ultimately come from feeling overwhelmed by guilt, shame, and anxiety. No longer able to tolerate these emotions, or the helpless and dependent feelings beneath them, we escape into anger, numbness, or both.

As much or more than any of our other instincts, anger can feel beyond our control. It can boil up inside us as a primitive drive that takes over and blinds us to the damage we are doing. But, remember, we can liberate ourselves from our Stone Age feelings. As we have seen through this book, even Charles Darwin, who taught us about our evolutionary heritage, believed in self-control, sympathy, and love as our highest achievements. Darwin saw that we can redirect and even transcend instinct and evolution through reason, free will, love, and higher ideals.[1]

Letting go of anger is a major step in liberating ourselves from primitive emotions. That is the mandate given to us—to make more of ourselves than our biological drives and to reach our highest potential as human beings.

THE LIMITED USEFULNESS OF ANGER

Anger can have useful, if limited, purposes. Anger can sometimes drive away a human or animal predator, but it poses the risk of dangerous physical escalation. Anger can indicate to others that their behavior is intolerable to us, and it may cause them to stop, but, again, there is the risk of our anger making things worse. Anger too often leads us to willfulness that results in conflict painful to everyone involved. It tends to drive people away, or to make them defensive and angry in return, without resolving anything.

Some people feel motivated by anger, and, undoubtedly, it can energize them. Unfortunately, while anger may give us energy and even direction, it often interferes with rational decision making. In sports, making an opponent angry is a technique for disrupting the other athlete's "flow" or focus. When we are required to fight, either verbally or physically, anger is not likely to make us more effective.

The best use of anger is as a signal that we feel threatened and vulnerable. If we identify our anger without acting on it, we can then focus on our underlying vulnerable feelings in a constructive fashion, such as communicating to a friend or loved one that we feel hurt. Anger can also signal to us that we need to figure out why we feel threatened. Despite these important exceptions, however, anger is expressed much too freely by most people, leading to considerable unnecessary or irresolvable conflict. It is almost always better to take a deep spiritual breath and to decide, instead, to express ourselves in a rational and caring fashion.

ANGER MAKES US IRRATIONAL

Anger usually disrupts clear thinking, putting us at the mercy of our impulses. Often, it forces us to persist at something that is irrational or even dangerous, such as acting vengefully despite obvious negative consequences to everyone involved.

Anger, as already emphasized, is most frequently driven by shame. We feel misunderstood or hurt and react back angrily. We can also feel irritable and resentful toward people who seem to make us feel guilty and overburdened. When anger is driven by anxiety, we tend to express it as frustration with ourselves or as vague irritability about nothing in particular. Our anxiety-driven frustration will probably not feel as extreme as the self-criticism and self-hate that result from guilt.

Expressing anger can provide a fleeting sense of power, and it can intimidate other people, but it destroys communication and trust and ultimately worsens conflict. Arguing is a thinly veiled power struggle. It readily deteriorates into anger and seldom improves relationships. When we feel angry, we can take it as a signal that we are feeling overwhelmed by guilt, shame, or anxiety. We tend to react angrily when we believe we have been teased, neglected, misunderstood, used, or abused, or when we feel we are not being taken seriously. We need to see through our anger to find out what has made us feel so vulnerable to harm.

It can be tempting to drink alcohol or take prescription or recreational drugs to control our anger. Caution is required because psychoactive substances, including psychiatric drugs, can erode our self-control, inflaming and unleashing frustration and anger.

Adults commonly use their anger to manipulate people. In contrast, when children express anger or have a temper tantrum, it is more likely that they are feeling desperate. Usually, they are mustering all their power to resist what feels to them like humiliation. However, if flying into a rage results in a positive outcome for them, children will cook anger up manipulatively. It is generally best for adults to ignore tantrums and, when the child is exhausted, to offer redirection. Children never need to be broken; they always need a judicious mixture of limits and love, as well as infinite patience from caring adults.

Many people mistakenly equate being angry with being "honest." They resent having to hold back what they "really feel." Instead, we need to recognize that our anger actually covers up how we really feel—which is vulnerable and threatened. We can tailor everything we say to build trust, express love, and improve our relationships. When we feel it necessary to speak painful truths, we can take a deep breath before saying a word. If we do decide to speak, it can then be done in a respectful and positive manner.

OUR ANGER ALWAYS FEELS JUSTIFIED

We rarely feel angry with other people without believing we are justified. Often, we have a seemingly unchallengeable rationalization. Sometimes, we are angry about genuine offenses or injuries. Someone has been insulting, neglectful, or threatening, or perhaps insensitive or uncaring. Often, however, despite our feelings of being harmed, the other person is often largely, if not wholly, innocent. Something they have done has stirred up painful past experiences and prehistoric emotions in us. Nonetheless, we are likely to justify our misdirected anger by finding some fault, regardless of how innocently the person is behaving. We believe and perceive that we are *fighting back* rather than initiating aggression. From our perspective, our anger and aggression is a counterattack, but the other person feels attacked.

Defensiveness is a good example of anger as counterattack. When we are feeling defensive, we rarely admit to being either hurt or angry. Instead, we deny having any negative feelings, or we say that we are "just frustrated." Nonetheless, the other person will usually experience our defensiveness as an expression of anger against them.

When we realize that anger is a superficial or surface emotion, we can ask ourselves what we are covering up. Why do we feel so vulnerable that we feel compelled to defend or to counterattack? We need to look beneath our anger to find out what has hurt our feelings. Most of the time, something will have happened that made us feel ashamed. This includes the whole range from feeling humiliated to feeling teased, neglected, misunderstood, used, or not taken seriously. At other times, something will have made us feel guilty or anxious.

It is always in our best interest—and the interest of those we care about—to think through our anger in order to identify our vulnerability and emotional pain. Then, the underlying painful emotions can be identified and overcome with a more rational and loving approach.

IMAGINING A LIFE WITH VERY LITTLE ANGER

Take a moment, and let your imagination explore the following possibilities for giving up active anger:

- Imagine almost never getting angry with anyone in your family.
- Imagine almost never getting angry with anyone at work.
- Imagine almost never getting angry with anyone who provides services to you, such as waiters or sales staff.
- Imagine almost never again getting angry or even annoyed with other drivers on the road.
- Imagine almost never reacting angrily in response to someone else's anger or stupidity.

- Imagine always thinking twice before you respond angrily.
- Imagine never trying to get your way by being angry or threatening.
- Imagine never again withdrawing into yourself to simmer with anger and to harbor mean or nasty thoughts.
- Imagine never again wasting any time thinking about how you could hurt, get even with, or confront people who have offended you.
- Imagine letting go of your long-held bitter feelings toward someone.
- Imagine giving up the idea of ever being outraged, enraged, or otherwise very angry.
- Imagine always finding a way to communicate without irritability and defensiveness.

If some of these fantasies seem preposterous, you may be harboring self-defeating anger. Purveyors of wisdom as varied as Jesus, Buddha, St. Francis of Assisi, George Washington, Benjamin Franklin, Abraham Lincoln, Martin Buber, Mahatma Gandhi, the Dalai Lama, Martin Luther King Jr., Mother Teresa, Jane Goodall, and Nelson Mandela have urged us to put away our self-defeating anger and resentment in the interest of a more rational and loving approach to life.

BEING ANGRY IS NOT THE SAME AS BEING HONEST

Anger can be meaningful when it is an expression of emotions that have been too long repressed. Sometimes, our anger informs us of our own frustrations and suffering; sometimes, it lets other people know they have hurt us. However, when we express anger without additionally expressing the underlying vulnerability, this will only build barriers. It is one thing to tell friends or loved ones that we *feel* angry with them; it is another to express anger toward them in a way that is frightening or threatening. We will accomplish more if we express anger in a way that emphasizes that we feel hurt. That can invite the other person to listen to us and to remedy the situation.

Especially when it is our dominant feeling, we may think anger is our most real emotion. This focus on anger being "real" can put us out of touch with ourselves. If we have too often felt vulnerable and victimized, expressing anger can make us feel as if we are finally taking charge or doing something about the situation. Instead, we need to find a rational way to handle our vulnerability and more effective ways to avoid victimization.

Anger is a signal that we feel endangered or threatened. It is important to get beneath our anger to understand what seems to endanger or threaten us. Then, we can evaluate our situation and determine if it is best not to express or act upon the anger. It is almost a mathematical formula: the stronger our anger, the stronger our underlying painful emotions and feelings of helplessness and dependence. Overwhelming anger requires us to take a time-out to consider what is making us feel so vulnerable.

VENTING ANGER IS LIKE FANNING A FIRE

In the 1960s, psychologists often thought that venting anger was good for people. They held sessions in which people shouted with rage, pounded pillows, or beat each other with padded sticks. It was not very useful. For one, expressing anger in such contrived and harmless ways tends to make people feel less powerful. They are playing at being angry. More important, venting anger tends to justify it. Couples who vent on each other are fueling a potential disaster of escalating aggression.

Because it borders on losing self-control, venting anger is often very self-destructive. Athletes in competitive sports sometimes "trash talk" in order to prod each other into becoming angry. The aim is to make the opponent lose self-control, including concentration, focus, or judgment. When the trash talks gets "inside the head" of the opponent, the angered player becomes less effective, sometimes committing an unnecessary foul or taking a penalty that harms the team.

ANGER MAKES US MORE DEPENDENT AND HELPLESS

Chronic anger at people close to us, such as our parents or spouses, can enslave us to bad relationships. I have worked with adults who continued to live with their parents in part because they could not give up their anger toward them. If they stopped being constantly angry with their parents, they would have to face reaching toward independence, which they did not feel ready to do.

Similarly, some couples stay glued together by their cycles of anger and sometimes violence. A partner who decides to give up being angry may lose any motivation for staying in the relationship. In this sense, chronic anger is similar to an addiction to alcohol or drugs: it blinds us to what is really going on in our lives and allows us to remain indefinitely mired in misery.

ANGER BANISHES LOVE

Anger tends to blot out feelings of love in both the person who is expressing the anger and the person who is the object of it. Love does not flourish amid anger. Love flowers within emotional safety and security. When we stop using anger as a way of getting what we want, we will find much better ways to achieve our goals through reason, sound ethics, and love.

WITHDRAWAL SYMPTOMS WHEN GIVING UP ANGER

Expect that you will go through emotional withdrawal after deciding to stop expressing anger in ways that hurt, manipulate, or frighten other people. When you stop yourself from expressing or acting on anger, you may discover that enormous guilt feelings have been fueling your anger. You may feel anxious and insecure when you can no longer blast people with anger. Most likely, you will discover you have been feeling considerable humiliation beneath the anger. You will discover your anger was trying to cover up hurt feelings over perceived slights, manipulation, or disrespectful treatment. Shame will very possibly dominate your withdrawal syndrome.

The goal is to go through this emotional withdrawal without returning to anger to handle your vulnerability. Then, you can begin to focus on being more reasonable, ethical, and loving. Keep in mind that angry feelings are the very surface of what we really feel. To stop these damaging emotions from ruining our relationships, we need self-understanding. In the initial withdrawal from being an angry person, we will discover we have been at the mercy of guilt, shame, anxiety, and underlying feelings of helplessness and dependence. Recognizing this, we can seriously begin our journey toward greater emotional freedom.

Chapter 21

BREAKING OUT OF NUMBNESS

Anger and numbness are closely related. Both are reactions to feelings of guilt, shame, or anxiety, as well as to the underlying feelings of helplessness and dependence. People who feel numb are often boiling with so much anger they are afraid to feel or express it. Numbness often alternates with anger and irritability. Both are last-ditch attempts to deal with underlying emotional suffering.

BENEATH NO FEELINGS ARE TOO MANY FEELINGS

People who have undergone an emotional battering often say, "I don't have *any* feelings." When that happens during therapy, I offer gentle reassurance: "You are having so *much* feeling that it seems unbearable."

Why would it be reassuring to hear that we are stifling enormously unbearable feelings? Chronic numbness makes us feel hopeless, inhuman, and spiritually dead. It can drive us to cut or burn ourselves, to bang our heads against the wall, or to take dangerous actions in order to feel something, if only physical pain or an adrenaline rush.

Emotional numbness manifests as unreality or weirdness, the blahs, and even physical coldness. We feel out of touch with ourselves and remote from other people. We lack motivation, and we no longer feel like active participants in our own lives.

We may say we are bored, but human beings are too full of vitality to feel bored. Instead, self-defeating, primitive emotions are suppressing us and sapping our vitality. Although there may be exceptions, I suspect that people who feel bored in tedious classes and meetings, or while traveling without their accustomed book, are actually having difficulties with the negative emotions that arise when left to their own imagination. An emotionally free mind and spirit are an endless source of entertainment and good company for oneself.

Finding a safe place or a trustworthy confidant can begin the process of emotional liberation. Although we may initially draw a blank about our feelings, talking can initiate the process of bringing them to the surface. We can also try to write down or verbally record our thoughts and feelings.

FEELING OUT OF TOUCH WITH OURSELVES

It is difficult to suppress one strong emotion without suppressing all of them. Either we are in touch with our inner signals, or we are not. If we suppress our anger, we suppress our feelings of love at the same time. Numbness comes in degrees, so we can be more or less numb at different times and in different situations, but, to whatever degree we are suppressing our painful emotions, we are probably also suppressing the rest of our emotions.

If a man comes home from work determined to stifle his rage at his boss, he will become less tender and sensitive with his wife and children. If a woman gets numb in the presence of her mother and father, then she will not be her spontaneous self with her children or husband, especially when she is around her parents. Whatever their source, our guilt, shame, anxiety, anger, and numbness render us less loving toward the people in our lives. Suppressing our emotions alienates us from those to whom we might otherwise feel close.

If you or loved ones are using psychoactive substances such as marijuana and alcohol, or *any* prescribed psychiatric drug, it is almost certainly contributing to or even causing your numbness. A general subduing or flattening of emotion is an extremely common adverse effect of short-term exposure to any psychiatric drug, and, with longer-term exposure, it frequently turns to crushing apathy.[1]

THE MANY FACES OF REMOTENESS FROM OUR FEELINGS

Like anger, emotional numbness hides much more vulnerable underlying feelings, including guilt, shame, and anxiety, as well as an ultimate sense of helplessness and neediness or dependence.

Feeling numb or out of touch with feelings can take many different forms:

- Henry wishes he knew what love meant and when he was feeling it.
- Jill feels attracted to her boyfriend, but she does not know if it is infatuation or the real thing.
- Carol does not seem to know she is angry until it is too late. By then, she has hurt someone's feelings.
- Caleb gets confused in tense situations with his wife. Only afterward does he figure out that she was making him feel guilty.
- Lynn feels like a kindergartner when it comes to emotions. She wishes she could take Emotions 101.
- Tiffany gets numb whenever her husband makes a sexual advance, but she does not know why.
- Tom goes blank sometimes when talking with his wife. Only afterward does he realize that he felt she was making fun of him and that he was getting angry.
- Anita spaces out when she is around her mother and father. It can take days for her to return to herself.
- Michael wants to scream, "What do you want me to say?" every time someone asks him what he is feeling.
- Maria wonders why people are always asking her what she is feeling. It would be much easier if they asked what she was thinking. She *knows* what she is thinking.
- Alex wishes his wife would explain to him what she means by "tenderness."
- Sam wonders why there is so much fuss about feelings. They don't seem so important.
- Terri has to study other people's faces to see how she is supposed to feel.
- Marilyn has been through a lot. She would just as soon not know her own feelings.
- Richard is so out of touch, it feels good to feel anything, even fear. He watches horror movies.
- Diane has felt remote from herself ever since she was sexually assaulted. She fears she cannot ever get her feelings back.
- Matt has felt "out of it" ever since his girlfriend left him. His emotions blend into a gray palette.
- Rita sometimes feels like a person from another planet, like Mr. Spock from *Star Trek*.

- Drew sees his wife or children get upset at him. That is when he realizes he must be in a bad mood.
- Lilly and David wonder what other couples mean when they talk about "being in love."

You may be slow to react emotionally. You muddle through situations until you have time to figure out what you are feeling. When someone is upset with you, you go blank. Even when a friend is being especially considerate or caring, you do not know how to respond.

In arguments or conflicts, your husband will say that you are getting angry or upset, but you deny it; or, perhaps, someone will say you are looking nervous or embarrassed. You feel so stupid about people noticing your feelings that you end up denying having feelings at all.

You may have trouble recognizing a particular emotion, such as anger, guilt, shame, or anxiety. You may not know you are angry, for example, until your stomach or head starts to ache. You may not realize you agreed to do a favor out of guilt until later on, when you find yourself feeling resentful. You may not realize how anxious you are until your hands begin to sweat or your heart pounds. You may have no idea that you are embarrassed until someone notices you are blushing.

You wonder how people can express their feelings so easily and spontaneously. For you, it is hard work, a major effort, to identify your feelings. It can be even harder to express them. You wonder if you are inhibited.

You may cycle between feeling out of touch and feeling irritated, frustrated, and angry. Feeling out of touch and feeling angry go together in part because they are both ways of avoiding more painful feelings, including underlying feelings of guilt, shame, and anxiety, as well as the helplessness that lies even deeper down.

IMAGINING BEING FREE OF EMOTIONAL NUMBNESS

The following imaginings may help you to appreciate how your possibilities in life can multiply as you give up being numb:

- Imagine that you have an unexpected burst of feelings, making you newly aware of a whole new aspect of yourself.
- Imagine that you can guide your life in part by recognizing your feelings of passion, joy, and love.
- Imagine that you almost never have to ask yourself, "What am I feeling?" because you usually know.
- Imagine checking with your feelings, as well as your thoughts, every time you have an important decision to make.
- Imagine doing some things simply because you feel like it.
- Imagine being able to sit safely with a friend while exploring your feelings.
- Imagine knowing when you are in love.
- Imagine knowing what kind of work you want to do for the rest of your life.
- Imagine no longer hiding from any of your feelings.
- Imagine being delighted when a loved one wants to share feelings with you.

NUMBING RESULTS FROM TOO MANY PAINFUL FEELINGS

Lack of awareness of our feelings—emotional remoteness, blunting, or numbing —can come from many sources. Irrational anger and numbing often result from severe stress and trauma. After being assaulted, going through a severe accident, or experiencing a sudden death of a friend, there is a tendency to undergo varying degrees of anger mixed with emotional withdrawal. This is a natural part of the healing or recovery process. If, however, the stress has been extreme, or if it has aggravated earlier trauma, these reactions may persist and become self-defeating. We can get emotionally stuck and fail to move on with a satisfying, productive life.

Unrelenting anger and emotional numbing often go together. People who are very angry often have little awareness of other feelings. Conversely, individuals who feel numb frequently also feel compulsively angry. When emotionally stressed or traumatized, an individual may cycle between self-defeating anger and numbness.

Fear of our own anger can cause us to feel out of touch or numb. Teetering on the edge of losing control over our rage, we may reflexively suppress our feelings.

Difficulty handling other people's anger is also a common cause of emotional withdrawal. As noted in the previous chapter, when anger is directed at us, we can become so threatened that we numb our own feelings and pull back emotionally from the angry person and from people in general. Bombarded with anger, we feel too vulnerable to let ourselves or anyone else know how hurt or frightened we feel. We want to shut down our feelings to reduce the suffering. Numbing ourselves in the face of someone else's seemingly uncontrollable anger is self-induced anesthesia.

Often, children—and sometimes adults—are belittled or rejected for having strong or seemingly unusual feelings. If, as children, we expressed our tenderness openly, we may have been abandoned or ridiculed. If we expressed justifiable anger, we may have been humiliated or rejected. We may have grown up in a family that feared and forbade strong emotions.

If we were taught while growing up that we would get in serious trouble for expressing anger, excitement, passion, or other strong feelings, we not only learned to hide these emotions from others, we began to hide them from ourselves. It was much too difficult to constantly inhibit disapproved emotions around other people while remaining in touch with those feelings in our own mind. We ended up losing touch with and suppressing the feelings that we are afraid to express.

THE DANGERS OF FEELING NUMB

Emotional numbness is a hazardous state. As a forensic medical expert, I have found that, prior to committing aggression, individuals have often lost contact with their own feelings as well as their empathy for others. Frequently, they have felt very numb immediately before acting violently. Witnesses to the violence commonly describe them as glazed in the eyes, robotic, and even unresponsive to the spoken word. They rarely show much feeling at the time, not even anger at the victim or satisfaction at having revenge. They do not go berserk or act wildly outraged but mute and stuporous. Especially if they have been under the influence of psychiatric drugs, they typically cannot recall or explain their feelings and often cannot even remember what happened.

Psychiatric medications, street drugs, and alcohol can cause or reinforce emotional numbness, but numbness can be also be apparent in people who are not under the influence of substances when they act violently.

Being numb is hazardous to the people around us. Even if our reactions fall short of violence, when we grow out of touch with our own feelings, we also lose touch with the feelings of the people around us. We can inadvertently inflict pain on our loved ones and associates. Our underlying anger makes us irritable, and our numbness makes us unaware of the harm we are causing to others.

It can be difficult to deal directly with the problem of remoteness from our emotions. Finding a safe place to be and a trustworthy companion to talk with can be helpful.

THE FIRST AND SECOND STEPS

Like all other self-defeating emotional reactions, numbness can be overcome by taking the three steps to emotional freedom. First, we need to recognize that we are feeling numb, withdrawn, blunted, or out of touch with ourselves. Second, we must reject and refuse to acquiesce to these self-deceptive feelings.

When we are feeling emotionally out of touch or numb, we can usually trace it back to demoralizing experiences with people in our lives that reactivated more remote assaults by primitive emotions in childhood. Feeling unable to handle the intense emotions, we withdrew our feelings from other people, became emotionally distant, and ended up lacking empathy for ourselves and others. To heal, we need to reverse the process to find people with whom we can communicate.

Reliving past traumatic experiences can be helpful, but there is always a risk that revisiting painful times will reinforce a sense of helpless victimization. In therapy, I avoid delving into emotionally charged issues until the individual feels able and willing to take charge of the process and make good use of the information.

We can assume there is a great deal of anger beneath our numbing. Anger lurks beneath our guilt, shame, or anxiety, or all three. Beneath that, expect to find significant helplessness and neediness. It takes considerable stress to drive us into feeling numb. We did not become emotionally flat or apathetic without enduring losses or harm at the hands of other people, often in childhood and again in adulthood. Getting in touch with our feelings is likely to require learning to trust people again.

The three steps to emotional freedom begin with identifying our painful feelings. At the same time, promise yourself not to act on painful feelings as they arise inside you. That will make it safer to get beneath the numbness. Remind yourself that, no matter how bad you feel, these emotional reactions have little or nothing to do with reality—with who you really are and what you can make of your life. They are primitive relics of biological evolution and childhood influences. After you have felt and identified them, you can begin the process of repeatedly refusing to obey them while you build or rebuild the pursuit of life, liberty, and happiness.

HOW FEELING NUMB MEANS YOU HAVE A GREAT DEAL OF FEELING

Remember that you would not feel numb if you did not have suppressed feelings crying for release. As numb as you feel, and as angry as you may also feel, that is how much potential you have for more positive feelings, including love. Think of it this way: The degree of your numbness reflects the degree of your suppressed passions. If you are very numb, you are also very passionate. You have so much emotional potential that it has caused a reactive shutdown.

No one is actually empty or devoid of feelings. Instead, we have so many feelings that we cannot stand it, so we take flight into anger and numbness. This is good news! You can peel back the layers of your painful feelings and, in the process, find what lies at the heart and soul of every human being: the desire to love and be loved, and to build a successful and meaningful life.

Chapter 22

HOW TO RUN OUR MINDS AND LIVES

The decision to reject subjective or emotional helplessness and to be in charge of ourselves is critical to our lives. It means we are responsible for our inner emotional and mental landscapes and for making the best possible decisions to direct our lives. It opens the way to living by means of reason and love. Rejecting helplessness is a choice, but it has such life-changing power that it feels like a momentous action.

Crises and challenges frequently demand a decision between helplessness and empowerment, between hateful and loving responses, between giving up and renewing our efforts, and between accepting defeat and embracing another heroic effort. Being autonomous entails rejecting our self-defeating emotions, our half-hearted efforts to be responsible, and our underlying feelings of child-like helplessness and dependence.

When we finally decide to take charge of our lives and to make the most of all our opportunities, something remarkable happens. We no longer harbor resentment and regret. Becoming able to experience emotional freedom, however briefly, is so satisfying in itself that we begin to look forward to the future without regret.

REAL FREEDOM

Our freedom to take actions can be gravely limited by outside circumstances and often requires us to make the most of the few opportunities available to us. These external limits on our freedom can motivate us to take liberating actions but are seldom the cause of grave emotional suffering. Nor are external limitations the most restrictive factor in most of our lives. Our negative legacy emotions are the most pervasive, persistent, and powerful impediments to our freedom. They prevent us from taking advantage of the choices available to us. Emotional freedom and freedom of choice go hand in hand, and both depend upon becoming as free as possible of guilt, shame, anxiety, and chronic anger or numbness. Real freedom begins within, with our emotional freedom to make rational and loving choices.

THE AUTONOMY TOGGLE SWITCH

Taking charge of our lives, or failing to do so, can be like throwing a toggle switch. Switch it once to the on position, and we no longer feel sorry for ourselves but, instead, welcome being fully in charge of our lives. Switch it off, and we are in trouble.

Almost exactly like that, a person can decide at one moment to take charge of his or her life no matter what and, at another moment, decide to surrender to emotions or circumstances that seem overwhelming.

When rejecting helplessness and self-destructive attitudes, we cannot leave any wiggle room. When we first begin to face this essential truth about life, we have to practice consciously choosing autonomy from minute to minute. Eventually, this choice can become second nature, although the commitment to personal autonomy will have to be consciously renewed at times of extreme stress and conflict, especially within our family.

The human spirit is so strong that people with brain injuries can learn to take charge of their lives. As described earlier, many people injured by head trauma, psychiatric and street drugs, and shock treatment can learn to live better, happier lives than before they were injured.

Life can be lived from a loving viewpoint, or not. We can make ourselves into a source of love and a gift to others, or not. It is a choice—not an easy choice, but a choice of vast significance.

We've had a tough time at the office. Now, at lunch, our waitress is having a tough time. She can't get anything to our table promptly. Do we make her miserable? Or do we empathize with her as we would with ourselves, help her through her tough time, and, incidentally, guarantee ourselves the best service she can deliver? Or do we turn on her, as we might on ourselves, and add our criticism to her already stressful day? The choice is always there. We can go either way.

One of our children is screaming for no apparent reason, and we've "had it up to here." Do we strike out in anger, humiliating and possibly hurting our child? Or do we take a deep breath and purposefully decide to exert firm yet loving discipline? Again, the choice is ours.

Our spouse has threatened to leave. We love him or her very much, but this threat is too frightening and humiliating. We could threaten back. Worse yet, we could leave as a preemptive strike, demolishing our loved one before we get demolished. Or we can remain in charge of our own feelings and spiritual state by rejecting our panic and humiliation. We can continue working toward more loving communication. We can look into our own hearts to see what contribution we are making to this pattern of failure in our relationship. Again, when we are relatively free of guilt, shame, and anxiety, the choices can become surprisingly clear.

TURNING THREATS INTO CHALLENGES

When we see something as a *threat*, we tend to feel anxious and even helpless. When we see the same thing as a *challenge*, we prepare ourselves to do everything we can to master it.

Guilt, shame, and anxiety are threats from the deep past of biological evolution and our childhood. They warn us that something bad is going to befall us if we do not obey them and suppress our autonomous self-assertion. They push us toward self-defeating actions. The creative response is to renew our autonomy and take charge of ourselves. At that point, we can identify our negative legacy emotions, reject their influence, and do everything we can to bring about an outcome based on reason and love.

I had known George and his wife Annette for years and loved them both. I also felt they loved each other, but George was always complaining about his wife. She wasn't feminine enough, she wasn't soft enough, and she wasn't devoted enough. He was often attracted to younger, more passive women, and this, of course, made his wife miserable. Despite these shortcomings, however, he was in many ways a devoted and loving husband and father.

I always questioned George's way of viewing his wife. Where he complained about her lack of femininity and softness, I saw independence and strength. I also suspected that George really loved her a great deal more than he was willing to admit. But he carried this burden of withholding his love. He'd always been this way with women, even before meeting Annette, and there was no reason to believe he'd be different with anyone else.

George developed a dangerous-looking growth on his skin and, in his fashion, tried to ignore it. Annette, in her fashion, took charge and made sure he had it biopsied. The fateful phone call came to her. Her husband had a malignancy that would most probably cause his death within the next year or two.

With great fear for his reaction, Annette took George aside to tell him the devastating truth. She chose a quiet place in the woods behind their house.

Let me continue the story in George's words: "I didn't know what my wife wanted. It really scared me, the serious manner in which she said she had something important to tell me, that we had to be alone, away from the kids, and all. I decided, 'This is it, George. You've finally done it. She's fed up with your crap, and she's going to leave you.'"

"Instead," George explained, "She told me I had a serious form of cancer. I might not survive two more years. Even then, I would probably need surgery and chemo."

Tears came to George's eyes as he told me, "Without a moment of hesitation, I blurted out, 'Cancer? Is that all? I was afraid you were finally leaving me! I was afraid you took me out here to say goodbye.'"

From that moment, both George and his wife agree that he became a changed man. Annette told me, "He finally loves and appreciates me the way I always wanted him to. Instead of rejecting me for my strength, he loves me for it. He is tender and passionate the way he never was before. And he's so much more open. He really shares his feelings with me."

George explained to me, "It just clicked. I'd been married to this woman for twenty years, and, for twenty years, I'd been playing games with her and with other women who came along. I'm almost glad I got sick. These last two years have been worth it."

The cancer was fatal, and George died three years later. He maintained until the end that these had been the best years of his life. He gave his family a positive legacy of love.

People can change. If the incentive is powerful enough, they can change overnight. Overnight? George changed in seconds.

People can change for the better or for the worse. Some, on finding they are terminally ill, bring out the worst in themselves and others. It can be heartbreaking to them and to everyone around them. Why do it that way when we can be a source of love until the end?

TAKING OUR LIVES INTO OUR OWN HANDS

In life, what seems like the easy way is usually the hard way, and what seems like the hard way is usually the easiest way in the long run. The individual who looks for the easy ways in life is doomed. He will never meet his potential at school, at work, or in his personal relationships and spiritual life. Life will only get harder and harder for him while he simultaneously makes life harder and harder for others. When we choose the easy way, it eventually becomes the hardest way of all, dragging us down, along with the people nearest and dearest to us.

One of the most seductive of the easy ways is conformity. We all sometimes find ourselves trying to be like others in order to stay out of trouble and be accepted. Our lives get smaller and smaller, and our very selves seem to shrink. By contrast, making the hard decisions, one after another, to pursue an ethical life will make that life as successful as possible.

Many people come to therapy with a determination to use every bit of help to improve their lives. They enjoy applying what they learn and are pleased with how they improve from day to day. Unfortunately, other people come for help with an attitude of "Save me" and "I can't help myself." They will make little or no progress until they recognize their helpless feelings and decide to reject them in favor of taking charge of their mental life and conduct. Overcoming subjective or emotional helplessness may be achieved slowly, one small increment at a time. It can also come quickly, like a news flash: "I can take much greater charge of how I think, feel, and act!" This realization that we do not have to be helpless is life changing. It is the basis for every other positive step.

BUT WHAT ABOUT THOSE OF US "HANDICAPPED" BY MISFORTUNE?

Learning to live a positive life is not limited to those of us with relatively positive childhood and adolescent experiences. David Pelzer endured a childhood so abusive that it is difficult to read his horrific descriptions. Nonetheless, and perhaps in part because of the huge effort it took to transcend the abuse, Pelzer went on to live a successful life and to become a powerful author of positive psychology. In his book *Help Yourself,* in a section titled "You Do Not Need to Be a Victim," Pelzer writes:

> All of us have had and will continue to face issues in our lives for the rest of our lives. Nothing and no one on this planet can stop it. It's a fact of life. Someone once said that it's not one's external but his internal environment that truly counts. So, *your* attitude is everything.[1]

Al Siebert survived involuntary commitment to a mental hospital with the diagnosis of paranoid schizophrenia. He rejected psychiatric treatment and went on to become a leader in the psychology of resilience. He concludes *The Survivor Personality* with these words:

> Thus it is that adversity can lead to the discovery of strengths you did not know you had. An experience emotionally toxic for others can be made emotionally nutritious, and a difficulty that almost breaks your spirit can be turned into one of the best things that ever happened to you.[2]

Similarly, Jerome Kagan observes:

> Put plainly, a conception of children as frail, helpless, passive pawns errs by disregarding their coping capacities and the power of a loss or frustration to provoke a thoughtful analysis and attempts to carve out a satisfying, productive life. Experts who write that all stressors permanently impair children run the risk of persuading victims of their impotence. . . . Rather, what I am suggesting is that children, like skilled actors and actresses, interpret the script they are given.[3]

If we were making life-changing decisions as children, then surely we can do so as adults—and with greater wisdom and love.

AUTONOMY GOES WITH SELF-RESPECT

Autonomy and self-respect go hand in hand. It becomes extremely difficult, if not impossible, to remain in control of our emotions and actions if we are being bombarded with disrespect. A key to successful living is to insist on being treated respectfully. As a therapist, when parents come for help with their out-of-control and emotionally distressed children, I first focus on creating an environment of mutual respect in the family, which starts when the parents begin to insist that all communications from their children be made respectfully. Once parents establish this standard and adhere to it themselves, then, and only then, does it become possible for parents and children to live together cooperatively.

Similarly, when couples come for counseling, I begin by teaching them to treat each other with respect. Although I believe love is the highest value, few of us are capable of expressing or even feeling love when being treated in a way that demeans us.

To be successful in our personal and professional lives, we need to carry ourselves with a sense of self-respect. This instantly affects other people, making them more cautious about acting disrespectfully and more eager to receive us positively. If these efforts fail to have the desired effect, it may become necessary to explain, as nicely as possible, that the other person's attitude or manner of speaking makes us feel disrespected. Most people will respond to this by apologizing and trying to change their behavior, at least temporarily.

If people continue to relate to us disrespectfully, we need to take it seriously. We may express more adamantly that we require mutually respectful conduct, or we may have to evaluate whether to remain in the relationship. Under most circumstances, if we insist in a kindly manner on respectful treatment, offenders will change their attitudes. Compulsively disrespectful people, when gently confronted by a person who insists on respect, are likely to become embarrassed and to back off or leave rather than escalate. On those rare occasions that someone insists on disrespecting us, we should do what is necessary and ethical to remove ourselves from the situation. Obviously, we would not abandon someone whose life was in danger because they were treating us disrespectfully, but, in general, it is possible to find or create a personal and work life in which people respect each other.

Of course, people deny that they are being disrespectful or demeaning. We've probably all been told at one time or another, "You're too sensitive," "I was only kidding," or, "You take everything I say too seriously." For this reason, it is important for us to set our own standards for what it means to be treated with dignity. We need to explain, "You may think that teasing is OK, but it doesn't feel good to me. So you need to stop."

Conversely, if people tell us that we are hurting their feelings or otherwise being disrespectful, we should do our best to relate to that person in a way that makes them feel comfortable. Without this simple rule of mutual respect, relationships can quickly deteriorate.

AN END TO ALL RESENTMENT AND REGRET

Resentment and regret are closely related. When we resent our current circumstances and anticipated future, we tend to regret our past. Resentment grows from the feeling that other people or unfair circumstances have irrevocably harmed us. When we feel so negative about our lives, it is no wonder we regret the past. We might say that regret is driven by resentment of the past and, even worse, by resentment of the sum total of our lives. When we resent and regret, we make the self-defeating assessment that our lives are flawed and beyond redemption.

The way out of resentment and regret is straightforward. First, we have to take responsibility for our present and future lives. Even if, in the past, we were trapped in ways that were out of our control—which is seldom the case beyond childhood—we always have to take full responsibility for our own actions. Put simply, when we become autonomous, we stop resenting our past.

Second, we need to express gratitude for everything we have. It is not possible to be grateful and resentful at the same moment.

Finally, we have to decide to make the most of our lives—to dedicate ourselves to principled living and the achievement of our highest ideals. In my personal and clinical experience, the moment we (1) take responsibility for all our actions, (2) become grateful, and (3) decide to go after what we truly value in life, all resentment and regret die of irrelevance and lack of sustenance, and we begin to prosper emotionally.

I want to make clear that leaving resentment and regret behind does not require great accomplishments or making up for what we have lost in the past. It requires a change in attitude and outlook—a determination to make the most of every present and future moment given to us.

We cannot control the greatness of our achievements. There is too much chance involved. Similarly, after a great loss, we may not be able to reclaim or rebuild everything we once had. Just as living in a physically healthy fashion does not guarantee perfect health, an emotionally healthy approach does not guarantee a perfect life. What we can guarantee is that a positive, principled approach to life reaps instant benefits of self-satisfaction and happiness, and it offers the best opportunity for success in anything principled we attempt.

We can choose at any moment to set aside our particular emotional handicaps in the interest of thinking straight, making positive choices, and loving. We will have additional work to do as we practice consistently recognizing, identifying, and rejecting our self-defeating emotions while promoting our life-enhancing ones. Meanwhile, we and everyone around us will quickly become aware of a major change for the better.

Whatever emotional ball and chain we carry, it is never too late to saw it loose. No matter how much we have handicapped ourselves, whatever time we have left will become infinitely happier.

Disappointment, betrayal, and losses may overwhelm us, but, once we decide to take charge of life and become a source of love, we will no longer be preoccupied with what has gone wrong in the past. We will realize that what matters is being the person we want to be in the present moment while planning to continue bringing out our best in the future.

Chapter 23

FACING REAL-LIFE CHALLENGES

This chapter offers a "Real-Life Challenges Chart" that compares helpless responses with self-determined responses. The chart can be used as an aid in identifying self-defeating approaches to life that are driven by guilt, shame, anxiety, and underlying helplessness and dependence. The chart also provides reminders to look toward love and higher ideals as guides for meeting every challenge.

Some of the "Self-determined responses and outcomes" below may seem unrealistic. For instance, can people really recover from serious mental crises and disturbances without resort to psychiatric drugs? The answer is a resounding yes. I have been in the private practice of psychiatry since 1968, seeing a full range of patients, and I have never started anyone on psychiatric drugs. People recover far better without impairing their brains and minds with drugs.

Is it possible for people with mental impairment from brain injury to go on to live better lives than before they were injured? Yes, it happens all the time. When the human spirit becomes inspired to live by the best principles, such as personal responsibility and love, the spirit can often shine through—even with a wounded brain—better than it did before the injury.

Of course, a summary chart has to be very simplified and cannot capture what life is all about, but it can be helpful for stimulating thought. Please review this chart in the spirit of getting from it whatever seems useful to you. Again in the interest of your privacy, you may not want to mark your answers directly into the book.

THE REAL-LIFE CHALLENGES CHART

Real-life challenges	Helpless or over-whelmed responses	Self-determined responses and outcomes
My marriage isn't working. We have become increasingly disappointed and angry with each other over the years. The spark is gone, and it's become dreary. We rarely enjoy each other anymore.	Most of my friends tell me I expect too much from marriage. So what if I don't feel loved? So what if sex is uncomfortable or nonexistent? I have to live with it. No one's marriage is perfect.	I remember how much we loved each other in the beginning. Our relationship felt blessed. Maybe this book can help us, and there are other good books and many qualified marriage counselors. I want to make our marriage loving and happy again.
My partner has ended our relationship. My partner has decided to leave me and says that this time it's final.	I'll die if she does that. I can't stand to go through another loss. It feels like the end—not only for the relationship but for me. I have to give up on love.	I am still in love and will work on reviving and improving our relationship. If it doesn't work out despite my best efforts, I can learn to love again, this time without holding back and without making the same mistakes again.
My lifetime partner has died. I never thought this would happen. Not so soon. My partner meant everything to me.	I feel guilty that I didn't give more love and ashamed of being so lost without my partner. I'm anxious about the future. I'm becoming angry and numb. I will never go through this again, even if I have to be alone.	I reject guilt, shame, and anxiety and grieve my loss without suppressing my feelings of love. I will keep my love alive in my heart and my memories and be grateful for the time we had. Perhaps, with time, I'll be open to new love.

My life lacks creativity. Whether it's writing, composing music, taking photographs, cooking, or traveling, I don't have much creativity in my life. Many people want more creativity, but very few actually achieve it.	I'll put my creative fantasies and dreams on the back burner. Everybody's got childish daydreams like mine. No sense trying for something so difficult that I end up disappointing myself again.	I will make time for my special creativity and actually complete some projects. Then, I can decide if I want to market my work, even to a limited audience, and if I want to devote more of my life to being creative.
Psychotherapy has not worked for me. I've been to psychotherapists and haven't gotten any useful help from them.	All psychotherapists are frauds. It's bought friendship. My problems can't be solved with anyone else's help. I'll learn to live with them.	I will continue to shop for a therapist who cares about me and my well-being, displays wisdom, and promotes my strengths. At the same time, I will take responsibility for my therapy experience and my emotional recovery.
I wish I could find work that interests and excites me. All the professions I'm interested in require training, are difficult to break into, and don't necessarily pay very well.	People who have great careers are lucky, have connections, or got a lot of help from their parents. For me, a job is a job, and I've got a family to support.	I will make a rational decision to take the necessary steps to finally do the kind of work I want to do. If I have to, I'll go back to school, or I'll figure out a happier compromise between making a living and doing what I feel destined to do.
I'm unhappy at my job. My boss is a bully, my colleagues are slackers, and the pay is lousy.	There's no sense trying to find a new job, especially not in this economy. There's no point even thinking about it. Among my friends, most of them don't like their work.	Many people hate their jobs, but that's no excuse for me. I can seriously look for a much better one. It's scary, but I can put myself out there again and see what I need to do to get a better job.

I have failed at finding romantic love. All my relationships have ended unhappily, and now I can't even seem to find someone I would like to date.	I'm done with the rat race. I've learned not to expect too much from relationships. I'm not going to get infatuated and hurt again. I'll be realistic.	I'm going to find love, even if I have to make some difficult or frightening changes in myself and my life. Love is too important to betray or to live without.
My elderly parent has died, and I can't stop feeling bad. I feel guilty all the time because I wasn't there when my parent died (even though I took care of him day in and day out). And I just can't seem to stop feeling that I didn't do enough.	My father loved me, even though he never said he loved me and never thanked me for taking care of him. That's just the way he was. I sacrificed my own family taking care of him, but I don't feel good about how he died without me there to tell him I loved him. I can't feel good about the way he died.	My father was ungrateful and repeatedly made me feel bad about myself. If he had loved me, he would have told me at least once. If he'd loved me, I wouldn't still be feeling guilty. It's time for me to focus on the people who really do love me.
I have become physically disabled. The pain is difficult enough to live with, but, even worse, I cannot do most of the things that used to come easily to me. I feel useless.	I feel so bitter and resentful. Why me? I can't feel worthwhile without working. And the pain—nobody could stand it! I have to blunt myself by taking all the drugs I've been prescribed.	I will devote myself to rehab and do everything I can to strengthen my mental powers. I will wring every bit of meaning that I can out of my life and focus on what I have to give to others. I'm not only going to survive—I'm going to thrive.

My brain was injured in an auto accident (or with psychiatric drugs or electroshock treatment). I feel so hopeless and depressed because my memory is so poor, my concentration is lacking, and it's harder to control my emotions.	I was the smartest person in my class and on my job. Now, I've lost my sharpness, and I'm still having trouble focusing and learning new things. I feel so cheated. How am I supposed to go on?	I'm so much more than my brain. With my new spiritual strength, my appreciation of life, and the knowledge that love is the source of happiness, I'm feeling better and doing more worthwhile things than before my injury. No, I'm not glad my brain was injured, but, every day, I'm more grateful than ever for my life.
My psychiatric drugs are no longer working for me. I've been taking psychiatric drugs for years, and my doctor says I need them for the rest of my life, but, no matter how many I try, they don't seem to be working. I'm not myself anymore. I'm tired; don't have much energy; and feel less engaged in my work, my family, and my life.	My doctor says I have a biochemical imbalance that is making me depressed, anxious, and bipolar. He wants to keep looking for the right combination of drugs. He says I have an illness, like diabetes, so psychotherapy or changing how I live can't work without psychiatric medication.	I've done my own reading and research: There's no such thing as a biochemical imbalance and no evidence of long-term help from drugs. Instead, the medications are making it harder for me to think and feel, so it's no wonder I'm not getting better. I will learn to safely withdraw from psychiatric drugs, and then I will focus on increasing my emotional freedom to embrace more positive approaches to life.
My life has no meaning. For some time now, I have been losing interest in my marriage, my work, and even myself. I keep going because of the kids, but what happens when they grow up and leave?	Why keep trying? No one would miss me. Ultimately, life has no meaning. I look all around me, and all I see is dishonesty, betrayal, and abuse. I don't think anything will make a difference, and I'm resigned to it.	Instead of focusing on my despair and encouraging my futility, I will finally deal with my guilt, anxiety, shame, and persistent anger and emotional numbness. The world is in desperate need of loving individuals, and I will become one myself.

How we respond to life is ultimately up to us. Winning the lottery or meeting our soul mate will not improve anything if we still cannot take the three steps to emotional freedom by identifying our negative emotions, rejecting them, and then transcending and triumphing over them.

In an earlier book in which I explored the lives of America's Founding Fathers and Mothers in order to seek the basis of sound principles of living, I formulated the Primary Principles for living as good a life as possible.[1] The Primary Principles are:

Protect freedom.

Take responsibility at all times.

Express gratitude for every gift and opportunity.

Become a source of love.

PART 3.

FREEDOM TO LOVE

INTRODUCTION TO PART 3

In chapter 5, I wrote, "A fundamental premise of this book is that the human spirit and free will can triumph over what nature has given us. Another premise is that there is no inherent contradiction between science and spirituality." In agreement with Charles Darwin, I do not believe that science can prove or disprove spiritual viewpoints or, conversely, that spiritual outlooks can invalidate science.[1]

I do not find that biological evolution can account for our highest aspirations or ideals. Darwin also doubted that "instincts" by themselves could ever have led to "the height of morality" he saw expressed in the Golden Rule. He not only believed that humans are biologically endowed with social instincts, including sympathy for one another, he also concluded that we are able to modify and cultivate these innate qualities "by the aid of reason, instruction, and the love or fear of God."[2]

Darwin unequivocally rejected institutional religious ideologies that terrorize believers and condemn nonbelievers, but, in his later years, he admittedly vacillated between a belief in intelligent design and agnosticism. His ambivalent agnosticism was not the product of scientific investigation. Darwin had always been a scientist. Instead, he said that his agnosticism resulted from his growing disillusionment with the attitudes and behavior of human beings in general, which he personally saw as incompatible with a rational, moral creator.[3]

As pointed out earlier, from every great spiritual leader and every ennobling philosophy and religion, including the views of Charles Darwin, the message has been given to us that we must learn to love.[4] To do this, we must triumph over our more willful and aggressive tendencies; we must shed guilt, shame, and anxiety; and we must transcend our primitive nature. Part 3 of this book leaves pure science behind to describe from my own viewpoint how to live life most effectively by these higher values. Regardless of differing opinions we may hold in respect to science, humanism, atheism, or faith in God, the key message we can all share is about becoming a source of love, enabling each of us to bring out the best in our social, moral, and spiritual nature.

Chapter 24

LOVE IS JOYFUL AWARENESS

Love is joyful awareness and makes us feel happy. To love is to be glad about ourselves or another person, about nature or art, about our higher purposes or the divine. To love is to embrace, to protect, to care, to nurture, to encourage. To love is to promote the expressions or manifestations of life that bring us joy and happiness.

When we meet new people, we can check out our inner signal system to see if we feel delight or even love toward them—joy over their existence, pleasure that they are alive, and happiness in recognizing their personality or spirit.

Love for others blends directly into happiness. We can base our actions on amplifying and fulfilling positive feelings. The best in life requires knowing how to identify our positive emotions so that we can act rationally in the pursuit of what we desire and believe in.

In a loving relationship, the most basic principle is to keep love alive. Never withdraw it when feeling angry or scared. Never threaten in an argument to withdraw it. We should make these hard-and-fast rules: Always work at being loving to the person you have chosen to love. Decide that love is real, that it is the basis of your relationship, and that you will always do everything possible to preserve and enhance it.

WHAT IF I'M UNABLE TO LOVE?

In some ways, this is a matter of faith, but it is also my experience: I believe that love is the core of our souls and that we can open ourselves to expressing that love. Certainly, anyone with the ability and motivation to read this sentence also has the capacity to love. Assume you can love and that guilt, shame, anxiety, anger, and numbness may be blocking you from doing so. Work on sweeping away the emotional darkness that shrouds your spiritual flame. Love is there inside you, ready to bestow its life-giving glow.

WHAT IF I NEVER FIND SOMEONE TO LOVE?

When we reject the stifling effects of our most painful emotions and open our hearts to love, we will find someone to love romantically. Put simply, when we become ready to give and receive love, we will meet someone who wants to share a loving life with us. I have seen this confirmed repeatedly in my personal and professional life.

On the off chance that we do not find a life partner not long after opening ourselves to love, there are an infinite number of ways besides a romantic partnership to express and receive love. Everywhere we turn, we see people who are in need and suffering from lack of attention. Community agencies, churches, and clubs provide many opportunities for volunteers. Child-mentorship organizations; soup kitchens; programs to help the blind, elderly, and chronically ill; and projects to help many others in need of special services are always looking for people willing to donate their time.

If we prefer to start by helping, protecting, rescuing, or adopting animals, we will find many opportunities. If none of these alternatives seem appealing, there are innumerable ways to express love for the earth through environmental and nature groups. And if we do not like joining organizations, we can always start our own group on behalf of deprived children, lonely seniors, or others who need companionship and love.

My point is simple: This world is and will always be in desperate need of people who are willing to care and to love. When we allow ourselves to become a source of love, the opportunities will seem endless and everywhere. Human beings who become a source of love, and who welcome and embrace love, will rarely have to be alone or lonely. Love is the world's most precious spiritual commodity. At the very core of our being lies the capacity and desire to love and be loved.

UNSMOTHERING YOUR LOVE RELATIONSHIPS

Love may have hurt you. Love may have disappointed you. Love may have betrayed you. Betrayals in your family or church may have made you distrust anyone who speaks the word "love" or refers to a loving God. Your pastor may have threatened you with hell, and your father may have told you that you were damned. A friend or family member may have used the word "love" to manipulate you and make you feel guilty. Having lost love one too many times, you may have descended into chronic anger or numbness. None of that is really about love; it is about losing hope when under assault by your negative legacy emotions.

Love did not hurt, disappoint, or betray you; people or circumstances did. Love is the most pure, unalloyed spiritual gold. Love is like the speed of light— an emotional or spiritual constant in the universe. Learn to trust it. Always attribute the good in your life to love. Never withhold your love in the midst of conflict. Let the sunshine of love continually bring warmth and light to your relationships. It will maximize the hope of successfully resolving conflicts and moving on together in life.

Is this Pollyannaish? Unrealistic? A setup for disappointment? We human beings are so conflicted and easily overwhelmed by self-defeating emotions that we need to take a strong stand on love.

You are the primary source of love in your life and your surroundings. Love is your beacon light, something you shine on others and on the world. So-called self-love doesn't work. It is the hope and refuge of wounded psyches. Love for others makes us feel strong and worthwhile.

Love relationships never fail because of love; there is no such thing as too much love. Relationships fail because love has not overcome our self-defeating emotions. Our whole package of negative legacy emotions—guilt, shame, anxiety, and chronic or extreme anger and numbness—stands in the way of love. When we fail to deal with them, our primitive emotions are expert at breaking our hearts. But we can become expert at *mending* our broken hearts by getting back in touch with our capacity to love and by once again treasuring the life that we have been given.

Chapter 25

LET'S TALK ABOUT SEX

The theory of natural selection is about individuals competing to reproduce and, ultimately, to survive long enough to pass on their genetic material. But evolutionary theory stumbles when it tries to explain and to take into account human consciousness and choice.[1] When we humans make conscious choices about our individual acts of sex and love, reproduction and the passing on of our genetic material is often the *last* thing on our minds.

What do human beings want when having sex? Sometimes to create new life, but more commonly to relieve sexual tensions, to have pleasure, to dominate or submit, to make up with each other, and so on. Decades of living and doing therapy have taught me that, when having sex, most people are trying to end the loneliness of physical separation, to share comfort and closeness, and to make each other satisfied and happy. In other words, they are trying to make love.

Sex is the most emotionally charged intimacy of all and, therefore, the most commonly corrupted by the whole array of negative legacy emotions. We are assaulted by negativity about sex absorbed from our parents and peers; by skewed portrayals of sex from pornography, television, movies, music, and advertising; by guilt-provoking religious concepts; by sexual abuses we have endured; and by the way our need for sex has previously entangled us in con-flicted relationships.

Since negative legacy emotions developed through natural selection to inhibit us from aggression in our closest relationships, they are bound to rear up during the most intimate relationships of all. When having sexual intimacy, we are especially vulnerable to being distracted, troubled, or disabled by guilt, shame, anxiety, anger, and numbing.

Negative feelings about sex prevent many people from knowing or accepting that they are looking for intimate love. I have previously written about how sexual dysfunction is rooted in emotional and spiritual problems.[2] I can now add that most "sexual dysfunction" results from the arousal of self-defeating primordial emotions that cause a failure to infuse the relationship with love. Except when individuals are impaired by psychiatric or recreational drugs or, occasionally, by known endocrine disorders, biological dysfunction is rarely at the root of sexual problems in men or women. The ability and willingness to love—not the bodily function of sex—is what needs repair or revival. The three steps to emotional freedom lead to fulfilling sex. When we have *identified* and then *rejected* our negative legacy emotions, and we *triumph* and *transcend* with love—when love flows through our every word, gesture, and touch—then lovemaking will never grow old but will grow richer and more satisfying with time.

Many people compulsively seek sexual relationships but find little satisfaction in them. In my clinical work, I have found that men and women who seek sex with many partners are often having trouble relating with genuine feelings to any individual person. For men, compulsive sex is often an attempt to prove their manhood or to allay their fears of women, but it offers little satisfaction. For women, compulsive sex often expresses a need for real love that they dare not seek because they feel unworthy or fear rejection. Some women boast about how they understand love much better than men do, but that is commonly a cover-up for their own fears of loving. Young men and women seeking sex in the bar scene often have little understanding and much guilt, shame, and anxiety about the prospect of a loving relationship.

For most people, sex without love quickly degenerates into an unsatisfying experience of physiological relief that is often accompanied by boredom or even disgust. The closeness between two human beings is what makes the bodily function of sex uplifting and beautiful. Loving intimacy is the spiritual flower of life that began to bud millions of years ago when that little shrewlike mammal first began to suckle her young and that fully blooms within human beings when they make love to each other.

Chapter 26

LOVE IS NOT THE SAME AS RELATIONSHIP

Love is not the same as relationship and should not be confused with it. Love is pure and good. Love emanates from our emotional or spiritual core. Love, like a smile, shines regardless of its reception and does not depend upon what others do in return.

Relationship is another matter. The *ideal* marital relationship involves two people who freely choose to love one another through all life's challenges. Unfortunately and inevitably, relationships, unlike love itself, are far from ideal. Relationships are plagued by every sort of negative human emotion. Our task in life—indeed, our privilege in life—is to love freely without attempting to coerce or control and without a guarantee about the outcome. That is the risk required in loving—offering ourselves with no demands or guarantees.

When we love someone, we do not necessarily live with or stay with him. We may find it unethical or impossible to live together. We may leave if she becomes abusive. Nonetheless, to maintain our own well-being, we do not stop loving. We simply make a painful decision to remain separate. We do not suppress the source of love within ourselves. This is the key to successful grieving—never to deny the strength of our love or the pain of missing our loved one.

LOVE IS NOT DEFENSELESS

It is important to remember and to live by the all-important principle of our inalienable right to emotional self-defense (see chapter 10). It is a corollary to our right to pursue life, liberty, and happiness. The right to emotional self-defense is one of the keys to a happy and productive life.

Being loving does not make us oblivious to how people hurt us. Instead, it usually makes us more aware of whether we are being treated in a disrespectful or unloving fashion. When we are feeling hostile and disrespectful, we are less sensitive to the same negative responses coming from other people. They will seem "natural." Our own negativity may feel justified by their negative behavior and unwittingly encourage it in a vicious circle. By contrast, when we are feeling love and acting in a loving fashion, we are much more likely to notice even subtle negativity from the other person because it so starkly clashes with what we are feeling.

Do not use love as an excuse for acting defenseless or submissive. In order to feel as loving as we can within a relationship, we need to feel safe, and we cannot feel safe while being emotionally bullied or manipulated. Love grows amid security and trust, and it tends to be withdrawn in their absence.

By requiring respectful and loving attitudes in our personal relationships, we help those close to us to bring out the best in themselves. By making the same demand on ourselves to be respectful and loving at all times in our personal relationships, we also bring out the best in ourselves. Conversely, if we accept or give disrespect, we bring out the worst in everyone involved.

In badly conflicted relationships within families, including both adults and children, it is common to see the participants enable each other by failing to reject disrespectful behavior or, worse, by responding to it with further disrespect, creating a downward spiral. Family members can also enable disrespectful conduct by responding to it in a positive way, such as giving in to a child's or spouse's demands when he or she whines, nags, or otherwise acts obnoxiously. Insisting upon mutual respect within the family is the single most important step toward resolving conflict and restoring or creating good relations.

When we set a high standard for the emotional quality of all our relationships, we begin the process of building happy and satisfying relationships. While we may end up pulling away from some friends or family members who refuse to be respectful, in the long run we will surround ourselves with wonderful relationships.

We do not need to be objectively correct when we perceive that someone is bullying or manipulating us. Our personal viewpoint is what counts. If we *feel* emotionally harmed, we have the right to act upon our feelings by demanding a stop to it or by removing ourselves. If we end up reevaluating the situation and deciding we were mistaken, we can apologize, but it is important to use our own judgment in regard to whether someone is being offensive toward us.

Someone who truly respects us will stop whatever communication we find offensive. Similarly, if possible, we need to stop or modify our own communications when other people feel offended. After deliberation, we may decide the communication needs to be made—for example, that we are concerned about being treated dishonestly—but our approach should remain as respectful as possible. Always being respectful creates the optimum emotional climate for being heard, and it also prevents us from making excuses for mistreating other people.

It is a truth: by insisting upon respectful and loving relationships, we create a life for ourselves in which we thrive while giving our very best to other people.

CONFLICT RESOLUTION REQUIRES LOVE

Because our interests become enmeshed with the interests of the person we love, loving relationships are above the ordinary experiences of jealousy and competition. Loving relationships exist beyond the realm of generosity and sacrifice. When another's existence and happiness matters to us as much as or more than our own, it is not "generous" to give to our loved ones, because we thrive on and embrace giving to them. When we love, it is not a sacrifice to share or to give to our loved ones because their happiness brings us happiness. For this reason, love is the ultimate source of conflict resolution.[1]

When we love, we place another person's interests at least on par with our own, and, therefore, we look out for his or her interests at least as much as or more than our own. For this reason, love erases conflict.

In practical and yet spiritual terms, when we look at others with love, it remains difficult to be in conflict with them. There are exceptions—for example, if the people we love are feeling self-destructive. We may have conflict with them when we refuse to support or enable what they falsely believe to be in their self-interest. These are fine points, and even arguable if we believe in unconditional love. Two people who love each other begin attending to each other's needs, and conflict becomes minimized.

Love especially thrives between equals who freely choose to relate to each other. When we coerce or force others to relate to us, we are likely to suppress our own feelings of love as well as those of the person we are trying to control. Emotional bullying or coercion suppresses love on both sides of the conflict. This is one reason why raising children can become so difficult. Sometimes we need to control or punish our children, and, at those times, it can become difficult for us and for our children to remember how much we love each other. In adult relationships based on love, there is little or no place for control or coercion.

EXAMPLE: A COUPLE FIGHTING OVER MONEY

Matt and Sarah love each other very much, but Matt, at times, reacts with guilt, and his wife tends to react with shame and anxiety. Sarah, who keeps track of the family finances, is telling her husband that they won't have the expected funds to pay for their children's upcoming college educations.

Matt immediately experiences a spasm of guilt; it feels as if Sarah is saying he is a bad husband. His mother was always making his father feel bad about money, and now Matt automatically blames himself. He feels like banging himself on the head.

Sarah is terribly ashamed she did not see the financial problem sooner. She sees Matt slightly clench his fist in his lap, and for the first time in their marriage, she imagines him slapping her across the face, the way her father used to do. Although Matt was thinking of hitting himself, Sarah becomes flooded with shame and anxiety.

Matt sees Sarah's face tighten up but has no idea why. His guilt tells him that she must be disappointed with him. He yells at her, "Damn it, it's not my fault!"

"So it's my fault!" Sarah screams back in fear, but to Matt, it sounds like anger. Both are now emotionally disabled and overwhelmed—Matt, by guilt, and Sarah, by shame and anxiety.

This is how it could have turned out better:

Sarah realizes she was reacting with shame and Matt was reacting with guilt. She reassures her husband, "Matt, I never meant to make you feel guilty. I love you so much. I just didn't realize that college costs had gone through the roof, but there are loans available."

Similarly, Matt realizes that Sarah's anger is usually driven by shame and anxiety. He tells her, "Sarah, I got so upset with myself that it scared you and made you feel worse. It's not your fault. I should have been working with you on the finances. I love you, Sarah."

They take a walk and afterward reexamine their financial plans together. A conflict originally destined to tear them apart brings them closer.

Matt and Sarah stopped their self-defeating legacy emotions from blocking out their love for each other. Reviving or staying in touch with love, as they did, is the necessary basis for resolving conflict.

EXAMPLE: A COUPLE FIGHTING OVER THEIR CHILD

Matt and Sarah get a call from school that their fourteen-year-old daughter, Chrissie, who never gets in trouble, was caught in a closet with a boy. The details are fuzzy, but the principal sounds very concerned, and they are driving to school for an emergency meeting.

As we know, Matt tends to be affected by guilt and rarely feels shame, but the idea of a boy taking advantage of his vulnerable daughter sends a shudder of primitive, prehistoric humiliation through his body. He imagines beating the daylights out of the young man.

He growls ominously at Sarah, "Call the principal, and tell him to get that boy and his father into the office with us."

Sarah is already anticipating being humiliated by the principal, and she's terrified about her daughter's reputation. Now, she fears that her husband will make things still worse.

Then, Sarah reminds herself how much she loves her daughter and her husband and identifies that she's reacting to this stress with her self-defeating shame.

She says, "Matt, I don't blame you for being angry, but let's not make anything worse for Chrissie. I'm sure she's already horrified."

"Do you know the boy?" Matt asks.

Sarah replies, "I know she's interested in someone. That's all."

Matt, to his surprise, feels a tear running down on his cheek. "I feel so guilty about how little time I spend with her. I've been too damn busy with work. Our kids need more of me."

Sarah adds, "Chrissie's such a good child. Both of us sometimes take her for granted."

Matt and Sarah are beginning to overcome their guilt, shame, and anxiety and now are working together as a couple to focus on their daughter's needs.

Matt decides, "When I see Chrissie, first thing I'm going to do is hug her."

"That would be great," Sarah agrees.

"I don't even care what happened in the closet." Matt rethinks his shame-driven anger. "I just don't want Chrissie getting more hurt than she already is. She must feel terrible!"

Sarah chimes in, "Chrissie's a wonderful kid, and we're on her side. Let's make that clear to her, the principal, and the boy and his parents, if they are there."

As it turned out, Chrissie and the boy went into the closet to text Chrissie's new boyfriend, who was at home sick for the day. Yes, it could have been more serious, and greater challenges will arise, but banishing guilt, shame, and anxiety—and replacing them with reason and love—will always provide the best opportunity for resolving conflicts.

Chapter 27

WHAT TO DO WHEN
LOVE IS LOST

Even if a relationship ends painfully, we will feel stronger and recover more quickly if we embrace our feelings of love for the person we have lost. The most self-defeating emotional reactions set in when we not only lose someone but suppress our love. Love is the glue of our relationships and the glue that holds us together. When we try to suppress our feelings of love, we risk tearing ourselves asunder.

Even when an unexpected loss of a loved one through separation or death seems completely overwhelming, we need to stay in touch with our love for that person. Mourning can be filled with love as well as loss. Maintaining our deepest feelings of love demonstrates the value of the person we have lost while keeping us as strong as possible.

Guilt, anxiety, shame, anger, and apathy hold in place our resentment and lack of forgiveness toward loved ones who have pulled away or been lost. We feel guilty about having failed them, so we want them to feel guilty about having failed us. We feel anxious about our own ability to love through thick and thin, and, therefore, we feel anxious about their abandoning us. We feel ashamed of ourselves and see them as shaming us. We feel angry toward them and are afraid they will be angry back. We feel apathetic and indifferent at times and are sure they have the same reaction to us.

If we remain fully loving to someone who has left us, or who threatens to leave, we remain in the best position to keep the relationship from ending against our wishes. First, we will be behaving as well as we can, and that will give us strength and courage. Second, people rarely leave a relationship in which they feel genuinely loved.

TAKING A RISK TO RESTORE LOVE

Many couples start out feeling strongly in love and gradually become mired in conflicts over the ensuing years. Supporting a family and raising children becomes trying. Economic problems cause strife and worry. Individuals can grow in different directions.

If a couple was once genuinely in love, stressful circumstances in themselves are not likely to ruin the relationship. Overstimulated negative legacy emotions destroy love and relationships. Remember that intimate relationships always stir up guilt, shame, and anxiety because these emotions are built-in reactions intended to control self-assertion and aggression in close relationships. Over time, many intimate relationships undergo slow strangulation by these negative emotions. Instead, through knowledge and work, couples can create increasing emotional freedom, in which love can continue to grow and prosper.

I like to reassure couples that if they once loved each other, they can love each other again if they have the desire and the courage to work on the relationship. This is because love is real and enduring and flows from our emotional or spiritual core. What is fragile is our ability to maintain relationships.

The first step in mending a relationship is to apply the inalienable right to emotional self-protection, not only requiring your partner or family member to be respectful but also requiring the same respectful attitudes and conduct from yourself.

In a more respectful context, it will be easier for you and your loved one to realize that your most stifling emotional reactions have nothing to do with your real merit or that of your loved one. Biological evolution, cultural evolution, and childhood imposed them on you. Applying the same principle to your marriage or partnership, the painful emotions stirred up within you and your loved one probably have much less to do with the current relationship than with primitive, prehistoric emotions that you can learn to recognize, resist, and surpass. However, this will only be true after both of you have resolved to treat each other respectfully and to put love at the center of your lives together.

Take the risk of loving again. Hold hands, share a hug, and then look into each other's eyes to see each other as you did in the beginning. Let the love glow once again. Inevitably, you will then be flooded with negative emotions, so fight them off, and return to letting the love surface again. The work is not in loving. Love generates spontaneously whenever given a chance. The work is in getting rid of our emotional impediments in order to achieve the freedom to love. Keep coming back to the realization that love, and love alone, is real—and that everything else is merely the complexities of being human that love can triumph over and transcend.

Chapter 28

GUIDELINES FOR MAINTAINING A LOVING PARTNERSHIP

Here are a few steps and guidelines for creating and maintaining happy, loving relationships and, ultimately, finding a partner to love and be loved by. The first guideline is fundamental to all relationships: approach relationships with an expectation of mutual respect, but maintain your inalienable right to emotional self-defense (chapter 10), which is your personal right to reject communications and actions that threaten or offend you.

If you start out expecting respect but alert for disrespect, you may quickly discover which relationships will go well and which will not. You may find that some of your initial contacts with people will be relatively brief, and some of your previous relationships will fall by the wayside. Usually, it only takes a few words or minutes to determine if someone is treating you with mutual respect. By having high expectations from the start for how you will be treated, you will weed out a great number of people, including all those who have a habit of trying to make people feel guilty, ashamed, or anxious in order to control them.

It may seem unrealistic or too idealistic to expect new acquaintances to treat you well from the start and to reject the relationship if they do not. What about giving people a break and a second chance? Won't we miss opportunities if we steadfastly expect to be treated well by the people we meet? To the contrary, if we start out accepting something less than a very respectful relationship, we are likely heading on a downhill course. Instead, setting a high standard from the beginning with everyone we meet is the way to build and maintain relationships on a high level. It is a key to a happy and productive life.

In addition to these basic principles of mutual respect and emotional self-defense, the following guidelines apply if you are seeking a romantic relationship:

- Motivate yourself by daring to let yourself feel how incomplete or, at times, lonely your life feels without love.
- Decide to take the risk of finding another person to whom you can offer a partnership with higher purposes, including principled living and love.
- Make clear to others that you are actively looking for a respectful and loving relationship, and actively look for places to meet people.

While looking for or improving a relationship, remember the true nature of love: joyful awareness and happiness over the existence of another person.

When you feel desperately in need of someone, remember this has little or nothing to do with love, which is a wonderful feeling. Rather, desperation has a lot to do with helplessness and dependence. Similarly, when you feel jealous, it says nothing about the real value of the other person to you, but it does indicate your insecurities. Also remember that it is potentially disastrous to try to build a loving relationship with someone who is not ready to do so. All this becomes much easier if you remember the criterion for love—that you feel happy and even joyful in the presence and awareness of another person.

If you have found someone with whom you want to try to build a life, then keep these additional guidelines in mind and be determined to act upon them:

- Treat the person you love as a treasure, someone to be nurtured and protected, and a reflection of all that is good.
- Connect your heart, mind, and soul with your loved one; become one in your interests, ideals, and purposes.
- Whenever you feel compelled to use force or to coerce your partner, or to compromise his or her autonomy in any way, think twice about it—or three or four times or as many times as necessary. Then, find an approach that is so loving and positive for your partner that he or she will *want* to accept your offer.
- Always remember that you are a source of love and that you have chosen your loved one as the chief recipient of the very best you have to give.

None of us manage to live by these standards all the time, but to the degree that we are thriving in a relationship, this is almost certainly how we are doing it.

GUIDELINES FOR LOVING COMMUNICATION

Living largely free of guilt, shame, and anxiety is possible. Keeping these emotions from turning your life into a shambles is even more possible. Although we will always have to fight off episodes of one self-defeating, primitive emotion or another, we can guide our overall decision making and, hence, our lives based on sound principles, reason, and love. This is how people build and maintain satisfying, happy, and productive lives. Here are some more specific suggestions aimed at using your capacity to love to rise above daily conflicts:

- Whenever you feel in conflict with your loved one, stop everything, and allow yourself to remember that your loved one's interests and happiness mean as much or more to you than your own. This, by itself, will end most conflicts with a loving and happy reunion, followed by resolution of the conflict.
- Never say a word that harms your relationship. Instead, whenever possible, make every word you say advance the relationship and the love. This may mean that you have to stop and think before you say a word when you are angry, but that will improve your learning curve for making good relationships.
- Never start a thought or statement tinged with hostility or resentment, such as, "OK, that's it, now I'm going to say what I really feel," or, "Now it's my turn," or, "I'm finally going to make him listen," or, "I have a right to express my feelings," or, "I'm not going to bottle up my anger anymore," or, "It's time to be honest." Instead, speak from love, and love only, when communicating about anything important to your loved one, and then when communicating about everything small and trivial as well.
- Never knowingly say or do something harmful to your loved one. That includes never coercing your loved one with guilt, shame, or anxiety. Negative legacy emotions should be outlawed by the Geneva Convention for Loving Relationships.
- Expressing anger is not all that it is cracked up to be by some authorities. Always search beneath your anger for what is making you feel hurt and leading you to fear that you have no other resort than willfulness and

anger. Then, express what is hurting you in a way that does not impose guilt, shame, or anxiety on your loved one.

- Tell your loved one how much you love him or her. How often? Once a day? Twice a day? If possible, say it all day long. Let your loved one decide when he or she has heard it enough. Make your important relationships a duet of love—even a symphony.

Are words like "never" too rigid when reminding ourselves not to say harmful things? I believe we need to give ourselves no slack when it comes to setting standards for our conduct, especially with our loved ones. Of course, we will fail sometimes, but knowing that we should never gratuitously hurt our loved ones can motivate us to improve ourselves.

Here is a key principle that I find useful, if difficult to follow, that has helped me and many of my patients in family situations, at work, and in everyday contact with other people: Make sure that every communication you make, your every word or physical gesture, advances your relationship with the other person and enhances their sense of worth. At our best, we can make all or nearly all our communications into expressions of care and love.

Is it too much to ask of ourselves to make *all* our communications loving? I doubt if anyone will ever meet that standard, but I believe it helps to set a high ethical bar that does not allow for loveless or otherwise negative communications in our closest relationships.

Imagine having a relationship with your loved one where you walk hand in hand through life as one, knowing you love each other in a way so special that it has become a sacred affirmation of your highest aspirations, principles, and ideals. This is the formula for a happy life.

Chapter 29

EMPATHIC SELF-TRANSFORMATION

When we relate in an empathic and caring manner in our personal or professional relationships, we tend to modify how we behave, and even how we think, to be more in concert with the other person. In my psychiatric practice, I am somewhat different with each patient I work with, and, to some extent, I'm different in varying sessions with the same person. I am not being a chameleon, nor does it feel artificial or manipulative. Instead, at my best, I am naturally receptive to the mood of the other person. Often without thinking about it, I find a mood within myself that will help the other person feel safer and more comfortable.

I call this *empathic self-transformation*—modifying ourselves in response to the other in a caring and positive fashion.[1] People who love each other and increasingly grow to trust and treasure each other will find, over the years, that they become more alike in how they think and feel and more able to anticipate each other's thoughts. A natural human process, this can be cultivated with awareness.

Empathic self-transformation is in marked contrast to conflicted, unhappy relationships in which people grow apart over time as they exaggerate and solidify their particular rigid ways of protecting themselves, often involving anger and numbness that stifle empathy. Partners who, in better times, felt like soul mates now feel miles apart.

PASSIONATE LOVE EXPANDS OUR CIRCLE AND UNIVERSE OF LOVE

There is a mistaken idea that people who love each other passionately will naturally become mutually dependent, self-centered, and exclusive. Couples who withdraw into themselves are probably reacting, at least in part, to negative legacy emotions. They may be hanging onto each other in a state of anxiety over losing the love they have tasted. Loving each other may have stimulated other feelings of guilt and shame, leading them to become self-protective. Their relationship may be stimulating dangerous envy in others that, in turn, activates guilt, shame, or anxiety. At the same time, they could have realistic reasons for wanting to avoid envious or otherwise destructive people who resent their love for each other.

Nothing is more important than asserting our right to love, and nothing is more likely to stimulate the negative legacy emotions of guilt, shame, and anxiety within us, as well as resentments and jealousies in others. When we overcome our self-defeating emotions and stand up to or avoid envious bystanders, love promotes courage, individuality, and independence while inspiring us to reach out to others.

When unencumbered by Stone Age emotions, love makes us feel worthwhile and expansive. If they come from loving families, people newly in love are likely to want to bring their new partner home to meet everyone. Coming from conflicted families ridden by misguided and destructive emotions, couples are likely to stay away from their families and perhaps from other people as well. They need to do so to protect and nurture their loving relationship.

Most people who fall in love experience the presence of something sacred—something above and beyond themselves—yet uniquely their own. Often, they feel blessed by God or enormously grateful for their good fortune. For those with a more secular outlook, what I have been saying about spirituality can become useful as a metaphor for seeking higher ideals and higher purposes. With or without a spiritual or religious faith, love can inspire us to become better human beings.

Before dismissing the possibility of a spirituality that permeates human existence, consider how unimaginable Wi-Fi would have been a few decades ago. Now, ask yourself what other connectivities could be going on in the not-so-physical universe that are infinitely more difficult to grasp and yet far more important to our lives. Think of love as universal connectivity—an ever-present Wi-Fi of emotional freedom and spiritual empowerment that we can tap into anytime, anywhere, at will and without cost.

Chapter 30

WHERE TO TURN WHEN *ALL* SEEMS LOST

This is what I have concluded about life: there is love—and everything else matters little in comparison. My second conclusion is that the greatest impediments to love are those primitive emotions of guilt, shame, and anxiety, as well as anger and numbness.

There is love, and then there is relationship, with all its complexities, including the arousal of painful emotions from the past. There is love, and then there are all the miserable remainders of interactions that go on among us human beings. There is love, and then the rest of human nature leaves much to be desired. There is love, and then there is everything else, mostly the negative legacy emotions of guilt, shame, anxiety, anger, and numbness that corrupt and misdirect us. We will be the happiest and the most fulfilled when we keep our hearts open to love throughout the vicissitudes of being human. It is a simple but oh-so-difficult task.

Life can be lived from a loving viewpoint, or not. We can make ourselves into a source of love and a gift to others, or not. It is a choice—not an easy or facile one but nonetheless a choice.

Love may have hurt us. Love may have disappointed us. Love may have betrayed us. We may have learned to feel guilt, shame, and anxiety at the very thought of love. The breaking of trust we experienced in the family, church, or elsewhere, and all the emotional suffering, was not really about love.

I hope you will give love the benefit of the doubt and hold in abeyance your distrust of the idea that you can live life as a source of love. Be reassured that what other people have called "love" is not necessarily love and that an understanding of real love—the stuff of your emotional or spiritual core and the goodness you have to share with others—can transform your life and the lives you touch. Love is at the heart of being the best we can be as human beings.

We will often have to call upon ourselves to work hard to avoid confusing love with the self-defeating emotional turmoil it can stir up in us. Keep this rule of life uppermost in your mind: love is happy and, ultimately, joyful.

Love is joyful awareness and treasuring of others and of life. All the pain and suffering seemingly associated with love has to do with the flawed ways in which we human beings relate to each other, including our bad choices and our compliance with harmful emotions.

Although love is at the core of being human, it is not all there is to human nature. Our task in life is to find our way through the complexities of our own human nature—including our self-destructive feelings and attitudes—in order to guide ourselves with reason, sound principles, and love.

NOWHERE TO GO BUT UP

It is impossible to be loving and insane at the same moment in time. This is because love connects us to people, and insanity is all about disconnections from people. It is impossible to feel and act destructively while knowing we are a source of love. This is because love makes us want to nurture and protect. Any attempt to find the exceptions to these principles is likely to bring us back to the truth that cleanses our hearts and minds and makes us emotionally free to pursue what we feel is important.

It is a fact of life that it is impossible to be filled with love and filled with regret at the same time. It is also impossible to be loving and resentful at the same time. Once you understand that you are a source of love, you will feel grateful for every moment you are able to feel and express it.

Love and gratitude, if practiced on a daily basis, make it impossible to be miserable and instead create endless possibilities for improving your life. This is because gratitude connects us to something greater than ourselves, and when making that connection in an appreciative fashion, we experience emotional freedom. Gratitude is a practical demonstration of spirituality. Expressing and feeling gratitude instantly brings emotional freedom.

When genuinely felt, love banishes guilt, shame, and anxiety, as well as chronic anger and numbness. When we experience ourselves as a source of love, and we look with love upon others and life, we are, at those moments, as free as humanly possible of self-defeating emotions and the most able to expand our potential for love and to live a deeply fulfilling life.

In a marvelously self-generating cycle, as we overcome our biological and childhood inheritance of negative emotions, we become more able to love, and as we become more able to love, we will find increasingly less negativity in our hearts and minds. Although we fear the vulnerability associated with being loving and loved, love in fact makes us stronger. Being a source of love is the most secure and emotionally sound way to be and to live. These observations about love are the essence of what I have distilled from nearly eight decades on Earth. The rest is detail.

A LIFE-CHANGING PERSONAL EXPERIMENT
THAT TAKES HARDLY ANY TIME

Here is a personal experiment you can conduct anytime and anywhere that will help you stay in touch with yourself—that is, to stay in touch with your psyche or soul as a source of love. In the beginning, you can try it for a few seconds or maybe a minute or two. You can do this anywhere you are, as long as it is safe for you to take a few minutes to relax your guard. You can do it as a spiritual refresher as often as you like for the rest of your life. The experiment is to prac-tice being a source of love.

Decide you are a source of love, then let yourself feel it. You can do this at first with your eyes briefly closed or with them wide open. As an aid, you can focus on something nonthreatening, such as a sunset, a flower, your pet, or someone you love.

Having become relaxed, look peacefully at everything around you in the room or the outdoors with a feeling that you are a source of love shining upon the world and the people around you. Imagine yourself as a spiritual lantern, adding a loving glow to all you see and experience. Bathe all you see with your feelings of love.

In this experiment of spiritual refreshment, let yourself think, "I am a being, soul, or spirit and a source of love." If you believe in something or Someone greater than yourself, you can add, "I'm participating with God or some greater purpose than myself." For a few minutes, keep bringing your mind back to that idea about yourself: "I am a source of love." If you let yourself experience that, you may find that the colors brighten around you, that sounds are clearer, and that life, however briefly, becomes invested with special or greater meaning.

At the same time, and this is almost a certainty, you will become distracted. Primitive negative legacy emotions like guilt can have a seductive quality. They may tell you that you are not good enough or do not deserve to think of yourself as a loving person. They may insist you will become a better person if you feel enough guilt. Identify and reject the guilt. Remind yourself that the feeling is nothing more than useless guilt and that you are simply practicing being a source of a love.

Then, shame may strike, beguiling your senses with ideas like, "Who do you think you are?" or, "People will think you are ridiculous." Again, remind yourself that you are listening to shame, that it has nothing to do with your real value, and that you are simply learning to be what anyone and everyone can be—a source of love.

Then, anxiety may start to overwhelm you, trying to make you feel dumb and inarticulate, confused and befuddled. Remind yourself you are feeling something implanted in you ages ago that you no longer need, and then return to thinking about yourself as a source of love.

During this personal experiment, you may find yourself going back into earlier experiences of guilt, shame, and anxiety, or you may find yourself feeling angry or numb. This is an opportunity for insight into what stops you from being as open and loving as you wish to be. You can use this as a self-educational moment, but remember to return to the goal—to being a source of love. Let yourself bask in the psychological and spiritual reality that there is meaning in the universe and that you most fully participate in that meaning when you actively become a source of love. Eventually, if only for a brief second or two at the start, you will experience yourself as a source of love—and everything will change for the better. In those few seconds or minutes, emotional and physical pain will go unnoticed or recede into the background, and you will feel yourself bringing love into the world. With hard work and practice over time, experiencing yourself as a source of love will become a greater and greater part of your relationships and your life. All the emotional burdens, those primitive and prehistoric legacies, will begin to lift. You will find that love is good—absolutely and purely good.

BURNED OUT BY CARING TOO MUCH?[1]

Do you want to be a sensitive, caring person? Be careful not to confuse love with feeling sorry for people. People who feel sorry for themselves are being overcome by helplessness. Do not accept that debilitating emotional contagion. When you feel sorry for them, you have been captured by their feelings of help- lessness. You will be more helpful to them if you can bring them hope, encour- agement, and self-empowerment.

Love, at times, may make us sad and disappointed because it contrasts so sharply with the emotional distress and the dismal conditions we see all around us. But love also fuels a powerful desire to become more grateful for what we have and to be more useful to others who can benefit from us. Negative legacy emotions, and not love, will always burn us out.

Do you want to devote part or even most of your life to making the world a better place? Be sure to love what you are doing and the people you are helping. Lacking that joyful experience, at least make sure you are gaining satisfaction from fulfilling a higher purpose. Much of what I do in my reform work is moti- vated by purposes that bring satisfaction even when they interfere with my hap- piness. Life is better lived by principles than by pursuing happiness. And, in a surprising way, living by principles brings more happiness than pursuing hap- piness for itself.

Do you want to be a helpful friend to those in distress? Do you want to become a professional counselor or therapist? Then do it out of empathy and love and not out of guilt.

Empathy is the ability to understand other people's experiences and view- points in a kind, thoughtful, and caring manner. It does not mean we agree with them or condone their thoughts and actions. Instead, we try to grasp other people's experiences, to understand their viewpoints, and to know what they are feeling without necessarily sharing or approving of the emotions.

Being empathic does not require us to experience others' painful emotions—and especially not their guilt, shame, and anxiety, their anger and numbness, or their helplessness. If we suffer in response to the suffering of others, we will eventually burn out and become angry or numb. In *The Heart of Being Helpful*, I call this "induced suffering." We will withdraw from being empathic in order to save ourselves emotionally. Empathy requires an openheartedness that cannot thrive while absorbing the suffering of others. Empathy requires staying in touch with loving other people while appreciating and knowing, to the best of our ability, what they are experiencing.

AN EMPATHIC NIGHTMARE

Sharing empathy feels like a worthwhile experience for me most of the time, including when I am helping someone who is suffering. I feel that my presence is healing and that I can provide understanding and comfort. By contrast, I feel very uncomfortable when watching people suffer on a movie or television screen. Perhaps it is because I have no personal opportunity to relate to the people. I think there is something universal in my experience—that it can be emotionally damaging to witness suffering while being helpless to do anything about it. This would make a great deal of television and film potentially harmful to the viewers.

Be kind to yourself in this regard. Being empathic does not require you to watch depressing videos, movies, or plays or to read depressing books. If you can make something useful from remotely viewing suffering—for example, if you can use the information to choose or to further a worthwhile cause—that could be life enhancing for you and those you help. Helplessly watching something that makes you feel depressed is much more about induced suffering than healthy empathy, and guilt usually drives it.

GREETING THE GOD IN EACH OF US

The Quakers speak of greeting "that of God in everyone" when they meet. The idea is that God is in all of us.[2] Think of the implications. The Quaker viewpoint could lead us to consider that every time we look into the face and eyes of another person, *God is looking back at us.*

Whether viewed as a metaphor or the actual truth, this stunning consideration makes clear the high regard and respect with which we can and ought to welcome each other. If we can do that, if we can see a deep sense of intrinsic worth shining back at us through the eyes of every human being we meet, we will be changed forever for the better. We will treasure the lives of the people we touch. We will know ourselves as able to love and to share the best we have to offer. We will lift off our emotional burdens and bring ourselves ever so much closer to being the happy and fulfilled human beings that all of us ultimately wish to be.

Right now, you may feel you have suffered so much internal emotional pain and external emotional abuse that you will never get over it. Yet this is guaranteed: when you identify and reject guilt, shame, and anxiety and allow yourself to become a source of love, you will no longer think or care about all the misery you went through in the name of love.

Genuine love, experienced as joyful awareness, has an emotionally and spiritually cleansing quality. Once we experience love, it no longer matters what went wrong along the way. What matters is that we are here right now, being a source of love and thriving with it.

Chapter 31

LAST RESORTS THAT SELDOM WORK OUT

In each of our lives, there are times when we feel desperate to control our emotional suffering or negative behaviors. Where do we turn as the discomfort and desperation increase? Our choice of a "last resort" can determine our success or failure in life.

Nowadays society encourages us to turn to psychiatric drugs. Many others turn to nonprescription drugs like alcohol and marijuana. Some seek relief through sex and gambling; others through meditation or prayer. Some seek out friends or family. We need to become consciously aware of our choice for a last resort, and then make sure that it genuinely meets our needs and expresses our values.

PROTECT YOUR BRAIN FROM PSYCHIATRIC DRUGS

Psychoactive drugs are a dead end. In the short term, they blunt emotional awareness and substitute for the important psychological work that needs to be done, including the three steps to emotional freedom—identifying, rejecting, and triumphing and transcending guilt, shame, and anxiety. In the longer run, they injure brain function and can physically harm the brain, and they tend to diminish overall quality of life.[1] There is no genuine happiness down the psychoactive-drug road. I have written dozens of books and articles about this and provided a source of further information in Appendix A. Here, I will simply remind you that information is available concerning how and why to stop taking psychiatric drugs.

Despite all the drug-company hoopla, and despite Food and Drug Administration (FDA) approval of specific drugs for treating specific "mental disorders," there is no scientific basis for such claims. From marijuana and alcohol to psychiatric medications, psychoactive drugs work by causing widespread dysfunction in the brain, sometimes initially causing a mild euphoria and always causing emotional blunting or anesthesia. This is what I call the *brain-disabling principle* of psychiatric drug treatment.[2] In addition, as noted earlier, all psychoactive substances cause what I call *medication spellbinding* by impairing the ability to realize how much the drug is reducing the quality of life and harming mental and emotional function.[3] People continue taking psychoactive substances because they do not realize the harm being done to them, and also because they confuse distressing withdrawal symptoms with a need for the drug.

By throwing multiple neurotransmitter systems out of whack, all psychiatric drugs vastly and unpredictably distort human emotions, making it difficult for the victim or anyone else to recognize or identify the individual's genuine emotions compared to those created or distorted by the drugs. It makes it impossible to determine whether an emotion is being driven by predrug normal brain function or by drug-soaked neurotransmitters. Psychiatric drugs also mute the motivational system of the brain, interfering with the personal determination and stamina to identify and reject negative emotions. By impairing the limbic system and frontal lobes of the brain, all psychiatric drugs make it much harder to generate or to focus on higher purposes, values, and spirituality. A brain exposed to psychiatric drugs is a brain swimming in toxins and, therefore, vastly impeded in its emotional recovery and growth. Months and years of exposure to psychiatric drugs work against emotional recovery and instead frequently cause apathy, cognitive deficits, and loss of quality of life.

Psychiatric drugs intrude into the innermost processes of the brain and are very damaging to the brain and mind. These days, choosing or being forced into psychiatric treatment is the most common cause of a downhill course in life for children and adults. Psychiatric drugs are shortening lives and leaving children and adults disabled.[4]

Physical interventions into the brain with psychoactive substances are shots in the dark that inevitably risk muting, disrupting, and destroying our essential psychosocial capacities and characteristics as human beings. Only holistic psychosocial and spiritual interventions are sophisticated and meaningful enough to heal the emotional problems that are the legacy of our biological and social evolution, our childhoods, and our adult experiences and decisions.

The biological basis of emotions does not logically lead to the conclusion that emotional problems are "diseases" or "mental disorders" or that they are genetic or biochemical in origin. Guilt, shame, and anxiety arise out of the normal brain functioning given to us by evolution. When these emotions become overwhelming or disabling, it is a result of *normal functional responses* to childhood neglect, abuse, or trauma, or to adult trauma, such as war, incarceration, domestic abuse and rape. These are the responses of a normal person with a normal brain to unusual stress.

Stopping psychiatric drugs can avoid further harm to the brain and mind and enable gradual recovery of intellectual and emotional capacities. However, stopping psychiatric drugs can be as dangerous as starting them and is best carried out consistent with the individual's desires and with guidance from experienced clinicians. Family or close friends need to be involved to help as much as possible and, if necessary, to protect the individual during the anguish that sometimes accompanies withdrawal from psychiatric drugs. I have described this process in *Psychiatric Drug Withdrawal: A Guide for Prescribers, Therapists, Patients and their Families*.

Each of us, however badly life has gone for us, has the ability to take command of our lives, to vastly enhance the quality of our lives, and to improve our chances of achieving our goals. This can be accomplished most readily and successfully with a brain and mind unencumbered by psychiatric drugs.

ANGER AND NUMBNESS ARE RUINOUS LAST RESORTS

For too many of us, outbursts of anger become our last resort. We go through the day secretly, or not so secretly, seething inside. We cultivate resentments to maintain our pride and sense of control in relation to others. We imagine becoming so angry that our boss, husband, wife, or children will finally listen to us. Meanwhile, our anger eats away at our physical, mental, and spiritual vitality.

Others of us turn to emotional numbness as our last resort. When the conflicts in our family seem unbearable, we withdraw emotionally and physically. We end up feeling isolated and lost.

Some of us embrace the identity of "survivor." This identity can help us to get by, but it discourages and limits genuine success and happiness. Rather than surviving, it is far better to work toward becoming triumphant and transcendent.

Psychiatric drugs have become among the most common escapes from facing the hard work of improving our lives through reason, ethics, and love. We obsess over how to manage our rollercoaster feelings by changing drugs, adding drugs, or adjusting doses. When nothing works or things get worse, we call the doctor again and resume the inevitable endless tinkering with medications that never leads to happiness but only to more numbness.

We no longer imagine that healing lies within ourselves, our relationships, our higher purposes, or our understanding of a higher power. We give up trying to control our emotions through the exercise of our reason and intellect and through better choices. Pills replace any hope for meaningful purposes. Drugs fill our consciousness as our first, last, and only resort. We live an unexamined life, wondering why we keep feeling worse and worse.

What if our last resort is *love,* a joyful awareness and treasuring of our partner, family, nature, work, higher ideals, or spiritual beliefs? No longer relying on pills, we seek purposes for our lives and adopt spiritually uplifting practices and ideals. Instead of subduing our brains, we muster our mental and spiritual power to improve our lives. Instead of stifling our emotions, we learn to identify them and sort them out as we take steps toward emotional freedom.

Chapter 32

LOVE AS OUR HIGHEST PURPOSE

Always remember that love is joyful awareness! Remember that it can be joyful awareness of any aspect of the world: family, friends, colleagues and coworkers, the people we serve through work and volunteering, companion animals, nature, music and art, principles and ideals, higher purposes, and spirituality, which, for many, includes a belief in God. This joyful awareness called love leads us to treasure others and life itself, and it provides direction and inspiration in all our choices. Especially in our friendships and family life, love and higher ideals draw us together and generate the best possible life for us and those we care about. If we decide to expand our love into the wider world, the very same principles apply when we are working with others at our jobs, in church, in our community service groups, or within reform or charitable organizations.

All the pain and suffering seemingly associated with love has to do with the flawed way we human beings relate to each other and with conflicts within ourselves as individuals. Relationships come and go, they turn out well or badly, they offer comfort or inflict suffering, but knowing we are a source of love will generate spiritual nourishment for us and those we touch. Handling personal conflict without losing sight of love is probably the most difficult challenge given to us as human beings. If the conflicts and calamities of life never dim our desire to love and be loved, then we have found a secret to life.

Unfortunately, and often tragically, love and higher ideals are not all there is to human nature. We easily become baffled by guilt, anxiety, shame, anger, indifference, and myriad other expressions of helplessness and destructiveness. We are, as the earlier chapters made clear, the most loving and the most violent creature ever to populate this planet. Each of us must find our own way through the complexities of our human nature to guide ourselves with reason, sound principles, and love.

EMPATHY AND LOVE WILL KEEP US SANE

Empathy is so closely related to love that it is difficult to consider them separately. Remember that love inspires us to be nurturing and protective of whatever or whomever we love. In relating to other living creatures and beings, from our pets to our intimate human relationships, love also encourages and enables us to be empathic. Love and empathy lead to a happy life.

As a psychiatrist and therapist, I have never experienced burnout. Of course, I occasionally have difficult times with patients, but they are the exception and usually turn into learning experiences, and they do not weigh down the overall work experience. I continue to enjoy and love working with patients.

There are a number of related reasons why I still enjoy my work as a therapist after so many decades:

- Because I do not start my patients on medications, I am not suppressing their emotions and causing them harm.
- Because they are not drugged (unless they come to me on medications and have not yet withdrawn from them), they can relate to me in a caring and meaningful way and can more easily work toward empowering themselves.
- Because I never lock up people against their will or otherwise coerce them, I can create free and respectful relationships with my patients.
- Because I work at respecting and encouraging my patients' autonomy and independence, I do not get caught up in feeling guilty, anxious, ashamed, frustrated, or angry as they struggle with the ups and downs of their lives.
- Because I love and feel empathy for the people I try to help, when I am with them, I am as free as possible of any guilt, shame, anxiety, anger, or numbing.

In other words, caring about and loving people, including my patients, keeps me happy and sane. Hence, I am even more enthusiastic about life in my seventy-eighth year than when I was in my youth.[1]

Modern psychiatry relies so heavily, if not exclusively, on drug treatment that young psychiatrists can go through their training without ever spending time with disturbed patients whose minds are not clouded or damaged by toxic chemicals. The only drug-free patients they tend to see are suffering from drug withdrawal or drug-induced brain damage. Because I work with my patients without resort to psychiatric drugs, I can get to know what they really think and feel and what actually helps them. My drug-free treatment approach has enabled me to make the observations and gain the knowledge I am sharing in this book.

A FEW BASIC LIFE-ENHANCING PRINCIPLES

Review the following principles and apply them to your own life. They can enormously enhance your life:

- Do not take psychoactive substances to solve emotional problems, and do not encourage loved ones to take them. You will be more in touch with your emotions and more fully able to relate to other people. Keep in mind that you or your loved ones may need to withdraw from psychiatric drugs carefully and with supervision to be safe and that no one should be coerced into taking or stopping psychiatric drugs.[2]
- Work together with loved ones, coworkers, and others toward mutual empowerment.
- Never bully or coerce other people; instead, create free and respectful relationships with everyone in your life.
- Respect and encourage each person's autonomy and independence, and you will avoid feeling guilty, anxious, ashamed, frustrated and angry, or numb because of them as they struggle with the ups and downs of their lives.
- Love and feel empathy for as many people as you can. It will help you to banish your self-defeating emotions and move forward with your life.

Caring about people and loving them as separate and independent human beings can keep us as sane and happy, and as beneficial to others, as possible, but it is not without challenges. There will be temptations to indulge our darker nature and do something for the sake of short-term advantage or power. There will be times when it will take courage to do what we know to be right. Often, it seems too risky to take the principled, honorable, and empathic road, but, as rocky as it can be, it remains the best road—and, really, the only one on which we can live a good life.

BECOME THE WONDERFUL EXCEPTION

Even casual encounters with people can affect the quality of their day. For many years, I had a number of flight attendants in my practice in the airline hub of Washington, DC. It was revelatory to see how even these highly paid, experienced, and well-trained men and women could feel that a few days of their lives had been "ruined" by one unruly, disrespectful passenger.[3] Similarly, many recalled kindnesses from individual unnamed passengers that had occurred years earlier. The same is true for nearly everyone who deals with the public, from physicians to store clerks and waiters.

Of course, when we are relating with people we know well and care about—including coworkers, clients, friends, and family—the spiritual stakes are even higher in regard to how we treat each other. Often, we can greatly undermine or greatly enhance the quality of their lives.

In any contact we have with other people, they will tend to feel affirmed as someone of worth—or not. Human encounters are seldom inconsequential, neutral, or objective. Every communication you make, however indirect, will either encourage or discourage the other person. The expression on our face—a scowl or a smile, a suspicious or a welcoming attitude—can have an instantaneous impact on the people we meet. Our promptness, our gestures, our tone of voice, our spoken words—what is said and what is not said—give others a sense of whether or not we take them seriously and value them. Especially in our cities, but to some degree everywhere, we human beings treat each other as something less than miraculous creations. That is, we anticipate nothing heartwarming or life enhancing in our everyday relationships or even in our more intimate ones. In contrast, if we want to spread comfort and happiness in our everyday living—and, especially, if we want to be a *good* friend, family member, coworker, or provider of services to others—we must do the unexpected. We must *treasure* the people whose lives we touch.

At times, the value we ascribe to other human beings may lead us to take stands that are unpopular or even dangerous. It may lead us to take actions that entail risks. In the process, courageous living increases our sense of personal value and can bring inestimable good into the world.

It is tragic that so few human beings value themselves and the people whose lives they touch. Too often, our routine interactions do nothing but add to this dismal experience of mutual daily indifference. Our task, as someone who wishes to feel personally fulfilled and who wants to positively influence others, is to become the exception—the person who treasures other human beings and acts on it.

LOVE AS OUR LAST AND EVERYDAY RESORT

Our ideals and higher purposes become clarified and fine-tuned when we ask ourselves on a daily basis how much these ideals and purposes promote the presence of love in our lives, in the lives of our families, and in the ever-expanding circle of humanity that surrounds all of us and responds to our actions. Make love and devotion to higher ideals your first, last, and only resort. Make it a part of your daily living, as well as the measure of the worth of all your important choices and actions. At times, living by these ideals may require extraordinary courage, but there is no other way to get and to give the most in our brief lifetimes.

Throughout our struggle to bring out the best in ourselves, we can keep our hearts open to giving and receiving love and pursuing meaningful values. We can implement love in our daily lives by treating each other as treasures. We can infuse all our communications with love, improving the lives of everyone we touch in our families and communities—and, with the help of the Internet, throughout the world. Through conflicts, crises, and catastrophes, we can continue to see love and sound values as our first, last, and ultimate resort. Not an easy task, but love offers a flawless moral compass to keep us pointed in the direction of the best possible life.

Decide for yourself what you believe in, what kind of ideals you have, what higher purposes you admire or wish to live by. Then, make them a central part of your emotional life. Nothing is more important than living by higher or greater purposes in life. Ultimately, make your highest purpose your last and only resort—the strength to which you return at all times in your life, good or bad, easy or difficult. Your last resort can be your daily resort. Becoming and being a source of love is the most basic purpose of all—one that can provide you with a constant source of strength.

The science in this book and the wisdom of the ages come together with a shared understanding that human beings must daily choose between their two natures: willfulness and aggression on the one hand, reason and love on the other. Simply, we must learn to live by our better nature. We can only do that if we triumph over and transcend our negative legacy emotions of guilt, shame, and anxiety, as well as chronic anger and numbing.

This book, at heart, is an invitation to love—to love not only people but also life, our highest values and purposes, and our spirituality, with an appreciation of something or Someone greater than ourselves. By becoming a source of love, we bring out the best in ourselves and in every person we touch.

Appendix A

ABOUT PSYCHIATRY AND PSYCHIATRIC DRUGS

As a physician and psychiatrist, I felt required to share my views and scientific opinions in this book about how psychiatric drugs can make it more difficult and sometimes impossible for people to overcome negative legacy emotions and to prosper in life. Please understand that you can benefit from this book without agreeing with my critical assessment of psychiatric drugs, but I want to provide everyone with the opportunity to become familiar with my clinical experience and research—and a large body of additional scientific opinion and research that indicates that psychiatric drugs often do more harm than good.

In my own psychiatric practice, I work with children, adults, and families without resorting to psychiatric drugs. I want my patients to become empowered to understand and to overcome whatever has held them back, and then to direct their lives in more satisfying and creative ways.

I wrote *Psychiatric Drug Withdrawal* (2013) for both professionals and the public. It documents the information in this book with many scientific references about the dangers and lack of effectiveness associated with every class of psychiatry drug. It describes how *medication spellbinding* prevents us from knowing how psychiatric drugs are harming our brains, minds, and quality of life. The book also documents the *chronic brain impairment* (CBI) that all psychiatric drugs can cause over months and years with progressive loss of mental acuity and quality of life.[1] My medical book *Brain-Disabling Treatments in Psychiatry* (2008), which laypersons can easily read, presents the most thorough analysis of how biopsychiatric interventions "work" by disabling the brain. It, too, presents scientific background for the views expressed in this book and the summary that follows.

The evidence that psychiatric drugs work in the short term is flimsy and largely contrived by drug companies and the researchers they pay. Meanwhile, there are few studies and no convincing evidence that the drugs are helpful after several months or years of exposure. Worse yet, there is mounting evidence that all classes of psychiatric drugs, especially when taken for months or years, produce chronic brain impairment and diminished enjoyment of life. Psychiatric drugs frequently prevent recovery and often lead to chronic or permanent disability.

All or nearly all psychiatric drugs can also produce serious and even life-threatening withdrawal reactions. Therefore, it is both unsafe to start taking psychiatric medications and dangerous to stop them. As my book *Psychiatric Drug Withdrawal* describes, withdrawal from psychiatry drugs can be hazardous and should be managed with judicious tapering, a support network, and experienced clinical supervision.[2]

Throughout *Guilt, Shame, and Anxiety*, I provide endnote citations of scientific articles about the hazards of psychiatric drugs. Some of my most relevant scientific studies are in the bibliography to this book and are available for reading on my website, www.breggin.com. In this appendix, I will draw attention to a few relevant books and several films. The following selection of my books documents the limits and dangers of psychiatric diagnoses and drugs, often with hundreds or thousands of scientific references:

Toxic Psychiatry: *Why Therapy, Empathy and Love Must Replace the Drugs, Electroshock and Biochemical Theories of the "New Psychiatry,"* 1991

Talking Back to Prozac (coauthored by Ginger Breggin), 1994; reprinted with a new introduction, 2004

The Antidepressant Fact Book, 2001

Talking Back to Ritalin, Revised, 2001

The Ritalin Fact Book, 2002

Brain-Disabling Treatments in Psychiatry, Second Edition: Drugs, Electroshock, and the Psychopharmaceutical Complex, 2008

Medication Madness: The Role of Psychiatric Drugs in Cases of Violence, Suicide and Crime, 2008

Psychiatric Drug Withdrawal: *A Guide for Prescribers, Therapists, Patients and Their Families*, 2013

Medication Madness gives detailed stories about individuals driven to act destructively for the first time in their lives and offers a scientific understanding of how drugs can change personality and behavior for the worse. It is very relevant to the mass murders in the news.

Another of my books, *The Heart of Being Helpful*, describes my approach to both psychotherapy and personal relationships. My *Empathic Therapy Training Film* is available on my professional website and on Amazon.com.[3]

My wife, Ginger, and I founded the Center for the Study of Empathic Therapy. Our nonprofit organization's website, www.empathictherapy.org, offers a set of Guidelines for Empathic Therapy that reflect the same principles of living as promoted in this book. The site also offers DVD sets of some of our best Empathic Therapy Conference presentations.

Recent years have seen growing criticism of what I call the *psychopharmaceutical complex* and the unethical partnership between the drug companies and organized medicine and psychiatry. In addition to my own, here is a sample of critical books that can be found in the bibliography: Angell (2004); Baughman and Hovey (2006); Corrigan (2014); Glenmullen (2001, 2006); Goldacre (2012); Kirk and Kutchins (1992); Kirsch (2011); Kutchins and Kirk (1997); Light (2010); Lynch (2005); Moncrieff (2007, 2013); Scott (2011); Watters (2010); Whitaker (2002, 2010); and Whitfield (2011).

There is also a large and growing literature on psychosocial approaches to healing daily human distress as well as the most disturbed individuals, including those diagnosed with schizophrenia. Again in addition to my own books, here is a sample: Cornwall (2012); Karon (2003, 2005); Lynch (2011); Maddock and Maddock (2006); Mosher (1996); Mosher and Bola (2004); Mosher and Burti (1989); Watkins (2008); Whitaker (2010); and Whitfield (1987). Seikkula and Arnkil (2006) describe "Open Dialogue" in Finland, a largely drug-free, very successful family-intervention approach to treating patients who might otherwise end up being diagnosed schizophrenic. Mackler's 2011 and 2014 films document the project.

Several excellent films document the harmful effects of psychiatric drugs as well as the socially corrosive operations of the psychopharmaceutical complex. Kevin Miller's *Generation Rx* and *Letters from Generation Rx* are two very fine films about the harmfulness of diagnosing and drugging children. Sasha Knezev's *American Addict* (2012) is an excellent film about the psychopharmaceutical complex, and there is a sequel coming soon.

Billions of pharmaceutical company dollars promote psychiatric drugs. Most people are aware of the television ads, but those are a tiny fraction of the marketing budgets. Drug companies support universities, medical centers, research facilities, journals, medical societies and their conferences, and individual researchers and opinion leaders. They pay well-regarded experts to put their names on supposed research papers ghostwritten by the drug companies. They even pay to expedite the drug approval process at the Food and Drug Administration (FDA)!

Within a few decades, the drug industry and its paid collaborators have managed to undermine a number of basic American values: the responsibility of parents for parenting and teachers for teaching; the importance of children learning to take responsibility for themselves; and the necessity of adults using their own psychological, ethical, and spiritual resources to overcome personal and emotional problems.

Fabricated biological theories and unfounded genetic speculations are heralded as truths across the spectrum of society, from medicine and academia to pop culture. A third or more of our active-duty military and nearly all veterans in the Department of Veterans Affairs (VA) with emotional problems become consumers of cocktails of harmful psychoactive drugs.[4] An estimated 20 percent of women are taking antidepressants at any one time, and many more are taking other psychiatric drugs, including benzodiazepine "tranquilizer" sedatives and sleeping aids.[5] According to the Centers for Disease Control and Prevention (CDC), parents report that 6.4 million children have received a healthcare provider's diagnosis of attention-deficit hyperactivity disorder (ADHD), including one in five high school boys.[6] The average American psychiatrist does little else than prescribe drugs, typically during ten- to fifteen-minute "med checks." Primary-care doctors spend a few minutes with their patients and then lavishly prescribe psychiatric meds to adults who feel nervous, tired, stressed, or a little sad. Family doctors and pediatricians inundate children with drugs when they really need improved discipline at home and more inspired educational approaches at school. Federal and state governments pay families for each child diagnosed with an emotional disability, such as ADHD or oppositional defiant disorder, and, almost invariably, their doctors require these children to take psychiatric drugs in order to stay on disability. Low-income families are very vulnerable to this medical abuse of children.

For us to prosper as individuals and for our society to regain its vitality, we need to turn back the onslaught of psychiatric drugs. In their place, we must promote a return to basic human values that empower individuals to raise their children and take charge of their own lives with their innate, personal, and spiritually rooted resources.

DARWIN WAS NO DARWINIST

How does a book that offers a new theory on the biological evolution of negative emotions find its way to discussing love? Is this scientific? Is it compatible with the basic thinking of Charles Darwin, who developed the theory of evolution?

These days, Darwin's name is often used to undermine concepts of free will, morality, spirituality, love, and the divine. Advocates of the theory of evolution give the impression that Darwin believed that all aspects of human life, including our highest ideals, are wholly determined by instincts, by natural selection, and by inexorable biological evolution. For example, E. O. Wilson characterizes Darwin's science and philosophy as opposing religion and God.[1] The coeditors of the classic Princeton edition of *The Descent of Man* praised the supposed "frank out-and-out materialism" of Darwin's views.[2] In possibly the worst distortion of all in respect to how we view ourselves, Darwin "experts" have led us to believe that evolution is a dog-eat-dog competition leading to the survival of the fittest. Yet, as David Loye thoroughly documents in *Darwin's Lost Theory of Love*, none of this is true.

DARWIN ON THE SOCIAL INSTINCTS AND LOVE

Darwin was an extraordinarily empathic and wise man who sought to warn against all the excesses we now call "Darwinism." His great book about human evolution, *The Descent of Man*, focuses on how natural selection favors the development of the social instincts into a flowering of mutual aid, sympathy, and love among human beings. Throughout his analysis of the evolution of human life, Darwin repeatedly confirms that we thrive not because we compete with each other but because we cooperate, care for each other, and love one another.

In *The Descent of Man*, Darwin uses the world "love" eighty times and "sympathy" fifty-two times. By contrast, he mentions "survival of the fittest" only three times.[3] More extraordinary, in one of those three mentions, he explains how he reedited the original published version of *The Origin of Species* to eliminate what he saw as his previously mistaken emphasis upon "survival of the fittest."[4] Darwin declares that great virtues are not developed by "having succeeded best in the struggle for life."[5]

What does Darwin cite as the highest moral achievement of humankind? He reminds us "To do good unto others—to do unto others as ye would they should do onto you,—is the foundation-stone of morality."[6] Notice that this alleged "out-and-out" materialist uses language reminiscent of the Bible to advocate for the Golden Rule. He uses the evocative and already antiquated "ye" and "unto" only three times in *The Descent of Man*, always in describing the Golden Rule—probably to emphasize the spiritual and religious nature of the principle.[7] Elsewhere, Darwin refers directly to "sympathy and the love of his fellow creatures" as one of man's "higher mental qualities."[8]

Darwin specifically rejects trying to improve the human race by allowing the seemingly less fit to fall by the wayside or to die. To do so would offend our more "tender" sympathies, leading to "deterioration in the noblest part of our nature." Furthermore, any attempt "intentionally to neglect the weak and helpless" for a future benefit to humanity would bring about a "certain and great present evil."[9] As we shall find again and again, Darwin was no Darwinist.

ETHICS TRANSCEND THE INSTINCTS

My view is consistent with that of Darwin, who saw the origin of morality in the "instinct for sympathy" that eventually leads to a moral sense in human beings. He, too, believed that we humans have developed morality beyond the instinctual level:

> Ultimately a highly complex sentiment, having its first origin in the social instincts, largely guided by the approbation of our fellow-men, ruled by reason, self-interest, and in later times by deep religious feeling, confirmed by instruction and habit, all combined, constitute our moral sense or conscience.[10]

In *Selection in Relation to Sex*, Darwin elaborates that each individual human being must ultimately rely upon his own conscience:

> The moral nature of man has reached the highest standard as yet attained, partly through the advancement of reasoning powers. . . . Ultimately, man no longer accepts the praise or blame of his fellows as his chief guide. . . . His conscience then becomes his supreme judge and monitor.[11]

Contrary to the Darwinist idea that human beings are wholly the result of biological evolution and instinctual drives, Charles Darwin found that we can and should guide our own lives with the conscience as supreme judge and monitor.

FREE WILL AND REASON EXIST

In *The Descent of Man*, Darwin asserts that "free will" does redirect and modify instincts, so, at times, individual determination and choice operate without regard for them.[12] He gives several examples of animals exercising reason and making choices that "can hardly depend on the modification of any instinct."[13] He states that these intellectual faculties are preeminent ("at the summit") in human beings.[14]

DARWIN REJECTS "BLIND CHANCE" IN EVOLUTION

E. O. Wilson, editor of a four-book compendium of Darwin's work, attacks critics who, on religious grounds, refuse to accept that natural selection acts on "blind chance."[15] But Darwin himself specifically rejected and revolted against the concept of "blind chance" dominating human evolution:

> The birth both of the species and of the individual are equally parts of that grand sequence of events, which our minds refuse to accept as the result of blind chance. The understanding revolts at such a conclusion . . .[16]

By distorting and misrepresenting Darwin's scientific and philosophic viewpoint, Darwinists in positions of authority do great harm to science and humanity. The theory of evolution, as Darwin confirmed, is compatible with free will, reason, God, and a universe with a purpose behind it. In stark contrast to Darwin, Wilson and other Darwinists stir up war between "science" and deeper understandings of human life with the aim of imposing their sterile viewpoints as the only reasonable ones.

For those who still wonder at the progression of this book from human instincts to the primary, transcending value of love, I return to Charles Darwin. In the second edition of *The Descent of Man*, he added a lengthy footnote to make unmistakably clear where he stood on the relationship between our biological instincts and our capacities for love and spirituality:

> To do good in return for evil, to love your enemy, is a height of morality to which it may be doubted whether the social instincts would, by themselves, have ever led us. It is *necessary* that these instincts, together with sympathy, should have been highly cultivated and extended by the aid of reason, instruction, and the love or fear of God, before any such golden rule would ever be thought of and obeyed.[17]

LIFE SHAKES DARWIN'S FAITH

Chapter 5 mentions Darwin's belief that evolution by itself could not have led to "the ennobling belief in the existence of an Omnipotent God."[18] To Darwin, this ennobling belief in God, like all morality, was a derivative of the social instincts, but it was not, in itself, instinctual and was, therefore, not a "universal" aspect of human cultures. He explains, "The highest form of religion—the grand idea of God hating sin and loving righteousness—was unknown during primeval times."[19] Belief in God required "the aid of active intellectual powers" to more fully develop "man's moral constitution" and, ultimately, the Golden Rule.[20]

In *The Origin of Species*, Darwin argues that the theory of evolution, in comparison to older theories, "accords better with what we know of the laws impressed on matter by the Creator."[21] He theorizes "that probably all the organic beings which have ever lived on this earth have descended from some one primordial form, into which life was breathed."[22] Were he alive today,

Darwin might speculate that, while the material universe originated from the Big Bang, life originated from the Big Breath.

Darwin's books and letters, and his son's observations (especially see the 1892 autobiography and collected letters), confirm that throughout his life, and especially as he grew older, Darwin was conflicted over whether he could find the presence of God or intelligent design in the natural world. He always remained awed by nature and yet felt increasing doubt about his ability to know its essence or the place of humankind within it. He definitely did not think of himself as an atheist. Because Darwin's quotes are often cherry-picked to advance a viewpoint, here is a relevant quote that shows, at some length, the complexity and inner contradictions he experienced as a thoughtful, complicated, and spiritually oriented human being:

> Believing as I do that man in the distant future will be a far more perfect creature than he now is, it is an intolerable thought that he and all other sentient beings are doomed to annihilation [by a cooling sun] after such long-continued slow progress. To those who fully admit to immortality of the human soul, the destruction of our world will not appear so dreadful.
>
> Another source of conviction in the existence of God, connected with the reason and not with the feelings, impresses me as having much more weight. This follows from the extreme difficulty or rather impossibility of conceiving this immense and wonderful universe, including man with his capacity of looking far backwards and far into futurity, as the result of blind chance or necessity. When thus reflecting, I feel compelled to look to a First Cause having an intelligent mind in some degree analogous to that of man; and I deserve to be called a Theist. This conclusion was strong in my mind about the time, as far as I can remember, when I wrote the *Origin of Species*, and it is since that time that it has very gradually, with many fluctuations, become weaker. But then arises the doubt—can the mind of man, which has, as I fully believe, been developed from a mind as low as that possessed by the lowest animals, be trusted when it draws such grand conclusions?[23]

Darwin also said, "In my most extreme fluctuations I have never been an atheist. I think generally (and more and more now as I grow older), but not always, that an Agnostic would be the more correct description of my state of mind."[24]

As so often happens, Darwin may have lost his original faith not because of any scientific or necessarily rational conclusions but because the misery and suffering he saw about him and that he experienced in his own life seemed to him inconsistent with a benevolent God.[25] In other words, much like many of us, Darwin struggled with faith not as a scientist but as a moral person seeking to understand life.

AFTERWORD AND ACKNOWLEDGMENTS

More than forty years ago, I first began sketching out in my mind the concepts that have evolved into this book. Earlier versions of these ideas are laced through many of my books and scientific articles. In retrospect, understanding guilt, shame, and anxiety may be the most daunting and strenuous intellectual task I have undertaken. The most important original insight involved seeing all three negative emotions as serving the same purpose of inhibiting or deflecting our willfulness and anger toward each other in close personal relationships.

The next most transformative insight occurred in recent years when I began to see the roots of these emotions in biological evolution and natural selection. That led me to develop the theory of negative legacy emotions, which appears for the first time in this book. Because the concepts are sometimes complicated and subtle, I have provided an abundant index to serve as a guide to the book.

Starting in 1984, my wife, Ginger, has been with me through much of this process. Over these thirty years, our many discussions about guilt, shame, and anxiety have helped me to sharpen, revise, and apply my ideas. Ginger edited the nearly completed manuscript and, as always, made very important observations and added new emphases. Ginger's mother, Jean Ross, read the entire manuscript and made many valuable suggestions and copyediting corrections. Missy McDermott is our outstanding office assistant in all things, including this book. Ian Goddard has been my research assistant for many years and as always provided valuable help.

Stanley Krippner, PhD, recipient of the 2013 APA Division 32 Award for Distinguished Lifetime Contributions to Humanistic Psychology, was kind enough to read the entire manuscript. Drawing on his extensive wisdom, knowledge, and experience, he made many useful suggestions for content and style. His foreword and his enthusiasm for the book mean a great deal to me. Dr. Krippner also introduced me to the work of David Loye, which showed me the consistency of my views with the actual writings of Charles Darwin, in contrast to the distortions of

Darwinism. Thomas Scheff, Professor Emeritus of Sociology at the University of California, Santa Barbara, also took the time to comment on the manuscript. He, too, added encouraging words and made useful suggestions.

Brooks Miner, PhD, a postdoctoral research fellow in ecology and evolutionary biology at Cornell University, took considerable time to review Part 1 of the manuscript. Before reading it, he was understandably skeptical about a theory that could root guilt, shame, and anxiety in biological evolution and natural selection, but he found the theory useful and scientifically sound. He made many detailed and useful suggestions for clarifying and sharpening my language. Jeanne Stolzer, PhD, a professor of child development at the University of Nebraska at Kearney, read the manuscript and reminded me to write more about attachment theory. Joanne Cacciatore, PhD, an associate professor in the School of Social Work at Arizona State University, Phoenix, helped to focus my observations on bereavement. Patient advocate Richard Lawhern, PhD, contributed to the copyediting.

I want thank Bob Nikkel, MSW, and Gina Nikkel, PhD, Foundation for Excellence in Mental Health Care, for their interest and great encouragement throughout the several stages of development of this book. I also appreciate therapist Michael Cornwall, PhD, and Howie Glasser, creator of the Nurtured Heart Approach, for their affirmation of its value.

As my book grew near to completion, students in my spring 2014 graduate school seminar on "Mental Health and Children" in the Department of Counseling at SUNY Oswego read it and made useful comments. I want to thank Theresa Kiernan, Domenica Robinson, Adam Schwartz, Hannah Wadsworth, Vicki Wolfe, John Randall, and Brenda McAuslan. McAuslan, who works in child protective services, made numerous useful editing comments and important suggestions that improved the book, especially the sections on abuse and neglect.

Over the years, many patients in my clinical practice have read versions of the evolving manuscript, applied it to their therapy work and their lives, and made comments that have influenced my thinking and writing. They have added immeasurably to the book in its final form.

I want to thank editor in chief Steven L. Mitchell and the entire staff at Prometheus Books for their support in this project. Literary agent Andy Ross generously volunteered to read the book contract and made many helpful suggestions.

ABOUT PETER R. BREGGIN, MD

For his many decades of successful efforts to reform psychiatry and mental health around the world, Peter R. Breggin, MD, is called the "The Conscience of Psychiatry." Dr. Breggin began working with state mental hospital patients as an eighteen-year-old college student at Harvard and eventually directed the Harvard Radcliffe Mental Hospital Volunteer Program (1954–1958). He has been in private practice continuously since 1968. His experience helping people in emotional distress spans six decades!

Author photo by Kevin Miller

A former Teaching Fellow at Harvard Medical School and a former full-time consultant at the National Institute of Mental Health (NIMH), Dr. Breggin continues to teach in a university graduate school and to act as a legal expert in criminal and malpractice cases and in product liability cases involving drug company negligence. He is the author of more than forty-five scientific articles and more than twenty books, including the best sellers *Talking Back to Prozac* and *Toxic Psychiatry*. Dr. Breggin's most recent books are *Brain-Disabling Treatments in Psychiatry, Second Edition*; *Medication Madness: The Role of Psychiatric Drugs in Cases of Violence, Suicide and Crime;* and *Psychiatric Drug Withdrawal: A Guide for Prescribers, Therapists, Patients and Their Families.*

Dr. Breggin's research and educational efforts provide the foundation for modern criticism of psychiatric diagnoses and drugs, leading the way in promoting more caring and effective therapies. His earliest reform efforts, in the 1970s, brought an almost complete stop to lobotomy in the Western world. In the 1990s, he and his wife, Ginger, prevented a eugenic federal project aimed at the nation's inner-city children, which they documented in their book *The War against Children of Color* (1998).

Dr. Breggin's research and educational projects and his testimony before Congress have informed the professions and the public about the dangers of psychiatric drugs and helped to push the FDA to upgrade the seriousness of its warnings about adverse drug effects for dozens of medications.

As a medical expert in legal cases, Dr. Breggin has unprecedented and unique knowledge about how the pharmaceutical industry too often commits fraud in researching and marketing psychiatric drugs. He frequently participates in criminal, product liability, and malpractice cases. He has been the psychiatric expert in landmark psychiatric cases, including the first malpractice jury verdict involving electroshock (ECT) treatment and the first jury verdict against a psychosurgeon. One of his earliest cases, *Kaimowitz v. Michigan Department of Mental Health* (1972), ended lobotomy and psychosurgery in all state and federal facilities in the United States.

From *Time* to the *New York Times*, his work has been cited innumerable times in worldwide media. He has appeared hundreds of times as an expert on television across the political and social spectrum—from the *Oprah Winfrey Show* (many times), *Larry King Live* (many times), *20/20*, *60 Minutes*, and *Good Morning America* to the *O'Reilly Factor* and the Fox Business Network.

Dr. Breggin's professional website is www.breggin.com. With his wife, Ginger, he founded the Center for the Study of Empathic Therapy (www.empathictherapy.org). The center holds annual conferences, provides a list of therapy resources, and offers a free e-newsletter. His weekly radio interview show, *The Dr. Peter Breggin Hour*, is live and archived on the Internet at www.prn.fm. He offers "The Weekly Breggin Report" on his own website and also blogs on the *Huffington Post* and on *NaturalNews*.

A list of Dr. Breggin's books, articles, and legal cases, as well as a summary of his accomplishments, can be found in his resume on his professional website, www. breggin.com.

NOTES

Foreword

1. M. Shermer, *Why Darwin Matters* (New York, NY: Henry Holt, 2006).

2. D. Loye, *Darwin's Lost Theory of Love* (San Jose, CA: toExcel, 2000).

3. S. Krippner, D. B. Pitchford, and J. Davies, *Post-Traumatic Stress Disorder: Biographies of Disease* (Santa Barbara, CA: Greenwood/ABC-CLIO, 2012).

PART 1: UNDERSTANDING NEGATIVE LEGACY EMOTIONS

Chapter 1. The Most Violent and Most Loving Creature on Earth

1. Cromie (2001).

2. Wenban-Smith et al. (2006). Also see "Giant Prehistoric Elephant Slaughtered by Early Humans" (2013).

3. Our humanlike ancestors are called *hominids* and, more recently, *hominins*.

4. See Keeley (1996). Even our nearest relatives, the chimpanzee groups, conduct warfare against each other (de Waal 2005; Goodall 1999), but not remotely on the scale of human carnage (Masson 2014). See further discussion in chapter 4.

5. See similar discussion in Churchland (2013), pp. 127–29.

6. For early insights into our social nature, see Kropotkin (1914) and Adler (2009). The best introduction to Adler is Ansbacher and Ansbacher (1956). For a review of some earlier social theorists, see Breggin (2002). For a social evolutionary analysis, see E. O. Wilson (1979). Darwin (1952, 1981), as documented in Appendix B, was ahead of them in his emphasis on love and sociability.

7. Brooks (2011). In the field of psychotherapy, empathy has long been understood as a central aspect of the healing process (Rogers 1961; Bohart and Greenberg 1997; Breggin 1997; Breggin, Breggin, and Bemak 2002; Staemmler 2012). Based on our conviction that empathy is the key to therapy, sound ethics, and good relationships, in 2010, my wife, Ginger Breggin, and I founded the Center for the Study of Empathic Therapy (www.empathictherapy.org), which offers conferences, a resource center, and a free e-newsletter.

8. Montague (1971).

9. Morrison et al. (2010).

10. Darwin defined natural selection as the "preservation of favourable variations and the rejection of injurious variations" (2006, p. 504).

11. Group selection remains a complex and controversial theory in biological evolution (e.g.,

Wilson and Wilson 2008) but is not required here because natural selection for guilt, shame, and anxiety is explainable without it.

12. Decades of speculation and scientific publications describing genetic causes for psychopathy or sociopathy (now called antisocial personality disorder) have not been consistently confirmed (Scott, Briskman, and O'Connor 2014). If it turns out some people are born without empathy or without guilt, this would be a rare genetic aberration that would not undermine the theory that guilt, shame, and anxiety are genetic and built into humans.

13. Psychologist Stanley Krippner's phrasing excerpted from his personal endorsement of this book.

Chapter 2. Our Human Legacy of Stone Age Emotions

1. Churchland (2011), pp. 16–18.

2. Anthropologic research confirms that every culture displays shame reactions as a major, if not *the* major, means of social control. It is less clear whether guilt is also universal or whether it derived from shame and mostly appears in more individualistic societies. Scheff and Retzinger (1991) view guilt as a derivative of shame. If so, this would not affect this book's analyses of guilt's function in biological evolution and modern childhood. However, guilt plays a significant social role as far back as the Hebrew Bible. Two classics in this discussion are Dodds (1951) and Benedict (1967). Meanwhile, anxiety seems so pervasive in life that researchers seem to assume it has always permeated all societies and generally fail to discuss it in the context of guilt and shame.

3. Herron and Freedman (2014), p. 780.

4. Goodall (1999).

5. Masson (2010); Masson and McCarthy (1996).

6. Tallis (2011).

7. On my bookshelves as a student, the titles of these books were a constant reminder that life can and should be lived by meaningful principles: Alfred Adler, *Understanding Human Nature* (2009, originally published 1927); Erich Fromm, *Escape from Freedom* (1941); Viktor Frankl, *Man's Search for Meaning* (1959); Gordon Allport, *Becoming: Considerations for a Psychology of Personality* (1955); Rollo May, *Man's Search for Himself* (1953); Carl Rogers, *On Becoming a Person* (1961); R. D. Laing, *The Politics of Experience* (1967); and Abraham Maslow, *Toward a Psychology of Being* (1962). Many of these books blended well with philosopher and theologian Martin Buber's inspiring spiritual reflections on human relationship, *I and Thou* (1958). Entering medical school and then beginning my psychiatric training, I was already imbued with these works, but, by the time I began my psychiatric training in 1962, books that meaningfully addressed human life were missing from most clinical psychological programs and nearly all psychiatric training programs, and fewer were being written. As I document in *Toxic Psychiatry* (1991), the pharmaceutical industry, in partnership with organized psychiatry, had changed the cultural climate so that both academics and the general population have been discouraged from examining inner personal resources for the solutions to emotional problems.

8. Seligman (1995, 2011, 2012), for example, gives little attention to the forces of guilt, shame, and anxiety that can overwhelm our best attempts to live according to better principles. Even scientists who look at human morality tend to ignore these basic emotions. For example, Greene

(2013) examines innate primitive morality in relation to modern life while mentioning guilt and shame only in passing, and anxiety not at all, and giving none of them any importance. His "scientific" approach leaves out most of what matters in painful human emotions, as well as the origins of primitive, prehistoric morality.

Chapter 3. Our Brains Are Made Up of People

1. The idea that we have a "social brain" is not new (e.g., Lieberman 2013; Graziano 2013; Churchland 2011, 2013; and Brooks 2011). Unfortunately, the concept has sometimes been a metaphor bolstered by overinflated neuroscience and misused neuroimaging, rather than solid evolutionary theory.

2. Martin (2013), p. 125.

3. Knickmeyer et al. (2008).

4. Martin (2013), p. 128. Like many other evolutionary scientists, Martin theorizes that the small size of the human birth canal put limits on the size of the head and, therefore, the size of the brain that could be safely delivered. This, in turn, required that humans be born with small, immature brains. I suspect natural selection also favored human brains that would grow in response to the environment.

5. Perry and Marcellus (undated), p. 1.

6. For an empathic view of an infant's life experience, see Levine and Kline (2007), pp. 275–322.

7. Farah et al.(2008).

8. Diamond (2001), p. 1.

9. Ibid.

10. Martin (2013), p. 186.

11. Block and Krebs (2005), p. 1234. This is an official "Guidance for the Clinician in Rendering Pediatric Care."

12. Petanjek et al. (2011), p. 13281.

13. If, as Pinker (2009) suggests, there have been some changes in our genetic makeup since evolving into *Homo sapiens*, our basic social nature and our built-in conflicts between aggressiveness and close social relationships go back hundreds of thousands, if not millions, of years.

14. Skutch (1996), p. 23.

15. Szalavitz and Perry (2010), p. 6.

16. Ongoing personal communications between husband and wife.

17. For example, Satel and Lilienfeld (2013); Legrenzi and Umilta (2011); Tallis (2011); and Logothetis (2008).

18. Seung (2013).

19. Breggin (1991, 2008a) and Lacasse and Leo (2011). Also see Appendix A.

20. Swanson (2012), pp. xii–xiv.

Chapter 4. The Social Carnivore Emerges from Africa

1. Van Arsdale (2013).

2. Wenban-Smith et al. (2006). Also see "Giant Prehistoric Elephant Slaughtered by Early Humans" (2013). The earlier description of the hunting scene is in chapter 1 of this book.

3. Stiner et al. (2009). Also see "Early Human Hunters Had Fewer Meat-Sharing Rituals" (2009).

4. Hare and Woods (2013), p. 27.

5. Ibid., p. 29.

6. Ibid., p. 27.

7. Ibid., p. 29.

8. Alper (2003), p. 8.

9. Whipps (2006). See Keeley (1996). Chimpanzees, our nearest relatives, also go to war against each other (de Waal 2005).

10. Bowles (2009).

11. Skutch (1996), p. 32.

12. Goodall (1999), p. 4. For violence among chimpanzees, also see de Waal (2005).

Chapter 5. Instincts for Language, Morality, and Spirituality

1. Van Arsdale (2013).

2. Herron and Freedman (2014), p. 807.

3. Ibid., p. 802.

4. Ibid., p. 805.

5. Kagan (2013), p. 219, fig. 7.4.

6. I discuss empathy as the root of ethical living in *Beyond Conflict* (1992).

7. Kagan (2013), pp. 21–22.

8. Churchland (2011), p. 12.

9. Ibid., p. 14.

10. Leroi-Gourhan and Michelson (1986).

11. "Domestication of Dogs May Explain Mammoth Kill Sites and Success of Early Modern Humans" (2014). The quote is from the picture caption at the top of the page.

12. Lieberman (1991).

13. Pettit (2002).

14. Alper (2003).

15. Spence (1989) and Josephy (1994).

16. Dawkins (2008), despite his vocal allegiance to science, is not beneath using fake neuroscience to bolster his attack on religion when he cites the possibility that "visionary religious experiences are related to temporal lobe epilepsy" (p. 196).

17. Dawkins (2008), p. 196. See Appendix B for further discussion.

18. E.g., the Inquisition conducted by the Catholic Church (Darwin 1981a, p. 179).

19. Darwin (1981a), p. 65.

20. Zweig (1971), p. 13.

21. Ibid., p. 14.

22. See Appendix B.

23. Numerous writers have supported the existence of free will based on the principle of indeterminacy in physics. There is no more validity to this than to arguments against free will based on the principle of cause and effect in physics. As a sophomore (or possibly a freshman) at Harvard circa 1955, I wrote a paper for a course on the history of science in which I may have been among the first to make the argument that the principle of indeterminacy supported the principle of free will. I now view that as a sophomoric idea.

24. Breggin (2008a). Also, see Appendix A.

25. In Breggin (1991), I coined the phrase and described the psychopharmaceutical complex. The complex is funded and controlled by drug companies, which influence and direct the recipients of their largesse—including medical and psychiatric associations, scientific journals, research institutions, universities, government agencies, insurance companies—as well as individual researchers, professors, and so-called thought leaders and experts. This is not a conspiracy theory but an openly acknowledged "partnership" (see Breggin 1991) about which a number of books have now been written (see Appendix A).

26. My most recent discussion of the brain-disabling principle of biopsychiatric treatments can be found in my medical text *Brain-Disabling Treatments in Psychiatry, Second Edition* (2008a) and in two articles (Breggin, , a concept I first described in a book chapter (Breggin 2008) and then in my medical book *Psychiatric Drugs: Hazards to the Brain* (1983). Moncrieff (2008, 2013) discusses the theory. Also, see Appendix A.

27. Newberg and Waldman (2006), p. 97.

28. Borg et al. (2003).

29. For an analysis of the serotonin system and the scientific impossibility of locating depression or any other human mood or behavior within any one neurotransmitter system, see Breggin and Breggin (1994); Breggin (1991, 2001a, 2008a); and Lacasse and Leo (2011). Also, see Appendix A.

30. For example, Churchland waxes eloquent on the vast implications of mirror neurons (2011, pp. 135ff.).

31. Newberg and Waldman (2006), p. xx.

32. Greenberg (2007); Hicks (1997); Parent (2003); Wang et al. (2011).

33. Nibuya et al. (1995). Fake neuroscience drives and corrupts some of this research on neurogenesis. For example, Bocchio-Chiavetto et al. (2006) suggest that the increase in serum BDNF during shock treatment indicates that the treatment is useful, when, in fact, it is a response to brain damage and confirms that shock treatment damages the brain. Also, see Bolwig and Madsen (2007), who take the same mistaken position. Similar claims are made for various psychiatric drugs—that the drug-induced increases in growth factors and neurogenesis are therapeutic, when, in reality, they are indicators that the brain is responding to drug-induced damage. See my website www.ECTresources.org for comprehensive analysis and bibliography about harm from shock treatment.

34. Breggin (2008a).

Chapter 6. We Are Born Helpless and Dependent

1. Breggin (1983, 1988, 1991, 1992). My concept of subjective helplessness is somewhat similar to Seligman's concept of learned helplessness (1995, 2011, 2012). Seligman associates learned helplessness largely with feelings of depression, whereas I believe it underlies most of what we call "mental disorders" and is the root disabling emotion beneath guilt, shame, and anxiety.

2. Hart (2014) and Klackl et al. (2013) are recent contributions to the theory of terror management.

3. Drug-free or mostly drug-free treatment programs for acute psychosis are described in Breggin (1991), including the programs I developed as a college volunteer leader in a state hospital in college, Loren Mosher's Soteria House, and the successful history of moral therapy in eighteenth- and nineteenth-century hospitals run by Quakers. Karon (2003, 2005) describes individual psychotherapy with patients diagnosed with schizophrenia. Mosher (1996), Mosher and Bola (2004), and Mosher and Burti (1989) describe a very successful, largely drug-free, program in residential settings for persons suffering from first-time psychotic breakdowns. Seikkula et al. (2003) describe family therapy interventions called "Open Dialogue," a Finnish program in Lapland that continues to be successful in almost all cases of "schizophrenia." For more references to drug-free therapies, see Appendix A.

Chapter 7. Why None of Us Escape Emotionally Free from Childhood

1. Kagan (2013), p. 161.

2. Several of my books have sections on parenting, including *Talking Back to Ritalin* (2001b) and *The Ritalin Fact Book* (2002). I believe most parents will also benefit from Howard Glasser's and Jennifer Easley's (2014) *Transforming the Difficult Child*.

Chapter 8. Nature's Anger Management

1. Many of my scientific articles and books deal with suicide. They also deal with the role of shame and humiliation and the role of psychiatric drugs in causing violence. My book *Medication Madness* (2008a) presents the most cases and the most thorough analyses available anywhere of how psychiatric drugs drive children and adults to commit suicide and violence. My book *Reclaiming Our Children* (2000) contains my most thorough analysis of the role of shame and humiliation in mass murders and spree shootings (two or more victims), including the Columbine shootings on which the book focuses. As I have frequently pointed out in my blogs and in the media (see www.breggin.com for blogs and videos of media appearances), nearly all recent perpetrators of spree and mass violence have had psychiatric treatment, and many were receiving psychiatric drugs, including antidepressants and benzodiazepines, which are known to be associated with violence. Some of the cases fitting the shame profile that I have reviewed for court cases, books, or media appearances include Stephen Leith (Chelsea, MI), Joseph Wesbecker (Louisville, KY), Eric Harris and Dylan Klebold (Columbine High School, Littleton, CO), Christopher Pittman (Chester, SC), Seung-Hui Cho (Virginia Tech, Blacksburg, VA), Nidal Malik Hasan (Fort Hood, TX), James Holmes (Aurora, CO), Adam Lanza (Newtown, CT), Aaron Alexis (Naval Yard, Washington,

DC), Ivan Lopez (Fort Hood, TX), and Elliott Rodgers (Santa Barbara, CA). I testified in trials involving Stephen Leith and Joseph Wesbecker and was a medical and legal consultant without going to trial in the Pittman case and in cases associated with Eric Harris.

    2. Breggin (2008b).

Chapter 9. When Abuse Overwhelms the Child

    1. Briere and Elliott (2003).

    2. A book my patients have found especially useful is *Toxic Parents* by Susan Forward (2010). Other classics about child abuse include Pelzer (1995, 2000); Miller (1996); and Whitfield (1987). Bazelon (2013) is a book that encourages empathy. There are varied useful resources on the Internet. A classic is Lenore Walker's (1984) *The Battered Woman Syndrome*.

    3. For one of many epidemiological studies connecting childhood stress and trauma to adult mental disorders, see Spataro (2004) and Breggin (1992). Clinical and biographical classics in the field include Pelzer (1995, 2000); Miller (1996); and Whitfield (1987). Levine and Kline (2007) have written an empathic textbook about child abuse.

    4. Feldman et al. (2002); Ferber and Makhoul (2004).

    5. Goodall (1971, 1999).

    6. Breggin (1991), pp. 130–33.

    7. E.g., Terr (1991) and Spataro (2004).

    8. Child maltreatment or abuse is commonly divided into several overlapping categories of physical, sexual, emotional, and psychological abuse, as well as neglect. Neglect is by far the most commonly reported category of abuse and includes the failure to provide adequate food, clothing, shelter, education, supervision, medical care, or safekeeping. In 2012, there were 678,801 individual children reported (9.2 per 1,000 children). The greatest number of reports were for children in the first year of life (21.9 per 1,000). The most frequent form of abuse, the emotional and psychological undermining of a child's sense of worth, is not included in this data but is unfortunately common. Data from U.S. Department of Health and Human Services (2012, p. xi).

    9. See Breggin (1991), *Toxic Psychiatry,* which has influenced many mental health professionals in their career paths. Remarkably, most of the professionals I interview on my weekly talk radio show, *The Dr. Peter Breggin Hour*, on www.prn.fm, tell me on the air that *Toxic Psychiatry* was one of the most influential books in their professional development. Also, see Breggin (2008a, 2008b, 2013) and Appendix A.

    10. Breggin (1991, 2000). Also, see Appendix A.

    11. Watkins (2008).

    12. Watkins (2008); Williams (2012).

    13. I borrowed the title of this section from filmmaker Kevin Miller (2008, 2014), who has directed two outstanding film critiques of the psychiatric diagnosing and drugging of America's children: *Generation Rx* and *Letters from Generation Rx*.

    14. Breggin (2002), *The Ritalin Fact Book*, and *Talking Back to Ritalin* (2001) as well as *Brain-Disabling Treatments in Psychiatry* (2008). Also see Appendix A.

15. Lagnado (2014).

16. CDC (2013); Schwarz and Cohen (2013).

17. Reviewed in Breggin (2013a). See Swanson et al. (2007a).

18. Reviewed in Breggin (2013a). See Swanson et al. (2007b).

19. Reviewed in Breggin (2013a). For an example of a study demonstrating these bad outcomes but blaming it on childhood ADHD (in this study, mild hyperactivity in school), see Proal et al. (2011). For an independent, long-term, controlled study showing that children given stimulants become prone to cocaine abuse in young adulthood, see Lambert (2005).

20. Breggin (1991, 2000, 2001a) and others examine the harm of diagnosing children.

21. Bolstered with the latest science, in a peer-reviewed article in *Children and Society*, I have recently called for professionals to work toward an eventual ban against giving psychiatric drugs to children (Breggin 2014b). The article provides a good introduction to harm associated with psychiatrically diagnosing and drugging of children and can be found on www.breggin.com. In addition, I have written many other relevant scientific articles and books, including *The Ritalin Fact Book* (2002), which is the easiest read, and *Talking Back to Ritalin* (2001b). Pharmacologically impairing and disabling the brains of children is not a rational or ethical approach to helping them develop self-discipline and mastery skills or to ameliorating the circumstances that are causing them emotional distress.

22. Whitaker (2010) documents how the disability rolls are swelling with children placed on psychiatric drugs.

23. See www.empathictherapy.org and Appendix A.

Chapter 10. Bullying, Domestic Violence, and Posttraumatic Stress

1. Centers for Disease Control and Prevention (2014).

2. Centers for Disease Control and Prevention (2012).

3. Szalavitz and Perry (2010), p. 190.

4. See my analysis of PTSD, TBI, and psychiatric drugs (Breggin 2014a).

5. I discuss subjective or emotional helplessness as the underlying cause of so-called mental disorders in Breggin (1991), *Toxic Psychiatry*, and Breggin (2002), *Beyond Conflict*, in which I formulate the basic stress paradigm as having a common childhood origin.

6. Krippner et al. (2012).

7. I have written extensively and testified before the Veterans Affairs Committee of the U.S. House of Representatives about the hazards of giving psychiatric drugs in the military (Breggin 2010a, 2010b, 2014a).

Chapter 11. Don't People Need Some Guilt and Shame?

1. Also see discussions of medication madness in Breggin (2007, 2009).

2. See further discussions of medication spellbinding in Breggin (2007, 2008a, 2008b, 2011, 2013). Also see concluding chapter of this book and Appendix A.

PART 2: ACHIEVING EMOTIONAL FREEDOM

Chapter 12. Taking the Three Steps to Emotional Freedom

1. The difference between love and relationship is more fully explored in the final chapters of this book.

Chapter 13. Identifying Feelings of Guilt, Shame, and Anxiety

1. Breggin (1991) and more recent books; Kutchins and Kirk (1997); and Appendix A.

Chapter 16. How Our Bodies Tell Us about Guilt, Shame, and Anxiety

1. Mellander et al. (1982) and Drummond (1997).

2. From the slang word *udgy*, meaning a strange, uncomfortable feeling, an inexplicably weird feeling.

3. Brown (2008), pp. 69–70.

4. Breggin (1964, 1965).

5. Trivedi (2004), p. 6.

6. Baughman and Hovey (2006); Breggin (1991, 2008a, 2008b, 2013); Lynch (2005); Moncrieff (2008, 2013). An increasing number of scientists and clinicians now realize the biochemical imbalance theory was a figment of drug-company imagination that was systematically spread by their paid collaborators in medicine and psychiatry.

7. See my special website about the hazards of electroconvulsive or shock treatment, www.ectresources.org.

8. See Appendix A.

9. A good start is Howard Glasser's and Jennifer Easley's (2014) *Transforming the Difficult Child* and also parenting sections in my books *Talking Back to Ritalin* (2001) and the *Ritalin Fact Book* (2002).

10. The antipsychotic drug clozapine is a possible exception in regard to causing tardive dyskinesia but has other potentially fatal adverse effects.

11. Breggin (2008a) contains an in-depth analysis of tardive dyskinesia. Also, see Breggin (2013a).

12. See Breggin (2008a) and Appendix A.

Chapter 18. Overcoming Shame and Defensive Feelings

1. Lynd (1958).

2. Schoeck (1987).

Chapter 19. Conquering Anxiety and Helpless Feelings

1. Breggin (2008a).

2. Breggin (1991) details the shenanigans, deceptions, and conflicts of interest surrounding the testing and marketing of Xanax for panic disorder.

3. It was not intuitively obvious how anxiety evolved through evolution, along with guilt and shame, as a way of controlling and suppressing self-assertion, willfulness, and aggression.

4. Breggin (1991, 2008a, 2013).

Chapter 20. Mastering Anger

1. See Appendix B.

Chapter 21. Breaking Out of Numbness

1. Breggin (2008a, 2008b, 2013).

Chapter 22. How to Run Our Minds and Lives

1. Peltzer (2000), p. 87.

2. Siebert (1996), p. 267.

3. Kagan (2013), pp. 122, 131.

Chapter 23. Facing Real-Life Challenges

1. Breggin (2009).

PART 3. FREEDOM TO LOVE

Introduction to Part 3

1. See Appendix B.

2. Darwin (1952), p. 312, footnote 27. I am indebted to David Loye's (2000) book *Darwin's Lost Theory of Love* for initially locating this important citation. See Appendix B for further discussion of Darwin's views.

3. See Appendix B.

4. See Appendix B.

Chapter 25. Let's Talk about Sex

1. Tallis (2011).
2. See Breggin (1987), "Sex and Love: Sexual Dysfunction as a Spiritual Disorder."

Chapter 26. Love Is Not the Same as Relationship

1. Love as the source of conflict resolution is a theme in my book *Beyond Conflict* (1992).

Chapter 29. Empathic Self-Transformation

1. Empathic self-transformation is described in Breggin (2007, 2009).

Chapter 30. Where to Turn When *All* Seems Lost

1. I discuss these issues, including burnout, in depth in *The Heart of Being Helpful* (Breggin 1997) and, more recently, in a book chapter, "Empathy, Woundedness, Burn Out, and How to Love Being a Therapist" (2013b).
2. Miller and Nakagawa (2002).

Chapter 31. Last Resorts That Seldom Work Out

1. Breggin (2013a) and Whitaker (2010) document that psychiatric drugs can shorten the lifespan and reduce the quality of life when used for months and years.
2. Breggin (2008a) presents my most thorough description and analysis of the brain-disabling principle of psychiatric drugs. The principle is also discussed and applied in Breggin (2008b, 2011a, 2013).
3. Breggin (2007, 2008a, 2008b, 2011, 2013).
4. Breggin (2013a) and Whitaker (2010).

Chapter 32. Love as Our Highest Purpose

1. For the Guidelines for Empathic Therapy, go to http://www.empathictherapy.org/Founding-Guidelines.html.
2. See Breggin (2013a), *Psychiatric Drug Withdrawal: A Guide for Prescribers, Therapists, Patients and Their Families.*
3. At the time, more than twenty years ago, flight attendants were highly paid, had great benefits, and were positively regarded socially.

Appendix A. About Psychiatry and Psychiatric Drugs

1. Also see Breggin (2011a) for scientific article.
2. Breggin (2013a).
3. Breggin (2011b).
4. Breggin (2010a, 2010b, 2014a).
5. Pratt et al. (2011).
6. Centers for Disease Control and Prevention (2013).

Appendix B. Darwin Was No Darwinist

1. Wilson (2006)—especially see the Afterword, pp. 1479–83. Darwinists like Wilson have fueled and possibly helped to create the conflict between evolutionary theory and religion by promoting a caricature of Darwin's views.

2. Bonner and May (1981), p. xi.

3. I derived the frequencies of these words and phrases from the concordance by Barrett et al. (1987).

4. Darwin (1981a), p. 152.

5. Ibid., p. 103.

6. Ibid., p. 165.

7. Ibid., pp. 106, 165. See Barrett et al. (1987).

8. Ibid., p. 156.

9. Ibid., pp. 168–69.

10. Darwin (1981a), pp. 165–66.

11. Darwin (1981b), p. 394.

12. Darwin (1981a), p. 37.

13. Ibid., p. 47.

14. Ibid., pp. 45ff.

15. Wilson (2006), p. 1480.

16. Darwin (1981b), p. 396.

17. Darwin (1952), p. 312, footnote 27. Italic added. I am indebted to David Loye's (2000) book *Darwin's Lost Theory of Love* for initially locating this important citation.

18. Darwin (1981a), p. 65.

19. Ibid., p. 182.

20. Ibid., p. 106.

21. Ibid., p. 182.

22. Ibid., p. 106.

23. Ibid., p. 55.

24. Darwin (1892), p. 53.

25. Ibid., pp. 235ff., the letter to Asa Gray dated May 22, 1860.

BIBLIOGRAPHY

Adler, Alfred. [1927]. *Understanding Human Nature*. London: Oneworld Publications, 2009.

Allport, Gordon. *Becoming: Considerations for a Psychology of Personality*. New Haven, CT: Yale University Press, 1955.

Alper, Joe. "Rethinking Neanderthals." *Smithsonian Magazine*, June 2003, http://www.smithsonianmag.com/science-nature/neanderthals.html.

Amat, J., M. Baratta, E. Paul, S. Bland, L. Watkins, and F. Maier. (2005). "Medial Prefrontal Cortex Determines How Stressor Controllability Affects Behavior and Dorsal Raphe Nucleus." *Nature Neuroscience* 8 (2005): 365–71. doi:10.1038/nn1399.

Angell, Marcia. *The Truth about the Drug Companies: How They Deceive Us and What to Do about It*. New York: Random House, 2005.

Ansbacher, Heinz, and Rowena Ansbacher, eds. *The Individual Psychology of Alfred Adler*. New York: Basic Books, 1956.

Barrett, Paul, Donald Weinshank, Paul Ruhlen, and Stephen Ozminski. *A Concordance to Darwin's* The Descent of Man and Selection in Relation to Sex. Ithaca, NY: Cornell University Press, 1987.

Baughman, Fred, Jr., and Craig Hovey. *The ADHD Fraud: How Psychiatry Makes "Patients" out of Normal Children*. Victoria, BC: Trafford, 2006.

Bazelon, Emily. *Sticks and Stones: Defeating the Culture of Bullying and Rediscovering the Power of Character and Empathy*. New York: Random House, 2013.

Beauregard, Mario, and Denyse O'Leary. *The Spiritual Brain: A Neuroscientist's Case for the Existence of the Soul*. New York: HarperOne, 2007.

Benedict, Ruth. *The Chrysanthemum and the Sword*. London: Routledge and Kegan Paul, 1967.

Block, Robert, and Nancy Krebs. "Failure to Thrive as a Manifestation of Child Neglect." *Pediatrics* 116 (2005): 1234–37. doi:10.1542/peds.2005-2032.

Bloom, Paul. *Just Babies: The Origins of Good and Evil*. New York: Crown, 2013.

Bocchio-Chiavetto, Luisella, Roberta Zanardini, Marco Bortolomasi, Maria Abate, Matilde Segala, Mario Giacopuzzi, Marco Andrea Riva, Eleonora Marchina, Patrizio Pasqualetti, Jorge Perez, and Massimo Gennarelli. "Electroconvulsive Therapy (ECT) Increases Serum Brain Derived Neurotrophic Factor (BDNF) in Drug Resistant Depressed Patients." *European Neuropsychopharmacology* 16 (2006): 620–24. doi:10.1016/j.euroneuro.2006.04.010.

Bohart, Arthur, and Leslie Greenberg. *Empathy Reconsidered: New Directions in Psychotherapy*. Washington, DC: American Psychological Association, 1997.

Bolwig, T., and T. Madsen. "Electroconvulsive Therapy in Melancholia: The Role of Hippocampal Neurogenesis." *Acta Psychiatrica Scandinavia* 115, suppl. 433 (2007): 130–35. doi:10.1111/j.1600-0447.2007.00971.x.

Bonner, John Tyler, and Robert M. May. Introduction to *The Descent of Man and Selection in Relation to Sex*, by Charles Darwin. Princeton, NJ: Princeton University Press, 1981.

Borg, J., B. Andree, H. Soderstrom, and L. Farde. "The Serotonin System and Spiritual Experiences." *American Journal of Psychiatry* 160, no. 11 (2003): 1965–69. doi:10.1176/appi.ajp.160.11.1965.

Bowlby, John. *A Secure Base: Parent-Child Attachment and Healthy Human Development*. New York: Basic Books, 1988.

Bowles, Samuel. "Did Warfare among Ancestral Hunter-Gatherers Affect the Evolution of Human Behavior?" *Science* 324, no. 5932 (2009): 1293–98.

Breggin, Peter. "The Psychophysiology of Anxiety." *Journal of Nervous Mental Diseases* 139 (1964): 558–68.

———. "The Sedative-Like Effect of Epinephrine." *Archives of General Psychiatry* 12 (1965): 255–59.

———. "Psychosurgery." *Journal of the American Medical Association* 226 (1973): 1121.

———. "Psychosurgery for Political Purposes." *Duquesne Law Review* 13 (1975a): 841–62.

———. "Psychosurgery for the Control of Violence: A Critical Review." In *Neural Bases of Violence and Aggression*, edited by William Fields and William Sweet. St. Louis, MO: Warren H. Green, 1975b.

———. "Brain-Disabling Therapies." In *The Psychosurgery Debate*, edited by Elliot Valenstein. San Francisco: W. H. Freeman, 1980.

———. "Psychosurgery as Brain-Disabling Therapy." In *Divergent Views in Psychiatry*, edited by Maurice Dongier and Eric Wittkower. Hagerstown, MD: Harper and Row, 1981.

———. "The Return of Lobotomy and Psychosurgery." Reprinted with a new introduction in *Psychiatry and Ethics*, edited by R. B. Edwards. Buffalo, NY: Prometheus Books, 1982. Originally published in the *Congressional Record*, February 24, 1972, E1602-E1612.

———. "Iatrogenic Helplessness in Authoritarian Psychiatry." In *The Iatrogenics Handbook*, edited by R. F. Morgan. Toronto: IPI, 1983.

———. *Psychiatric Drugs: Hazards to the Brain*. New York: Springer, 1983.

———. "Sex and Love: Sexual Dysfunction as a Spiritual Disorder." In *Sexuality and Medicine*, edited by E. E. Shelp. Boston: D. Reidel, 1987.

———. "A Hierarchy of Values for Evaluating Human Progress on an Individual, Institutional and Societal Basis." In *Ethical Individualism and Organizations*, edited by K. Kollenda. New York: Praeger, 1988.

———. *Toxic Psychiatry: Why Therapy, Empathy and Love Must Replace the Drugs, Electroshock and Biochemical Theories of the "New Psychiatry."* New York: St. Martin's Press, 1991.

———. *Beyond Conflict: From Self-Help and Psychotherapy to Peacemaking*. New York: St. Martin's Press, 1992.

———. *The Heart of Being Helpful*. New York: Springer, 1997.

———. "Empathic Self-Transformation and Love in Individual and Family Therapy." *Humanistic Psychologist*, 27 (1999): 267–82.

———. *Reclaiming Our Children: A Healing Plan for a Nation in Crisis*. Cambridge, MA: Perseus Books, 2000.

————. *The Antidepressant Fact Book*. Cambridge, MA: Perseus, 2001a.

————. *Talking Back to Ritalin*. Cambridge, MA: Perseus, 2001b.

————. *The Ritalin Fact Book, Revised*. Cambridge, MA: Perseus, 2002.

————. "Intoxication Anosognosia: The Spellbinding Effect of Psychiatric Drugs." *International Journal of Risk and Safety and Medicine* 19 (2007): 3–15.

————. *Brain-Disabling Treatments in Psychiatry*, 2nd ed. New York: Springer, 2008a.

————. *Medication Madness: The Role of Psychiatric Drugs in Cases of Violence, Suicide and Crime*. New York: St. Martin's Press, 2008b.

————. *Wow, I'm an American: How to Live Like Our Nation's Heroic Founders*. Ithaca, NY: Lake Edge Press, 2009.

————. "Antidepressant-Induced Suicide, Violence, and Mania: Risks for Military Personnel." *Ethical Human Psychology and Psychiatry* 12 (2010a): 111–21.

————. "Peter R. Breggin, MD - Antidepressants & Suicide - Congressional Testimony." YouTube video, 26:11. From a congressional hearing on February 24, 2010. Posted February 12, 2011. Video available on www.breggin.com. 2010b.

————. "Psychiatric Drug-Induced Chronic Brain Impairment (CBI): Implications for Long-term Treatment with Psychiatric Medication." *International Journal of Risk & Safety in Medicine* 23 (2011a): 193–200.

————. *Empathic Therapy: A Training Film*. Available from www.breggin.com. DVD, 2011b.

————. *Psychiatric Drug Withdrawal: A Guide for Prescribers, Therapists, Patients, and Their Families*. New York: Springer, 2013a.

————. "Empathy, Woundedness, Burnout, and How to Love Being a Therapist." In *Chimes of Time: Wounded Health Professionals: Essays on Recovery*, edited by Bruce D. Kirkcaldy, 261–71. Leiden, Netherlands: Sidestone Press, 2013b.

————. "TBI, PTSD, and Psychiatric Drugs: A Perfect Storm for Causing Abnormal Mental States and Aberrant Behavior." In *The Attorney's Guide to Defending Veterans in Criminal Court*, edited by H. Brock and R. C. Else, 251–64. Minneapolis, MN: Veterans Defense Project, 2014a.

————. "The Rights of Children and Parents in Regard to Children Receiving Psychiatric Drugs." *Children & Society* 28 (2014b): 231–41.

Breggin, Peter, and Ginger Breggin. *Talking Back to Prozac*. New York: St. Martin's Press, 1994.

————. *The War against Children of Color: Psychiatry Targets Inner City Youth*. Monroe, ME: Common Courage Press, 1998.

Breggin, Peter, Ginger Breggin, and Fred Bemak, eds. *Dimensions of Empathic Therapy*. New York: Springer, 2002.

Breggin, Peter, and E. M. Stern, eds. *Psychosocial Approaches to Deeply Disturbed Persons*. New York: Haworth Press, 1996.

Briere, J., and D. M. Elliott. "Prevalence and Psychological Sequelae of Self-Reported Childhood Physical and Sexual Abuse in a General Population Sample of Men and Women." *Child Abuse and Neglect* 27 (2003): 1205-22.

Brooks, David. *The Social Animal: The Hidden Roots of Love, Character, and Achievement*. New York: Random House, 2011.

Brown, Brené. *I Thought It Was Just Me (But It Isn't)*. New York: Gotham Books, 2008.

———. "Listening to Shame." Filmed March 2012. TED video, 20:38. http://www.ted. com/talks/brene_brown_listening_to_shame.html.

Buber, Martin. *I and Thou*. New York: Charles Scribner's Sons, 1958.

Cacciatore, Joanne. *Dear Cheyenne: A Journey into Grief*, 6th ed. Phoenix, AZ: MISS Foundation, 2002.

Centers for Disease Control and Prevention (CDC). "Facts at a Glance: Youth Violence, 2012." 2012. http://www.cdc.gov/violence prevention/pdf/yv-datasheet-a.pdf.

———. "Attention-Deficit / Hyperactivity Disorder (ADHD). Key Findings: Trends in the Parent-Report of Health Care Provider-Diagnosis and Medication Treatment for ADHD: United States, 2003–2011." 2013. http://www.cdc.gov/ncbddd/adhd/features/key -findings-adhd72013.html.

———. "Featured Topic: Bullying Research Youth Bullying: What Does the Research Say?" 2014. http://www.cdc.gov/ViolencePrevention/youthviolence/bullyingresearch/index.html.

Churchland, Patricia. *Braintrust: What Neuroscience Tells Us about Morality*. Princeton, NJ: Princeton University Press, 2011.

———. *Touching a Nerve: The Self as Brain*. New York: W. W. Norton, 2013.

Cook, Gareth. "History and the Decline of Human Violence." *Scientific American*, October 4, 2011. http://www.scientificamerican.com/article/history-and-the-decline-of-human-violence/.

Cornwall, Michael Warren. "Alternative Treatment of Psychosis: A Qualitative Study of Jungian Medication-Free Treatment at Diabasis." PhD diss., California Institute of Integral Studies, 2002. ProQuest.

Corrigan, Michael W. *Debunking ADHD: 10 Reasons to Stop Drugging Kids for Acting like Kids*. Lanham, MD: Rowman & Littlefield, 2014.

Cromie, William J. "Oldest Mammal Is Found: Origin of Mammals Is Pushed Back to 195 Million Years." *Harvard University Gazette*, May 24, 2001. http://news.harvard.edu/ gazette/2001/05.24/01-mammal.html.

Darwin, Charles. *Charles Darwin: His Life in an Autobiographical Chapter, and in a Selected Series of His Published Letters*. Edited by Francis Darwin. London: John Murray, 1892.

———. [January 1860, 2nd ed.]. *The Descent of Man and Selection in Relation to Sex*. Chicago: Encyclopedia Britannica, 1952.

———. [November 1859, 1st ed.]. "On the Descent of Man." In *The Descent of Man and Selection in Relation to Sex*. Princeton, NJ: Princeton University Press, 1981a.

———. [November 1859, 1st ed.]. "Sexual Selection—Continued." In *The Descent of Man and Selection in Relation to Sex*. Princeton, NJ: Princeton University Press, 1981b.

———. *The Origin of Species*. In *From So Simple a Beginning*, edited by E. O. Wilson, 441–760. New York: W. W. Norton, 2006.

Dawkins, Richard. *The God Delusion*. New York: Houghton Mifflin, 2008.

Diamond, Marian. "Response of the Brain to Enrichment." *New Horizons for Learning* (2001). http://education.jhu.edu/PD/newhorizons/Neurosciences/articles/Response%20of %20the%20Brain%20to%20Enrichment.

Dodds, E. R. *The Greeks and the Irrational*. Berkeley, CA: University of California Press, 1951.

"Domestication of Dogs May Explain Mammoth Kill Sites and Success of Early Modern Humans." *Science Daily*, May 29, 2014. http://www.sciencedaily.com/releases/2014/05/140529154155.htm.

Drummond, P. D. "The Effect of Adrenergic Blockade on Blushing and Facial Flushing." *Psychophysiology* 34 (1997): 163–68.

"Early Human Hunters Had Fewer Meat-Sharing Rituals." *Science Daily*, August 18, 2009. http://www.sciencedaily.com/releases/2009/08/090813142506.htm.

Farah, Martha J., Laura Betancourt, David M. Shera, Jessica H. Savage, Joan M. Giannetta, Nancy L. Brodsky, Elsa K. Malmud, and Hallam Hurt. "Environmental Stimulation, Parental Nurturance and Cognitive Development in Humans." *Developmental Science* 11 (2008): 793–801. doi:10.1111/j.1467-7687.2008.00688.x.

Feldman, R., A. Eidelman, L. Sirota, and A. Weller. "Comparison of Skin-to-Skin (Kangaroo) and Traditional Care: Parenting Outcomes and Preterm Infant Development." *Pediatrics* 110 (2002): 16–26.

Ferber, S., and I. Makhoul. "The Effect of Skin-to-Skin Contact (Kangaroo Care) Shortly After Birth on the Neurobehavioral Responses of the Term Newborn: A Randomized, Controlled Trial." *Pediatrics* 113 (2004): 858–65.

Forward, Susan. *Toxic Parents*. New York: Transworld, 2010.

Frankl, Victor. *Man's Search for Meaning*. Boston: Beacon Press, 1959.

Franklin, Benjamin. [1771]. *The Autobiography of Benjamin Franklin*. New York: Dover, 1996.

Freud, Sigmund. *Civilization and Its Discontents*. New York: W. W. Norton, 2010.

Fromm, Erich. *Escape from Freedom*. New York: Henry Holt, 1956.

Fry, Douglas, and Patrik Söderberg. "Lethal Aggression in Mobile Forager Bands and Implications for the Origins of War." *Science* 341 (2013): 270–73.

"Giant Prehistoric Elephant Slaughtered by Early Humans." *Science Daily*, September 19, 2013. http://www.sciencedaily.com/releases/2013/09/130919085710.htm??utm_source=feed burner&utm_medium=email&utm_campaign=Feed:+sciencedaily/plants_animals/animals+%28ScienceDaily:+Plants+%26+Animals+News+—+Animals%29.

Glasser, Howard, and Jennifer Easley. *Transforming the Difficult Child: The Nurtured Heart Approach*. Tucson, AZ: Nurtured Heart Publications, 2014.

Glasser, William. *Choice Theory: A New Psychology of Personal Freedom*. New York: Harper Perennial, 1999.

Glenmullen, Joseph. *Prozac Backlash*. New York: Simon & Schuster, 2001.

———. *The Antidepressant Solution*. New York: Free Press, 2006.

Goldacre, Ben. *Bad Pharma: How Drug Companies Mislead Doctors and Harm Patients*. London: Fourth Estate, 2012.

Goodall, Jane. *In the Shadow of Man*. Boston: Houghton Mifflin, 1971.

———. *Jane Goodall: 40 Years at Gombe*. New York: Stewart, Tabori & Chang, 1999.

Gould, Stephen J. "Sociobiology and the Theory of Natural Selection." In *Sociobiology: Beyond Nature/Nurture?*, edited by G. W. Barlow and J. Silverberg, 257–69. Boulder, CO: Westview Press, 1980.

Graziano, Michael. *Consciousness and the Social Brain*. London: Oxford University Press, 2013.

Greenberg, D. A. "Neurogenesis and Stroke." *CNS & Neurological Disorders - Drug Targets* 6 (2007): 321–25.

Greene, Joshua. *Moral Tribes: Emotion, Reason, and the Gap between Us and Them*. New York: Penguin, 2013.

Haaken, Janice, and Paula Reavey, eds. *Memory Matters*. London: Routledge, 2010.

Hales, Robert, Stuart Yudofsky, and Glen Gabbard. *Textbook of Psychiatry*, 5th ed. New York: American Psychiatric Publishers, 2008.

Hare, Brian, and Vanessa Woods. *The Genius of Dogs*. New York: Dutton, 2013.

Hart, Joshua. "Toward an Integrative Theory of Psychological Defense." *Perspectives on Psychological Science* 9 (2014): 19–39.

Herron, Jon C., and Scott Freedman. *Evolutionary Analysis*, 5th ed. Boston: Pearson, 2014.

Hicks. R., S. Numan, H. Dhillon, M. Prasad, and K. Seroogy. "Alterations in BDNF and NT-3 mRNAs in Rat Hippocampus after Experimental Brain Trauma." *Molecular Brain Research* 48 (1997): 401–6.

Hotz, Robert Lee. "Skull Shakes Up Humanity Family Tree." *Wall Street Journal*, October 18, 2013.

International Center for the Study of Psychiatry and Psychology, eds. *The Conscience of Psychiatry: The Reform Work of Peter R. Breggin, MD*. Ithaca, NY: Lake Edge Press, 2009.

James, William. [1907]. *Pragmatism*. Minneapolis, MN: Hackett, 1980.

Joseph, Jay. "Genetic Research in Psychiatry and Psychology: A Critical Overview." In *Handbook of Developmental Science, Behavior, and Genetics*, edited by Kathryn E. Hood, Carolyn Tucker Halpern, Gary Greenberg, and Richard M. Lerner, 557–625. New York: Blackwell, 2010.

Josephy, Alvin, Jr. *500 Nations*. New York: Alfred A. Knopf, 1994.

Kagan, Jerome. *The Human Spark*. New York: Basic Books, 2013.

Kandel, Eric. "The New Science of the Mind." *New York Times*, September 6, 2013. http://www.nytimes.com/2013/09/08/opinion/sunday/the-new-science-of-mind.html??emc=edit_tnt_20130906&tntemail0=y&_r=1&.

Karon, Bertram. "The Tragedy of Schizophrenia without Psychotherapy." *Journal of the American Academy of Psychoanalysis and Dynamic Psychiatry* 331 (2003): 89–118.

———. "Recurrent Psychotic Depression Is Treatable by Psychotherapy without Medication." *Ethical Human Psychology and Psychiatry* 7 (2005): 45–56.

Keeley, Lawrence. *War before Civilization: The Myth of the Peaceful Savage*. London: Oxford University Press, 1996.

Kirsch, Irving. *The Emperor's New Clothes: Exploding the Antidepressant Myth*. New York: Basic Books, 2011.

Klackl, Johannes, Eva Jonas, and Martin Kronbichler. "Existential Neuroscience: Neurophysiological Correlates of Proximal Defenses against Death-Related Thoughts." *Social Cognitive and Affective Neuroscience* 8, no. 3 (2013): 333–40. doi:10.1093/scan/nss003.

Knezev, Sasha, and Gregory A. Smith. *American Addict*. DVD, 2012. http://www.amazon.com/American-Addict-Sasha-Knezev/dp/B00FXSI9IY.

Knickmeyer, Rebecca, Sylvain Gouttard, Chaeryon Kang, Dianne Evans, Kathy Wilber, J. Keith Smith, Robert M. Hamer, Weili Lin, Guido Gerig, and John H. Gilmore. (2008). "A Structural MRI Study of Human Brain Development from Birth to 2 Years." *Journal of Neuroscience* 28, no. 47 (2008): 12176–82. doi:10.1523/JNEUROSCI.3479-08.2008.

Krippner, Stanley, Daniel B. Pitchford, and Jeannine Davies. *Post-Traumatic Stress Disorder.* Westport, CT: Greenwood, 2012.

Kropotkin, Petr. *Mutual Aid: A Factor of Evolution.* Boston: Porter Sargent Publishers, 1914.

Kutchins, H., and S. A. Kirk. *Making Us Crazy: DSM: The Psychiatric Bible and the Creation of Mental Disorder.* New York: Free Press, 1997.

Lacasse, J. and J. Leo. "Serotonin and Depression: A Disconnect between the Advertisements and the Scientific Literature." *PLoS Medicine* 2, no. 12 (2011): e392.

Lagnado, Lucette. "Drugged as Children, Foster-Care Alumni Speak Out: Use of Powerful Antipsychotics on Youths in Such Homes Comes under Greater Scrutiny." *Wall Street Journal,* February 23, 2014. http://online.wsj.com/news/articles/SB10001424052702 303442704579361333470749104.

Laing, R. D. *The Politics of Experience.* New York: Pantheon, 1967.

Lambert, N. "The Contribution of Childhood ADHD, Conduct Problems, and Stimulant Treatment to Adolescent and Adult Tobacco and Psychoactive Substance Abuse." *Ethical Human Psychology and Psychiatry* 7 (2005): 197–221.

Legrenzi, Paolo, and Carlo Umilta. *Neuromania: On the Limits of Brain Science.* Oxford: Oxford University Press, 2011.

Leroi-Gourhan, Andre, and Annette Michelson. *The Religion of the Caves: Magic or Metaphysics?* Boston: MIT Press, 1986.

Levine, Peter, and Maggie Kline. *Trauma through the Eyes of the Child.* Berkeley, CA: North Atlantic Books, 2007.

Lewis, Helen. *Shame and Guilt in Neurosis.* New York: International Universities Press, 1971.

Lieberman, Matthew. *Social: Why Our Brains Are Wired to Connect.* New York: Crown, 2013.

Lieberman, Philip. *Uniquely Human: The Evolution of Speech, Thought and Selfless Behavior.* Cambridge, MA: Harvard University Press, 1991.

Light, Donald. *The Risks of Prescription Drugs.* New York: Columbia University Press, 2010.

Logothetis, Nikos. "What We Can Do and What We Cannot Do with fMRI." *Nature* 453 (2008): 869–78. doi:10.1038/nature06976.

Lordkipanidze, David, Marcia Ponce de León, Ann Margvelashvili, Yoel Rak, G. Phillip Rightmire, Abesalom Vekua, and Christoph P. E. Zollikofer. "A Complete Skull from Dmanisi, Georgia, and the Evolutionary Biology of Early *Homo.*" *Science* 342, no. 6156 (2013): 326–31. doi:10.1126/science.1238484.

Loye, David. *Darwin's Lost Theory of Love.* San Jose: toExcel, 2000.

Lynch, Terry. *Beyond Prozac.* Cork, Ireland: Mercier Press, 2005.

———. *Selfhood.* Limerick, Ireland: Mental Health Press, 2011.

Lynd, Helen Merrell. [1958]. *On Shame and the Search for Identity.* London: Routledge, 2013.

Machluf, K., J. Liddle, and D. Bjorklund. "An Introduction to Evolutionary Developmental Psychology." *Journal of Evolutionary Psychology* 12 (2014): 264–72.

Mackler, Daniel. "Jaakko Seikkula Speaks on Finnish Open Dialogue, Social Networks, and Recovery from Psychosis." YouTube video, 8:24. Posted July 28, 2011. http://www.youtube.com/watch?v=ywtPedxhC3U.

———. "Open Dialogue: An Alternative Finnish Approach to Healing." YouTube video, 1:13:59. Posted April 8, 2014. http://www.youtube.com/watch? ?v=HDVhZHJagfQ.

MacLean, Paul D. *The Triune Brain in Evolution: Role in Paleocerebral Functions*. New York: Plenum Press, 1990.

Maddock, Mary, and Jim Maddock. *Soul Survivor: A Personal Encounter with Psychiatry*. Stockport, Ireland: Asylum, 2006.

Martin, Robert. *How We Do It: The Evolution and Future of Human Evolution*. New York: Basic Books, 2013.

Maslow, Abraham. *Toward a Psychology of Being*. New York: Van Nostrand, 1962.

Masson, Jeffrey Moussaieff. *The Dog Who Wouldn't Stop Loving: How Dogs Have Captured Our Hearts for Thousands of Years*. New York: Harper, 2010.

———. *Beasts: What Animals Can Teach Us about the Origins of Good and Evil*. New York: Bloomsbury, 2014.

Masson, Jeffrey Moussaieff, and Susan McCarthy. When Elephants *Weep: The Emotional Lives of Animals*. New York: Delta, 1996.

May, Rollo. *Man's Search for Himself*. London: George Allen & Unwin, 1953.

Mellars, Paul. "Why Did Modern Human Populations Disperse from Africa ca. 60,000 Years Ago?" *Proceedings of the National Academy of Sciences* 103, no. 25 (2006): 9381–86. doi:10.1073/pnas.0510792103.

Mellander, S., P. O. Andersson, L. E. Afzelius, and P. Hellstrand. "Neural Beta-Adrenergic Dilatation of the Facial Vein in Man: Possible Mechanism in Emotional Blushing." *Acta Physiologica Scandinavia* 114 (1982): 393–99.

Mender, Donald. *The Myth of Neuropsychiatry*. New York: Plenum, 1994.

Miller, Alice. *The Drama of the Gifted Child*. New York: Basic Books, 1996.

Miller, John P., and Yoshiharu Nakagawa, eds. Nurturing Our Wholeness: Perspectives on Spirituality in Education. Brandon, VT: Foundation for Educational Renewal, 2002.

Miller, Kevin. *Generation Rx*. DVD, 2008. http://www.amazon.com/Generation-RX-Kevin-P-Miller/dp/B001UKZGQ2.

———. *Letters from Generation Rx*. Film, 2015. http://www.lettersfromgenerationrx.com/.

Moncrieff, Joanna. *Myth of the Chemical Cure: A Critique of Psychiatric Drug Treatment*. New York: Palgrave Macmillan, 2008.

———. *The Bitterest Pill*. New York: Palgrave Macmillan, 2013.

Montague, Ashley. *Touching: The Human Significance of the Skin*. New York: Columbia University Press, 1971.

Morrison, I., L. Loken, and H. Olausson. "The Skin as a Social Organ." *Experimental Brain Research* 204 (2010): 305–14. doi:10.1007/s00221-009-2007-y.

Mosher, Loren. "Soteria: A Therapeutic Community for Psychotic Persons." In *Psychosocial Approaches to Deeply Disturbed Persons*, edited by Peter Breggin and E. M. Stern, 43–58. New York: Haworth Press, 1996.

Mosher, Loren, and John Bola. "Soteria-California and Its American Successors: Therapeutic Ingredients." *Ethical Human Psychology and Psychiatry* 6 (2004): 7–23.

Mosher, Loren, and Lorenzo Burti. *Community Mental Health: Principles and Practice*. New York: W. W. Norton, 1989.

Newberg, Andrew, and Mark Robert Waldman. *Born to Believe*. New York: Free Press, 2006.

Nibuya, M., S. Morinobu, and R. Duman. "Regulation of BDNF and trkB mRNA in Rat Brain by Chronic Electroconvulsive Seizure and Antidepressant Drug Treatments." *Journal of Neuroscience* 75 (1995): 7539–47.

Olson, Cheryl K. August 10, 2012. "Those Alluring Brain Images!" Brainlink. http://www.drcherylolson.com/health-and-science-videos/brainlink/those-alluring-brain-images.

Pam, A. "Biological Psychiatry: Science or Pseudoscience?" In *Pseudoscience in Biological Psychiatry*, edited by C. Ross and A. Pam, 7–84. New York: Wiley, 1995.

Papez, J. W. [1937]. "A Proposed Mechanism of Emotion." *Journal of Neuropsychiatry and Clinical Neuroscience* 7, no. 1 (1995): 103–12.

Parent, J. M. "Injury-Induced Neurogenesis in the Adult Mammalian Brain." *Neuroscientist* 9 (2003): 261.

Pelzer, Dave. *A Child Called "It": One Child's Courage to Survive*. Deerfield, FL: Health Communications, 1995.

———. *Help Yourself: Finding Hope, Courage, and Happiness*. New York: Penguin Putnam, 2000.

Perry, Bruce, and John Marcellus. Undated. "The Impact of Abuse and Neglect on the Developing Brain." *Teachers*. Accessed June 1, 2014. http://teacher.scholastic.com/professional/bruceperry/abuse_neglect.htm.

Petanjek, Zdravko, Milos Judas, Goran Simic, Miaden Rasin, Harry Uylings, Pasko Rakic, and Ivica Kostovic. "Extraordinary Neoteny of Synaptic Spines in the Human Prefrontal Cortex." *Proceedings of the National Academy of Sciences* 108, no. 32 (2011): 13281–86. doi:10.1073/pnas.1105108108.

Pettitt, Paul. "When Burial Begins." *British Archaeology*, August 2002. http://www.archaeologyuk.org/ba/ba66/feat1.shtml.

Pinker, Steven. *How the Mind Works*. New York: W. W. Norton, 2009.

———. *The Better Angels of Our Nature*. New York: Viking, 2011.

Pratt, Laura A., Debra J. Brody, and Qiuping Gu. "Antidepressant Use in Persons Aged 12 and Over: United States, 2005–2008." *NCHS Data* Brief No. 76 (October 2011). http://www.cdc.gov/nchs/data/databriefs/db76.htm.

Proal, E., P. Reiss, R. Klein, S. Mannuzza, K. Gotimer, M. Ramos-Olazagasti, J. Lerch, Y. He, A. Zijdenbos, C. Kelly, C. Milham, and X. Castellanos. "Brain Gray Matter Deficits at 33-Year Follow-Up in Adults with Attention-Deficit/Hyperactivity Disorder Established in Childhood." *Archives of General Psychiatry* 68 (2011): 1122–34.

Richerson, Peter, and Robert Boyd. *Not by Genes Alone: How Culture Transformed Human Evolution.* Chicago: University of Chicago Press, 2005.

Rogers, Carl. *On Becoming a Person.* New York: Houghton Mifflin, 1961.

Satel, Sally, and Scott Lilienfeld. *Brainwashed: The Seductive Appeal of Mindless Neuroscience.* New York: Basic Books, 2013.

Scheff, Thomas, and Suzanne M. Retzinger. *Emotions and Violence: Shame and Rage in Destructive Conflicts.* Lexington, MA: Lexington Books, 1991.

Schmahmann, J., and D. Caplan. (2006). "Cognition, Emotion and the Cerebellum." *Brain* 129, no. 2 (2006): 290–92. doi:10.1093/brain/awh729.

Schoeck, Helmut. *Envy: A Theory of Social Behavior.* University Park, IL: Liberty Fund, 1987.

Schwarz, Alan, and Sarah Cohen. "A.D.H.D. Seen in 11% of U.S. Children as Diagnoses Rise." *New York Times*, March 31, 2013. http://www.nytimes.com/2013/04/01/health/more-diagnoses-of-hyperactivity-causing-concern.html?_r=0.

Scott, Stephen, Jackie Briskman, and Thomas G. O'Connor. "Early Prevention of Antisocial Personality: Long-Term Follow-Up of Two Randomized Controlled Trials Comparing Indicated and Selective Approaches." *American Journal of Psychiatry* 171 (2014): 649–57.

Scott, Timothy. *America Fooled: The Truth about Antidepressants, Antipsychotics and How We've Been Deceived.* Victoria, TX: Argo, 2011.

Seikkula, Jaakko. "Five Year Experience of First-Episode Nonaffective Psychosis in Open-Dialogue Approach." *Journal of Psychotherapy Research* 16 (2006): 214–28.

Seikkula, Jaakko, Birgitta Alakare, Jukka Aaltonen, Juha Holma, Anu Rasinkangas, and Ville Lehtinen. "Open Dialogue Approach: Treatment Principles and Preliminary Results of a Two-Year Follow-Up of First Episode Schizophrenia." *Ethical Human Sciences and Services* 5, no. 3 (2003): 163–82.

Seikkula, Jaakko, and Tom Erik Arnkil. *Dialogical Meetings in Social Networks.* London: Karnac Books, 2006.

Seligman, Martin. *The Optimistic Child.* New York: Houghton Mifflin, 1995.

―――. *Flourish: A Visionary New Understanding of Happiness and Well-Being.* New York: Free Press, 2011.

―――. "PERMA." In *This Will Make You Smarter*, edited by John Brockman, 92–93. New York: Harper Perennial, 2012.

Seung, Sebastian. *Connectome: How the Brain's Wiring Makes Us Who We Are.* New York: Mariner Books, 2013.

Shipman, Pat. "How Do You Kill 86 Mammoths? Taphonomic Investigations of Mammoth Megasites." *Quaternary International* (2014). doi:10.1016/j.quaint.2014.04.048.

Siebert, Al. *The Survivor Personality.* New York: Perigee, 1996.

Siegel, Allan, and Hreday Sapru. *Essential Neuroscience.* New York: Wolters Kluwer, 2011.

Skutch, Alexander. *The Minds of Birds.* College Station, TX: Texas A&M Press, 1996.

Smith, Margaret. *Ritual Abuse: What It Is, Why It Happens, and How to Help.* San Francisco: HarperSanFrancisco, 1993.

Spataro, Josie, Paul Mullen, Philip Burgess, David Wells, and Simon Moss. "Impact of Sexual

Abuse on Mental Health: Perspective Study in Males and Females." *British Journal of Psychiatry* 184 (2004): 416–21. doi:10.1192/bjp.184.5.416.

Spence, Lewis. [1914]. *The Myths of North American Indians*. New York: Dover Publications, 1989.

Staemmler, Frank. *Empathy in Psychotherapy*. New York: Springer, 2012.

Stiner, Mary C., Ran Barkai, and Avi Gopher. "Cooperative Hunting and Meat Sharing 400–200 kya at Qesem Cave, Israel." *Proceedings of the National Academy of Sciences* 106, no. 32 (2009): 13207–12. doi:kn10.1073/pnas.0900564106.

Stolzer, Jeanne. "Breastfeeding in the 21st Century: A Theoretical Perspective." *International Journal of Sociology of the Family* 31 (2005): 39–55.

Sun, D., M. Bullock, M. McGinn, Z. Zhou, N. Altememi, S. Hagood, R. Hamm, and R. Colello. "Basic Fibroblast Growth Factor-Enhanced Neurogenesis Contributes to Cognitive Recovery in Rats Following Traumatic Brain Injury." *Experimental Neurology* 216 (2009): 56–65.

Sun, L. *The Fairness Instinct: The Robin Hood Mentality and Our Biological Nature*. Amherst, NY: Prometheus Books, 2013.

Swanson, J., G. Elliott, L. Greenhill, T. Wigal, L. Arnold, B. Vitiello, L. Hechtman, J. Epstein, W. Pelham, H. Abikoff, J. Newcorn, B. Molina, S. Hinshaw, K. Wells, B. Hoza, P. Jensen, R. Gibbons, K. Hur, A. Stehli, M. Davies, J. March, C. Conners, M. Caron, and N. Volkow. (2007a). "Effects of Stimulant Medication on Growth Rates across 3 Years in the MTA Follow-Up." *Journal of the American Academy of Child and Adolescent Psychiatry* 46 (2007a): 1015–27.

Swanson, J., S. Hinshaw, L. Arnold, R. Gibbons, S. Marcus, K. Hur, P. Jensen, B. Vitiello, H. Abikoff, L. Greenhill, L. Hechtman, W. Pelham, K. Wells, C. Conners, J. March, G. Elliott, J. Epstein, K. Hoagwood, B. Hoza, B. Molina, J. Newcorn, J. Severe, and T. Wigal. "Second Evaluation of MTA 36-Month Outcomes: Propensity Score and Growth Mixture Model Analyses." *Journal of the American Academy of Child and Adolescent Psychiatry* 46 (2007b): 989–1002.

Swanson, Larry. *Brain Architecture: Understanding the Basic Brain Plain*. New York: Oxford University Press, 2012.

Szalavitz, Maia, and Bruce Perry. *Born for Love: Why Empathy Is Endangered and Essential*. New York: Harper, 2010.

Tallis, Raymond. *Aping Mankind: Neuromania, Darwinitis and the Misrepresentation of Humanity*. Durham, UK: Acumen, 2011.

Terr, L. C. "Childhood Traumas: An Outline and Overview." *American Journal of Psychiatry* 148 (1991): 10–20.

Tinbergen, Nikolaas. [1951]. *The Study of Instinct*. Oxford, UK: Clarendon Press, 1989.

Trivedi, Madhukar H. "The Link between Depression and Physical Symptoms." *Primary Care Companion Journal of Clinical Psychiatry* 6, suppl. 1 (2004): 12–16.

U.S. Department of Health and Human Services, Administration for Children and Families, Administration on Children, Youth and Families, Children's Bureau. "Child Maltreatment 2012." 2013. http://www.acf.hhs.gov/programs/cb/research-data-technology/statistics-research/child-maltreatment.

Van Arsdale, A. P. "*Homo erectus* — A Bigger, Smarter, Faster Hominin Lineage." *Nature Education Knowledge* 4, no. 1 (2013): 2.

de Waal, Frans B. M. "A Century of Getting to Know the Chimpanzee." *Nature* 437, no. 7055 (2005): 56–59. doi:10.1038/nature03999.

Walker, Lenore E. *The Battered Woman Syndrome*. New York: Springer, 1984.

Wang, C., M. Zhang, C. Suna, Y. Caia, Y. Youa, L. Huang, and L. Liua. "Sustained Increase in Adult Neurogenesis in the Rat Hippocampal Dentate Gyrus after Transient Brain Ischemia." *Neuroscience Letters* 488 (2011): 70–75.

Wang, Shirley S. "Psychiatric Drug Use Spreads: Pharmacy Data Show a Big Rise in Antipsychotic and Adult ADHD Treatments." *Wall Street Journal*, November 16, 2011. http://online.wsj.com/article/SB10001424052970203503204577040431792673066.html.

Watkins, John. *Hearing Voices: A Common Human Experience*. South Yara, Australia: Michelle Anderson, 2008.

Watters, Ethan. *Crazy like Us: The Globalization of the American Psyche*. New York: Free Press, 2010.

Wenban-Smith, F. F., P. Allen, M. R. Bates, S. A. Parfitt, R. C. Preece, J. R. Stewart, C. Turner, and J. E. Whittaker. "The Clactonian Elephant Butchery Site at Southfleet Road, Ebbsfleet, UK." *Journal of Quaternary Science* 21 (2006): 471–83.

Whipps, Heather. "Peace or War? How Early Humans Behaved." *Live Science*, March 6, 2006. http://www.livescience.com/640-peace-war-early-humans-behaved.html.

Whitaker, Robert. *Mad in America: Bad Science, Bad Medicine, and the Enduring Mistreatment of the Mentally Ill*. Cambridge, MA: Perseus, 2002.

———. *Anatomy of an Epidemic: Magic Bullets, Psychiatric Drugs, and the Astonishing Rise of Mental Illness in America*. New York: Crown Publishers, 2010.

Whitfield, Charles. *Healing the Child Within: Discovery and Recovery for Adult Children of Dysfunctional Families*. Deerfield Beach, FL: Health Communications, 1987.

———. *Not Crazy: You May Not Be Mentally Ill*. N.p.: Muse House Press/Pennington, 2011.

Williams, Paris. *Rethinking Madness: Towards a Paradigm Shift in Our Understanding and Treatment of Psychosis*. San Rafael, CA: Sky's Edge, 2012.

Wilson, D. S., and E. O. Wilson. "Evolution 'for the Good of the Group.'" *American Scientist* 96, no. 5 (2008): 380–89. doi:10.1511/2008.74.1.

Wilson, E. O. *On Human Nature*. Cambridge, MA: Harvard University Press, 1979.

———, ed. *From So Simple a Beginning: The Four Great Books of Charles Darwin*. New York: W. W. Norton, 2006.

Zweig, Connie. *The Holy Longing: The Hidden Power of Spiritual Yearning*. New York: Tarcher/Putnam, 1971.

INDEX